Character - Aspect of life which is dominated
by principles.
Temperament - Activi[ty] [based on]
special condition [physio]logical,
chemical condition)
Temperament = Constitution

How We Influence One Another

The Psychology of Social Interaction

By

VINCENT V. HERR, S.J.
Loyola University, Chicago

THE BRUCE PUBLISHING COMPANY
Milwaukee

To His Excellency
THE MOST REVEREND SAMUEL A. STRITCH
Psychologist, Sociologist, and Beloved Pastor

PREFACE BY THE GENERAL EDITOR

The title of this book sufficiently indicates at a glance its practical aspect. The purely scientific approach maintained throughout is no less definitely implied in its supplementary description as a psychology of social interaction.

The effort of social psychologists in recent years has been largely directed toward eliminating in their theories the rational element in man's nature, or else giving it but scant acknowledgment in proportion to the vast importance attached by them to irrational and unconscious factors. Against such harmful tendencies we have here the sane and constructive doctrine set forth by the author, vindicating the rationality of man, without prejudice to any lesser elements.

Advisedly, the question of revealed religion is not touched upon in this book, except for passing allusions. The author's appeal is exclusively to the reason of man. His approach is technical throughout and purely scientific. His main purpose is to show the necessity of man's power of reason, and of the right use of voluntary attention on his part for the attainment of successful and smooth social relations.

Observation and controlled experiment, aided by inductive reasoning, are legitimate means of the objective worker in this specific field. These the author employs to their full possibility. By them he effectively shows how our most emotional reactions and emotionally toned attitudes involve an active choice on our part — a choice not made perhaps at the present instant, but at some stage or other in our previous human development.

In a word, the object of the book is to promote a return to sanity in our social psychology and in our social views of life. Its message is sounded as a timely blast against the ubiquitous suggestions of present-day social psychologists who would attribute to unconscious factors our differences of opinions and attitudes, ascribe to mere emotional thinking the rooted convictions of our race, and claim to see in our freest motivations the irrational acceptance of mores.

All this speculation conflicts with the common sense of mankind.

It is best repudiated in the very lives of the social psychologists themselves whose phantasmal conceptions are inculcated in American classrooms. Not in this way can we hope to produce a race of sterling men and women, conscious of their sacred responsibilities and heroically living up to them in the name of God, of country, and of home. But to the hidebound followers of false philosophies all this is heresy. To such materialistic teachings in the schools the world owes its Hitlers and its Mussolinis.

Add, then, to this confusion of thought the thoroughly motivated social psychology of high-pressure advertising and the effects of movie display, which alike help to create still further a state of dissatisfaction in countless minds by the artificial stimulus of needs that are entirely unreal. If people will be carried away by the splendors of costly dresses, the latest devices of indoor plumbing, and the most recent models of automobiles and aircraft, the fault does not lie in a supposed absence of reason, but in the lack of adequate use of men's human powers of self-reflection and self-determination. What is true of the masses is no less true of the rich with their cravings for still further developments of their already giant ventures or heedless displays of wealth. The most pitiable of all mortals was Alexander, King of Macedon, with no more worlds to conquer.

Wise, indeed, was the English poet who sought to bring home the great psychological truth that man never *is* blessed" (in a complete sense) but always *to be* blessed." Yet to achieve that last to the fullness of our measure we must wait for eternity. Rightly to comprehend this fact we must listen to the promptings of our reason and to what religion has to teach us.

But to make this plain is not the purpose of our book. We are concerned here rather with matters of a very specific kind: with special techniques and rating scales; with motives and mechanics in the process of social learning; with criteria of instincts and the classification of drives; with protective behavior and social incentives; with psychological bases of emotion, social temperament, and dispositions; with suggestibility and the reality of hypnotism; with attitudes and their measurement; and so we might continue, until we finally arrive at the confutation of that supposed discovery of modern social psychologists who proclaim that our human nature has been conferred on us not by God but by society!

Such, then, is the tempting study proposed here, so far as it can be gauged by the display of a select handful of its offerings. The book is accommodated for either private reading or for classroom text. What renders it still more distinctive is the unusual richness of its numerous aids and its pithy descriptive characterizations of the present-day writers on this subject. But to these things special reference is made in the "Author's Note."

We come, now, into direct contact with the writer of this book. A few words descriptive of his preparation for this undertaking will not be out of place here. It will suffice to confine ourselves to his studies abroad.

Leaving the university classroom in our own country, he attended courses at Vienna and Bonn, procuring his doctorate at the latter place. Particularly helpful to him were the travels in Europe that brought him into close contact with such noted psychologists as Lindworsky of Prague and Froebes of the Gregorian and of Falkenburg. Particularly thought provoking, however, were certain courses in social and theoretical psychology taken by him under the well-known Karl and Charlotte Buehler. Owing to suggestions made by the former he was able to secure requisite material for the experimental work of measuring the effect of "set" upon unconscious processes involved in perception. It was Karl Buehler, too, who commented that it was singularly inspiring to see an American psychologist who would attempt to combine the European philosophical with the typically American methods of research in a study of personality and attitudes.

In recent years Father Herr has been engaged in the teaching of social psychology at Loyola University, Chicago, where his own students have proved highly cooperative in the preparation of material on leadership and group activities, as well as on the measurement of attitudes and personality. With this introduction, the reader may now find himself on intimate terms with the author in the study of a subject which we hope will be of common interest.

JOSEPH HUSSLEIN, S.J., PH.D.
General Editor, Science and Culture Series

St. Louis University
May 16, 1945

AUTHOR'S NOTE

The following explanations will help to make clear the arrangement of this book:

In Chapters 1 and 2 special attention is given to supplying a general background for such as desire to become better acquainted with the variety of psychological literature, and with the technical and philosophic aspects of social psychology itself.

Similarly, in Chapter 11, a fundamental exposition will be found regarding human nature and the qualities of human persons.

Chapters 3, 8, 9, and 10, were written chiefly to clarify the respective roles of emotion and reason, as presented in such interactions as may occur in language situations, in the formation of attitudes and not least of all in the relation between leaders and followers.

Finally, Chapters 4, 5, 6, and 7 definitely sketch the factors underlying all social learning, motivation, and emotionality. We shall here find that no little of man's actual social behavior might well be styled irrational and stereotyped. Moreover, no secure hope of changing this state of affairs exists outside an appeal to reasoned reflection and unselfish motives.

In addition, for the benefit of such as are interested in the application of psychology to modern educational and political problems, a critical bibliography of authors has been appended, arranged in chronological order. This method of presentation brings out quite clearly the fact that there is much disagreement among earlier psychologists, but that later writers pronouncedly tend to accord with one another.

The points on which the greatest uniformity of thought exists among our modern social psychologists are their acceptance of the principles of Gestalt psychology and their desire to expound a psychology based solely upon empirical evidence and experiment. Gestalt psychology, as is known, stresses the importance of the group rather than of the individual, and consequently aims at adjusting the social field so that the individual may react to it in a more desirable way. Criticism of this will be found in its proper place in the volume.

To the authors and publishers of literature cited in this book, the writer wishes to express his sincere appreciation for permission to do so. He is greatly indebted to Professor John J. Wellmuth, S.J., for invaluable literary and textual criticisms; to the Rev. Charles I. Doyle, S.J., for correcting the proof; and to Mr. James Royce, S.J., and Miss Mary Brimberry for preparing the manuscript and the index.

VINCENT V. HERR, S.J., PH.D.

Loyola University, Chicago
May 17, 1945

CONTENTS

CHAPTER 1

SOCIAL PSYCHOLOGY AND RELATED FIELDS

The Subject Matter of Social Psychology. Purpose and Objective of Social Psychology. Relation of Social Psychology to the Science of Ethics. Relation to Physical Science. Relation to Biological Science. Experimental Social Psychology. Kinds of Social Reactions.

THE SUBJECT MATTER OF SOCIAL PSYCHOLOGY

Social psychology deals with the individual in his relation to other human beings. General psychology studies the nature, actions, and habits common to all men. Social psychology uses the data of general psychology as a starting point but investigates the way in which actions and habits are modified by the social interaction of many individuals. Hence the subject matter for both general and social psychology is really the same; namely, the human being. The aspect or phase of this subject which is stressed in *social* psychology in contradistinction to *general* is man's way of reacting to other human beings. This particular way of reacting will usually account largely for the great individual differences between one person and another, or between groups of persons. When many persons possess a certain trait we are able to regard them as belonging to a class in regard to this one characteristic and so may study this class more intensively.

Whenever we compare many human beings with one another, certain basic similarities can be observed in all of them throughout the world. These similarities are the properties of the whole human race and may be considered the special field of general psychology. Thus, for instance, all human beings possess sensory powers by means of which they may become aware of external reality. They also possess inner bodily impulses or tendencies toward certain

1

biologically necessary or useful modes of action, such as eating, sleeping, and taking bodily exercise. Besides these powers and tendencies, all human beings possess in some degree the rational powers of judging and reasoning, deliberating and choosing between alternatives presented to them on the basis of their value or desirability. All these powers and their interrelations are studied in detail in general and rational psychology.

But in spite of the fact that all human beings possess the same fundamental rational nature, we shall find great differences both between individuals and between groups, not only in the degree to which their powers are developed, but also in the ways in which they make use of them under specified social conditions. Thus, one person may be retiring and timid, another may be naturally quite aggressive and communicative. We often call the latter kind of person an extrovert. Both these types of persons have been affected by the conditions of society, probably the same conditions, but in widely different ways. Both have built upon their native endowments a particular superstructure or system of habits which might be called their sociability, and this is one of the main topics to be dealt with in social psychology. The acquired sociability of both these types is to some extent the result of the interaction between many rational social beings in a particular time, place, and group. Thus the effect of the group life upon the individuals who compose the group becomes the secondary interest of the social psychologist. We study the process of socializing which the individual undergoes and try to understand in what sense this process is the consequence of group life upon the individual.

By group we mean more than one person, but not, of course, all the individuals in the world. And since a group is obviously made up of separate and different individuals, when we say that our interest lies in the group effect upon the individual, we do not mean to imply that this group is a sort of new person who takes hold of the individual and fashions him. On the contrary, separate individuals make the group what it is. We have, then, just as much right to speak of the ways in which an individual can affect his group as we have to speak of the effect of the group upon the individuals.

Various kinds of groups that might be studied are the family, the community, the state, and the school. Every situation wherein human means of communication are used is a fruitful field of investigation for the social psychologist. Where many individuals of the same age can be selected we have an opportunity of studying the effect of age level upon the social behavior of individuals. Thus we might also investigate the work group, the play group, the audience group, and the political group.

Social psychology studies the reactions of rational social beings upon one another in all the various ways possible to them. A man may react to the presence of an acquaintance by a friendly salutation or by silently snubbing him and passing on. He may react to the sound of an air-raid warning by preparing to seek shelter or by seeking to aid others in distress. He may react to an officer of the law by argument, apology, or by attempts to escape. In all these cases he is using in some way his sensory and rational powers against a background of social and emotional habits. Most of these habits are of immense importance to him, but they may escape his attention just because they are habits, and they are therefore the most difficult of all human reactions to understand fully.

PURPOSE AND OBJECTIVE OF SOCIAL PSYCHOLOGY

Our declared purpose is twofold. First of all we shall aim to discover by observation and generalization what uniform modes of behavior, mental behavior as well as external bodily behavior, characterize social beings as individuals who are at the same time members of a group. In order to do this we shall be obliged to consider the particular situations which were present when the particular behavior was manifested. Second we shall show how this knowledge may be useful in fostering and attaining the primary end of social groups of all sorts, namely, the real good of the individual and of the group. Armed with a true knowledge of the nature of man and of his tendencies, we can reasonably hope to be of assistance in improving his lot. We can suggest means of making him happier and more successful in business and in the home, and need not fear that our suggestions will be opposed to the final end of man, the full development of his true nature.

Our purpose is more than merely to aid the student in acquiring certain social abilities, such as a charming manner or social prestige. On the other hand, there seems to be no particular harm in thus aiding the student unless one were to urge upon all the unlimited pursuit of honors, wealth, and position regardless of the consequences of such actions. Some writers put down as the purpose of our study the attaining of social graces and the adjusting of oneself to the difficult circumstances encountered in everyday life. M. Krout, for instance,[1] insists that the student of social psychology should acquire aids to personal adjustment and certain social graces. Here he seems to be encroaching upon the fields of clinical psychology and mental hygiene. Perhaps he feels that his students may never take those courses and thus may profit in social psychology by the suggestions derived from them.

We prefer to limit our subject to the socializing process, calling attention to its peculiar difficulties as we go along. We shall be particularly cautious in the use of the term "adjustment." Perhaps the authors who use it mean what we do but it is not at all clear that they do. By adjustment we mean not only the ability to solve one's problems efficiently and readily but also the ability really to profit by them. And we must not forget that a human being does not profit by his reactions in the long run if they are immoral in themselves or injurious to the rights of others. In other words, some consideration for the true good or advantage of an individual must necessarily be made in discussing his adjustments. Then too, the good of the group may not be overlooked. Many writers disregard the real happiness or good of a person when they talk of adjustments. They talk as though man had no other purpose in life than to gain supremacy over others. They instruct their readers to solve their conflicts and become adjusted to their surroundings by avoiding friction and by removing their inhibitions. Some even state, ignoring the contradiction, that each individual should seek to get the most of personal advantages for himself in our competitive society, but that he should not make his personality disagreeable by too much aggressiveness. The dilemma is not always stated so baldly, but it is contained by implication in such advice as this: follow the approved conventions and do the thing which is expected, but see that you gain social prestige for yourself, if you can, without appearing to be too selfish.

RELATION OF SOCIAL PSYCHOLOGY TO THE
SCIENCE OF ETHICS

From what we have just said it ought to be evident that no study of social reactions in all their implications can be made without presupposing some reliable knowledge of the real end of the individual and of society. If the reader is not warned of this fact, he may get a false impression from our later discussions. Let him consider the consequences of ignoring the existence of the true nature and destiny of man and all that they imply in the moral order. The student of society who ignores or denies man's true purpose in life will grope about blindly in search of a norm or rule according to which human actions are to be judged. He may eventually decide that man's actions are suitable if society does not object to them, or if the person acting is fortunate enough to avoid being detected in actions of which others disapprove. In a word the student may get the impression that social behavior is well adjusted and desirable in the highest and best sense of the term, provided that no one around us finds fault with it.

This way of stating the meaning of the desirability of actions exposes the fallacy of those who, as a matter of fact, do not have any convincing ultimate norm or rule to guide their thought and action. Failing this, the only thing they can do to improve individuals is to tell them to make personal convenience or mere convention the deciding norm. According to these norms any kind of action which would not come to the notice of others or react unfavorably upon oneself could not be termed improper or unsuitable. To act for undue praise or to deceive others could not be called undesirable, unless it were engaged in to the detriment of self. Any impropriety which would not affect other persons or come to their attention would have to be considered suitable. Hence undetected transgressions of the moral order would not be transgressions.

It is the thesis of this book that the approval and disapproval of society are not the only norms for all behavior. Yet that they should be the only norms is the inevitable conclusion of those writers who scoff at philosophy and overlook the inherent value of man's inner aspirations and secret intentions. Such writers destroy the possibility of any universally binding norms of behavior in their scheme of

things. They make custom and convention the real norms of behavior and then hope to discover what conventions are useful in the
long run by cataloguing the various reactions of people in specific
situations called "stimulating."

We shall attempt to prevent any such misunderstandings on the
part of our readers by assuming at the outset that there is a true
and certain ethics which tells us wherein the real desirability or
morality of human acts consists. This discipline alone can dictate to
us the immutable moral principles which must guide all behavior.
Human behavior is more than bodily response to stimulations. There
are interior acts of free choice, and habits resulting from them. These
we possess in addition to the externally observable behavior patterns
which the scientists are able to describe.

With this preliminary warning we can transmit the further ethical
questions at issue and make our study of this one aspect of human
behavior, namely, its conventionality, our chief objective also. We
can ambition improvement according to conventional and socially
approved norms just as well as the other writers. In acting so, we
do not, as they often do, deny the existence of ethical principles, or
make them all relative to some particular time and place. Further,
we make no pretense of trying to discover the universal laws of
morality by a mere observation and report of the outward behavior
patterns of civilized and of uncivilized peoples. We assume that the
laws of morality which are general were discovered by man before
this. The differences in customs for this or that place do not touch
the arguments for a universal moral law and order.

RELATION OF SOCIAL PSYCHOLOGY TO
PHYSICAL SCIENCE

Much ink has been spilled over this question: can psychology or
any other social study be a science? The answer is that it all depends upon what is meant by the word *science*. Competent writers
today[2, 3] claim that the essence of any science is predictability. That
is to say, when we can predict with physical certainty just what will
occur in the future in regard to certain phenomena, then we may
have a science with regard to that group of phenomena. Thus it
appears that a study of the laws governing the sequence of events is
an essential feature of science. Knowing the laws we are able to

predict future events reliably. Thus, when we know that a change in temperature will contract or expand certain substances by given amounts, we can predict what contraction will occur in the various parts, say of a bomber, operating in the stratosphere. Of course, we need to know what temperature prevails there as well. Social scientists have at times expressed the belief that all human behavior takes place in just such a determined fashion. They then claimed that, given a full knowledge of the inner forces and motives of each person, and of the outer resistances which he encounters, they could treat all of his behavior as something to be predicted with mechanical accuracy. In a word they thought that they could predict men's actions and that therefore investigations of social behavior ought to be called science.

Now no scientist can predict and control all the actions of men in the same way in which the movements of physical bodies can be predicted. J. J. B. Morgan[4] says this is not possible because people intentionally deceive us as to their motives, and that they are really not aware of their true motives. On the contrary, the real reason for the unpredictability lies in man's freedom of choice. He always has and not infrequently exercises the power of determining his own course of action in ways known only to him. This does not mean that no predictions at all are possible. It may actually happen that man will act in a way which suggests the uniformity, and hence the predictability, of the actions of brute beasts or of inanimate objects. That is to say, a man may sometimes actually fall in line with the current manner of behavior of others, voluntarily or just mechanically. In either case an observer like a social psychologist could succeed in predicting future behavior from a knowledge of this uniformity. But if we take science to mean a body of laws which enables us to predict all the actions of men, then it is clear that social psychology can never claim the dignity of a science.

But we hear it objected that an economist, with experience of the trends of the times and of the character of a group of people, can generally predict, for example, when there will be a run on a bank or a boom. It is also said that labor leaders can predict the outcome of a called strike, students of geopolitics can predict the cycles of history, etc. These predictions will be true only in cases in which the dominant habit tendencies of the people in question are known to the observers. Hence the real problem for social psychology is to find out why and how people develop certain habits, notably those which make them amenable to the suggestions of others, liable to be caught in an epidemic of insecurity, or to be carried along with the tide of the times. Our problem is not to take away their freedom in any of these circumstances but to help them perfect it.

It is evident that no deterministic science of human behavior is possible, and no one knows this better than the leaders of governments. If all of man's actions were strictly determined and predictable down to the last act of each individual, then we would need no laws to regulate behavior and no courts to hunt out violators of the law. We could calmly sit down and watch the stream of behavior flow on. We do not in this treatise hold to the thesis so commonly proposed by others, namely, that man is determined by the two factors of heredity and environment. Man is able to determine himself, and in a very true sense it is he who will determine how his native endowments will be utilized in his own particular environment. This is merely saying that man, though free, needs to live out his existence among many other persons and things which will exert a certain directive influence upon him.

There is another legitimate meaning to be attached to the word *science*. A scientific study is one which is systematic, that is, based upon accurate observation and correlation of observed events. We shall use the word in this sense from now on, and need make no further assumptions as to what these correlations indicate in the way of establishing causal sequence. We believe that such observation and correlation will be profitable, simply because so much of our external behavior is of the conventional sort described above. But we are convinced that no deterministic science of human behavior is possible. And moreover science itself can never make a declaration as to what the moral value of man's actions should be. Strictly speaking, positive science should never approach the question of moral values. It should stick to the observable events in nature and aim to discover their connections. Deterministic science generalizes from the observed uniformities of the past. By studying what has happened, it can tell what will happen in the future in regard to physical events. It can never hope to discover what man's ideals and moral values ought to be.[5]

But it is hard to find social psychologists today who make any distinction between man's moral convictions and his habitual external behavior. Perhaps they, like Morgan, doubt the ability of any human being to discover and truthfully report his actual intentions and motives.[6] Some writers declare that science cannot deal with moral values,[7] while others aver that only science can arrive at the objective truth about anything.[8] If you inquire of them whether there are any moral principles or values which hold for all men at all times, they either answer in the negative or they equivocate. A few more audacious ones will also take pains to explain how moral consciousness has evolved quite naturally out of the superstitions, dreams, and fears of primitive peoples.[9] It rather appears to the writer that such scientists fear to face the fact of moral law and justify their apprehensions on the assumption that human nature is always changing in essentials.

It would seem that during periods of unrest in the world, many thinkers are inclined to reconsider their views about the ability of science to control the wishes and destinies of men. Soon after the beginning of World War II, *Scientific Monthly* published a series of articles on the relation of science to human values. In September of 1941 Professor Jensen of Duke University evidently felt constrained to refute the charge that science has been destructive of higher human values. He wrote: "Science as such is morally neutral. It has no concern with value. It is interested in quantities, not qualities. It only studies what is, not what ought to be. It can tell us only what is true, not what is right or good or wise or beautiful or holy. For knowledge of these things we should turn, not to the scientist, but to the philosopher."[7] This kind of statement is to be found often enough in the writings of unbiased scientists, rarely indeed in those of unreflecting psychologists and pseudo philosophers.

RELATION OF SOCIAL PSYCHOLOGY TO BIOLOGICAL SCIENCE

Here the relationship is the same as that between general psychology and biology. The human being is both a social being and a biological organism, though not merely a "food-consuming mechanism of thought," as the behaviorists claim. Man's needs must be supplied and his cravings for food satisfied through the use of substances taken from the material world. He feeds, clothes, shelters, and protects himself in order to survive. He establishes customs in these matters, formulates laws, and governs the distribution of material commodities as occasion demands. Such laws are necessary and useful, but often short-lived because of the changing nature of the environment and of fluctuations of supply and demand. Economic problems often give rise to problems of social behavior which are most puzzling. Changing economic conditions may lead to changes in conventional ways of behavior, especially in matters of food, dress, recreation, and work. Even man's real biological needs for food and clothing admit of many variations and in times of emergency he may be satisfied with rationing. Needs are artificially created when people set their hearts on a certain quantity or kind of commodity. Scarcity of materials or lack of suitable means of transportation can be responsible for the creation of new and peculiar customs, the development of new tastes with the older ones temporarily disappearing. Man's biological nature must therefore be recognized as a factor in giving rise to social stresses, but it cannot be separated from his life of thought and feelings adequately. Sometimes the material needs and satisfactions can be subordinated to other and nobler ends, and this shows that the conscious factors are at least as important as the biological ones in directing group behavior. A psychology which neglects to consider these conscious factors, the life of ideals and motives, will merely mumble meaningless platitudes when it recommends adjustment of needs to the available means of satisfying them.

EXPERIMENTAL SOCIAL PSYCHOLOGY

Is such a thing as experimentation possible in the matter of social processes? It all depends upon what meaning we attach to the word *experiment*. Experimentation differs from mere observation only in the fact that relevant conditions must be controlled. The same situation must be duplicated again and again and accurate reports of the average results must be made. All these precautions are needed in order to keep constant, as far as may be possible, the various factors which enter into the making of a social response. If we could keep all the factors, such as interest and attention, just the same through a series of tests or readings of scores, then we would be able to get an average which is reliable for a given set of conditions. Thus we might wish to see if the mere presence of a second person in the room will change the performance of a child who is trying to solve a puzzle. The record of the time taken for the solution, before and after the introduction of another person, would give us some indication of the effect of this new person upon the child, provided we can assume that all the other contributing factors in the child's make-up remained the same.

But can we duplicate social events and control all the factors which enter into the process of reacting socially to other persons? Obviously we cannot, but we can control some of them, or we can allow for those which we are unable to control. We can systematically study those situations which are similar enough to justify calling them repetitions, and we can put individuals into them who are of equal intelligence, training, and age. Then the differences in their performance can be ascribed to the peculiar way in which they react to the new situation, the presence of other persons. The most reliable results concerning the facilitating effect of the group upon individuals, and the cooperative or competitive tendencies of types of individuals have come to us from this method of approach. Strict procedures of this nature have already done much to eliminate guess work and to dispel ignorance with regard to many social reactions. Of course, it goes without saying that we cannot duplicate mobs, strikes, and panics in our laboratories. Nor can we fully penetrate into the depths of personality structure, or compel a person to manifest his naïve spontaneous tendencies under conditions of laboratory experiment.

The Murphys and Newcomb have given us[10] a good account of the advantages and limitations of laboratory methods in social psychology. But, as we shall see, strict laboratory procedure, joined with the techniques of the statisticians, has given us very reliable results in studies of attitudes and interests. Applied psychologists today expect the same degree of success in the matter of trait measurement as has accompanied the measurement of intelligence. Their expectations have not yet been fully realized, but fortunately they do recognize the fact that intelligence alone is not sufficient to guarantee success in business for anyone. Hence many present-day employers would like to have the personnel directors fully equipped to classify their workers according to social as well as intellectual accomplishments. The ability of the directors to do this will depend upon the success attained in the statistical analysis of data regarding personality, attitudes, interests, and special aptitudes. Special tests for all these things have been and are being perfected, and there is reason to hope that, after enough subjects have been tested, they will be able to take more effective measures to fit persons into a profession or occupation. There is some hope also that these methods will be of service in breaking down prejudices between races and persons of different religions, economic levels, or education.

KINDS OF SOCIAL REACTIONS

In this introductory chapter we shall sketch only those broad headings under which all social responses may be subsumed. Our division is not meant to be either clear cut or essential to the understanding of a given reaction. It merely gives us a convenient means of classifying actions. There are the external or overt responses, and the internal or secretly mental (implicit or covert) responses. Examples of external reactions would be talking, gesticulating, or fighting, or all together. The internal responses are not so easy to describe because they are chiefly subjective, that is to say, they are capable of being looked at only by the person who has them. They include attitudes of all kinds, the secret thoughts, opinions and convictions, desires and sentiments of a person. The attitudes or the habitual frame of mind of a person are of great importance in any study of the individual in relation to others.

Examples may show what is meant by a mental or implicit response. One may have witnessed a lynching scene. His external response may be the very action of remaining at the scene, of pushing others aside to get a better view. The mental response might well be a decision to take stern measures to prevent such abuses in the future. One may have suffered some reverses of fortune in regard to his investments. Besides buying a cheaper car and home, he will ponder ways and means of safeguarding his property in the future. He might find himself developing a friendlier attitude toward persons of the middle class, as well as habits of greater economy and thrift. Again, one may be driving along a broad boulevard when someone crowds him into the curb. His mental response may be first anger, then remorse for similar offenses of his own in the past, or revenge for the personal insult with supreme confidence in his own faultless manner of driving. The external response will probably be to run up and scold the other party. Thus overt gross behavior at any given moment will depend upon the inner tendencies and impulses which may have escaped the attention of the person himself in the past. Much confused thinking in psychology arises from the fact that "internal" responses are often looked on as being merely "inside the body." Actually a person may not know himself whether there is response in body or mind or both, and hence the distinction is valueless unless we restrict the meaning of "internal" to mental or conscious.

Another way of responding to situations is to pause and to react to the present situation negatively, so to speak; that is, to turn our attention to something else. This method is often the best one, especially when we are inclined to be emotionally upset. One could scarcely say, for example, that a person is really responding to the teasing situation, if that person realizes that a show of anger would only aggravate the annoyance and then calmly turns his mind to thoughts of his own. Dale Carnegie, popular writer on problems of personality, recommends such pauses for reflection in all cases in which impulsive action has been harmful in the past. Spiritual writers tell us that deliberation and anti-impulsive decisions are in order whenever an ingrained undesirable habit has to be overcome.

Both external and internal responses may be either sudden or else delayed for various lengths of time. This is the modern technical way of saying that sometimes we ponder and think out a course of action; sometimes we begin to act or continue to act unreflectingly for a long time because of some habit formed in the remote past. The best instances of sudden reactions are to be found in the so-called irrational actions of the excited mob or gang. Slower or delayed reactions are generally the result of deliberation, desire, opinion, and conviction. Then too, one may possess emotional tendencies of which he is unaware and hence do nothing to change them. In this case the emotional habit, once formed, may be accountable for much seemingly irrational behavior. Thus we see clearly that all the inner and outer responses of any persons are complexly related to each other and to the situations which we call stimulations to response. Judgments and decisions can and do result in the formation of definite inner tendencies. The emotions, when inadvertently attached to a certain way of thinking and acting, can render much thinking faulty and ineffective. There are emotionally toned opinions and convictions which are more unreasonable than the irrational behavior of mobs or of infants. A fuller study of social interactions of all these sorts must be made later.

A theoretical classification of all reactions may again be made into those of one person upon another person, those of a person upon a group, and those of the group upon the person. This last kind of reaction includes what is known as public opinion. In practice we never know whether the total effect of a given reaction stops with one person or extends to the whole community. Gossip and rumors make it possible to extend the reaction indefinitely. Public officials need to be reminded that their actions may elicit reactions from persons far removed in time and space. Their reaction to the just criticisms of their charges is as important for the good of society as the reaction of the subjects to the officials. The inferiors can be censured for their behavior, but the higher official is less easily checked. Since he has been chosen to serve the needs of others, he at least must be able to plan future projects coolly, deliberately, and effectively, no matter what may be the disturbed sentiments of the masses.

FOR ACCELERATED READING

SHORT SUMMARY OF THE CHAPTER

Social psychology deals with human interactions and the differences existing in types of reactions. It considers group similarities, and the effects of group action on individuals and the reverse.

The *purpose* is to find uniformities in behavior tendencies for given situations. It will outline certain desirable goals or objectives for group and individual striving. It should help the reader to make profitable as well as efficient adjustments to his social environment.

Social psychology has a necessary connection with *ethics* because suitable or approved reactions are not the only desirable ones for a rational human being. Relativists in morals think that different groups prescribe the desirable reactions for a given time and that there is no invariable norm of morality binding on all human beings. Our study will avoid passing judgment upon the morality of certain actions, but supposes that there is a norm of morality.

Certain methods proper to the *physical sciences* may be used in social psychology, but prediction of future events is never very reliable in the latter discipline. This study can systematically correlate uniformities of behavior and describe apparent tendencies, but it cannot and should not try to control human behavior in the sense of dictating moral values.

Social psychology is related to *biology* because social needs overlap with biological needs. Conscious processes are involved in regulating bodily needs.

Certain types of *experiment* are profitable in this study because the results indicate a more objective treatment of facts than would casual observations. Many social situations cannot be duplicated in laboratories. Social reactions are given tentative *classifications*.

Find Review Questions and Supplementary Reading at the end of the book.

CHAPTER 2

METHODS OF INVESTIGATION

Historical Antecedents — Earliest Investigations; Later Agreement as to Proper Methods; Requirements for a Satisfactory Method. *Some Special Techniques* — Skill in Observation and Report; The Case History; The Interview and the Questionnaire; Rating Scales. *Serviceable Mathematical Concepts, Their Interpretations* — Correlation — The Mean and Its Deviation.

HISTORICAL ANTECEDENTS

EARLIEST INVESTIGATIONS. The effect of the group on individual behavior was one of the earliest phenomena to be investigated in a separate branch of study called social psychology. In 1860 Steinthal and Lazarus postulated a "group mind" as the carrier of that intangible all-pervading unity of spirit proper to a race or people. Suggestion was studied systematically by Braid, from 1841 to 1860. Psychologists paid little attention to his findings, even after Binét and Feré had used them successfully for the treatment of hysteria and loss of memory. Probably workers like Braid were suspected of dealing in occult science, as were the followers of Mesmer. But Braid soon showed experimentally that there was nothing mysterious about either suggestion or hypnotism.[1] He reduced both these phenomena to the simpler one of attention. He showed that during a state of fixed attention automatic responses of various sorts would be made when certain actions were suggested. Braid was the first to secure recognition by the medical profession for this type of work. It was not until 1890 that Tarde and LeBon, the real founders of social psychology, utilized the knowledge that had accumulated thus far in a study of imitation as a factor in crowd behavior and in popularizing the concept of the "Group Mind." Unfortunately subsequent writers were too much inclined to apply to all kinds of suggestion and imitation the principles which LeBon had derived from a study of morbid clinical cases and the revolutionary behavior of groups.

In 1908 William McDougall redirected the minds of social psychologists to the important problem of instincts. He believed that human behavior could be fully explained by establishing the existence of certain innate mainsprings of action or instincts. He was never quite sure about the number of these instinctual-emotional inner endowments and changed his views about them very frequently when confronted with adverse criticisms. From the time of his book until the publication of Knight Dunlap's criticisms in 1918 and later, a long and fierce debate ensued on the now famous question of instincts. Since 1918 there seems to be agreement that the concept of instincts should be dropped and the concept of motive or drive be put in its place. There is agreement also on the fact that both innate and acquired properties (nature versus nurture) are important, and that the exact proportion of each cannot be determined because it is probably not a fixed quantity. Some writers even state that the whole question is futile, but in our opinion there will always be an intense desire on the part of human beings to know just which abilities are born in them and which are not.[2]

Much of the bad feeling against social psychologists in general has been occasioned by this dispute over instincts. Although the sociologists had no more convincing answer to give than had the psychologists on the questions of instincts and of heredity versus environment, they soon parted company with the psychologists and built up their own working concepts. These were heavily weighted with the notions of motive, attitude, drive, and adjustment.[3] All of these processes were said to be active only in relation to a particular environment, and thus utterly dependent upon training and tradition. The sociologists have generally agreed with the psychologists in an attempt to eliminate the concept of purpose or finality from all study of human behavior. Along with purpose went the concept of rational motive and will, since both were said to involve metaphysical difficulties which were insoluble. The sociologically minded psychologists now speak almost entirely about the effects upon the individual of environment and learning and adaptation to the ever changing conditions of society. They rarely if ever concern themselves with such factors as ideals, purposes, or rational convictions in shaping the course of change.

McDougall's chief lasting contribution to social psychology, apart from his attempt to defend purposive instincts, lay in the new emphasis placed upon the "Group Mind." This mystical or superindividual unifying principle or soul has evoked another series of disputes which would have been avoided altogether had the disputants agreed upon their definition of the nature of society and of the human individual. We shall discuss this important topic after studying group phenomena in general. The question is intimately linked up with speculations in Gestalt psychology, as well as with the applications of this brand of psychology to theories of government and of state.

LATER AGREEMENT AS TO PROPER METHODS. Cultural anthropologists took advantage of the unrest created by the instinct debate to further their own interests. They sponsored what is called the cultural or historical method for interpreting complex behavior patterns and social changes. For them the problem of social behavior becomes a matter of explaining social tradition among different peoples in terms of geographic diffusion of culture through learning, imitation, or independent invention. In general they consider that the original needs of human organisms are satisfied in a manner which is determined solely by the total environment. Thus they agree with the sociologists against the psychologists in stressing the role of acquired traits. Many of them revive the older concepts of Tarde and LeBon as explanatory principles. Some also accept without criticism the principles of Gestalt psychology and psychoanalysis. From the former they derived the notion that the group is primary and individuals count little if at all in social process; also the notion of a group-soul or higher generic unity creative of culture patterns, which must be studied in their entirety. In so doing one may not treat isolated elements of culture, such as religion or art, independently of the total culture complex. From the psychoanalysts they borrowed the notions of repression, conflict, and unconscious mind.[4, 5]

The ethnologists and anthropologists have not as yet reached an agreement on the basic problems of social change. They do not even seem to be sure of their basic facts. Witness the dispute as to whether primitive people suffer from repression resulting from social conflicts, or whether they are unrestricted in behavior and hence suffer no "nervous breakdowns."[6] Practically all the very modern authors minimize the role of individual action in social processes. LaPiere and Farnsworth, Britt, and Krout are instances of this tendency. In place of reason and choice they postulate attitudes and impulses, passive but adaptive response to the environment. Along with the rejection of reason goes the denial of a moral law binding on all and recognizable as such. Such authors assume without proof that social behavior is determined by the environment, acquired and transmitted through habit and custom and imitation, so that an appeal to history and the laws of learning will suffice for an understanding of all cultural process and change. A few follow Spengler in picturing the process as one of rises and falls, rhythms which no human being is able to change in the least. This plainly fatalistic doctrine leads to despair of ever bringing social trends into line with the inspirations and ideals of rational beings.

The present tendency of observers, as one may learn by studying the chronological list of authors at the end of this book, is to be anti-instinctivist, environmental determinists, with a weakness for seeing only the irrational or emotional (subconscious and unconscious) side of human nature as directive of all social process and change.[7] There is generally an appeal to the study of primitive peoples for a solution of the problem of morality and change of original customs. Klineberg, Krout, and LaPiere-Farnsworth do agree in allowing that this field has not yet been fully explored. There are still a few writers who reject environmental determinism, among whom may be mentioned Gurnee, Ewer, Bird, and L. G. Brown who is a character determinist.

THE ONLY SATISFACTORY METHOD AND ITS REQUIREMENTS. Bearing in mind the substantial unity of the human individual, that is, his essential constitution of physical body and spiritual soul, the methods of investigation become easy to outline. In the first place physiological conditions existing in a human being, such as the state of health, nutrition, and general efficiency, can modify his conscious and hence his social reactions. Such bodily conditions are also important in a study of the impulsive and emotional life of man. Also hereditary factors may play a part in supplying the bodily basis for, and in giving direction to, future development of social dispositions and temperaments. Hence whatever methods are needed to measure these bodily accompaniments of mental life in any individual become applicable also to a study of his external social reactions. We must never forget that body and soul are substantially united in one complete being and that our study of the bodily basis for behavior does not mean that we conceive of the body as actually cut off from the organization of the total man. It acts with and is perfected by the conscious life of man, and both together have to be socialized, because both taken as a unit make man a person and a responsible individual among many.

Second, patterns of interaction and changes in these patterns are known to exist among individuals of a group, where no ascertainable bodily or biological basis for them can be found. An example might be a declared attitude toward another race. Such patterns are not purely biological mechanisms, on the one hand, nor are they isolated conscious phenomena with no relation to physical organisms. They are action-patterns attributable to many separate responsible agents. The collective activity of many persons may result in attitudes which are rather characteristic of a whole group. Such mental activity is not to be explained in terms of the physiology of each individual organism, nor in terms of a separate group spirit or "group mind." Every attempt to explain conscious life in such terms is bound to lead to confusion of thought and to false conclusions in regard to what is desirable for man and for society. A. Myerson,[8] a neurologist, exemplifies this confusion of thought when he tries to reduce certain social phenomena to the social psychology of the nervous system.

Changes in the institutions, laws, language, styles, customs, beliefs, and attitudes of a group bear no known relation to conditions or changes in the nervous system of any individual. They arise and take their course because of the activities of human minds, although each individual mind will function always in dependence upon certain bodily needs. These changes, as well as the mental activities themselves, can be the subject matter for social psychology. The sum total of all the social mental processes of any group may be called the nonmaterial elements of a culture. These elements as manifested by a living group at a given time constitute what is often called the social milieu or social environment. This milieu places a certain limitation upon the action of individual minds, but at the same time it is capable of being modified by them, since it comes from them and not from chance or necessity. And there is no other way of finding out what constitutes the milieu than to investigate the mental character and accomplishments of the people of a given period as handed down through tradition. When we propose to make this investigation, we are compelled to describe and compare the public opinions, convictions, preferences, habits, and dispositions of *individuals,* as well as the factors which operate to produce them. And in so doing we may at times be able to predict what the majority of men will elect to do under given circumstances, for example, in a national election.

Human minds exist in human bodies, and both together exist in a physical and social environment as unified individuals. The complexities of their minds cannot be profitably studied by analyzing their bodies alone. We cannot tell why a man is a fascist, a protestant, or a liberal simply by examining his emotional and physical make-up or his reflexes. There are special methods required for such investigations. The culture-historical method of investigating traditions and culture complexes is legitimate in its place, but only in the event that the reported facts are reliable. The only method which can give permanent results is one which leaves room for human ideals, rational motives, and free choice, even though men do act emotionally often enough to justify a study of their habitual impulses and attitudes.

The social psychologist is concerned today mostly with the process by which the individual becomes socialized, not with the gross changes in the group, no matter what sociologists may think about the culture process versus culture change controversy. We must put down as exceptions those who do not believe that the individual really exists in his own right, but that only the group has reality (the Gestaltists). This latter type of investigator stresses the group reactions, hence the social changes or crises become the leading topic. This one-sided view of society and of the individual cannot be very acceptable to the people of a democracy and is perhaps merely a reaction against the exaggerated individualism of older writers. And in actual practice the Gestaltists in this country prefer to investigate the group attitudes by administering tests to separate individuals.

American writers like O. Klineberg[9] are wise in pointing out that the "elements" of a configuration or group, that is the persons, must not be lost sight of in our investigations, even though the totality of the group gives the individual certain characteristics by the mere fact of his belonging to it. Klineberg appears to have grasped the real meaning of Gestalt philosophy in its relationship to theories of state.

Hence the immediate object of investigation in social psychology is the individual and the processes whereby he becomes socialized. This object specifies the methods to be applied. The individual becomes socialized (not humanized, as some writers say) when he utilizes and expresses the group patterns of thought and action in his own life, builds up his own typical mental attitudes, takes part in the group life, and makes his own little addition to the achievements of the group. In doing this he will make use of his native endowments and tendencies, modifying these in various ways by his own thought and decision. Ultimately he may become so formed or established in certain stereotyped ways of behaving that the psychologist is able to classify his traits and those of his group. Our study, then, of the process of socialization will include three main aspects of the individual: (1) his learning in social situations; (2) his instinctive and emotional tendencies under the influence of group life; (3) his own individual make-up with all the special habits, powers, and attitudes which characterize him in his group. In making this study it will be necessary to use some special techniques or tools of investigation.

SOME SPECIAL TECHNIQUES

CAREFUL OBSERVATION AND REPORT. Any student of human beings must possess or acquire skill in making accurate and unbiased observations, and in discounting factors which are irrelevant to the question in hand. Nor should whim or caprice dictate which factors are significant. There must be planning in advance, lest energy be wasted in collecting details which are useless. The accurate reporter gives such an account of an action or event that this account can be verified by another independent observer who has simultaneously made the same observation. In laboratory terms we say that the report must be so clear that any other observer could set up an identical situation and make the same observation without fail. This technique requires some practice and patience because we all tend to omit little details from our accounts of simple occurrences. The perception tests in the "test your facts" columns show us how easy it is to overlook salient features in describing an event such as an accident.

An example from a study of group behavior will illustrate what is meant by this first requirement. Suppose we wish to discover whether "razzing" has any effect upon mental performance. We must take care to have a standard task to be performed and scored. We must have a control group and an experimental group both of which are equal in mental ability. And we must produce the razzing in exactly the same way for all individuals in the experimental group. Lastly we must try to eliminate the element of individual competition in both groups by telling each individual that the group score alone will be made use of.

All this may be summed up by saying that every experiment in social psychology should be conducted according to the principles laid down for scientific induction. These rules reduce to the following: keep all the factors which enter into a situation constant (the test itself, the mental ability, attitudes, etc.), then vary only one factor at a time (introduce razzing in the above example) for the experimental group. The carrying out of this procedure will require the skills of observation mentioned above. An unskilled observer might fail to notice, for example, that some of the individuals in the experimental group were so angry that they did not try to make any score at all. This "negative" behavior would vitiate the results of the whole experiment.

The collection of data may seem a tedious process to a beginner in psychology, but it is the only scientific way in which to get at the facts. The case which I have chosen as an example is put down by various authors as giving very different results, probably because of varying procedures in the situation and because of the uncontrollability of certain factors such as the attitude of cooperation with the experimenter. It is well to notice here that we may sometimes wish to know merely the fact that there is such and such an effect, without inquiring into the reasons for the occurrence. After a number of similar observations have been made in which similar results have been obtained, speculators may begin to suggest reasons for what has been observed to happen.

It is unfortunate that so many of the so-called scientific observations and reports in the past have not been accurate. This is particularly true as regards the behavior of excited groups and of primitive peoples. Accounts are published pretending to give us the last word on the intelligence, customs, and attitudes of the group and these reports are contradicted by later observers.[10] If the full nature of the test given or the exact conditions under which customs had been observed were reported by each observer, the literature dealing with primitive man and mobs would be less extensive but much more reliable.

THE CASE HISTORY. This tells us the salient features in the life and times of the person whose social behavior is being investigated. Such histories are worse than useless if the writer does not or cannot obtain the facts. Accurate reporting of facts involves skill in perceiving as well as in narrating. It presupposes a sincere desire to include all relevant features whether they fit in with the expectations of the observer or not. Artistic biographies are open to suspicion from a factual point of view because of the writer's intention to make his account attractive. In these biographies and sometimes even in a report card written for a student in school, we often find what is called the "halo" effect. This means that the reporter has judged, intentionally or otherwise, that because a person is skilled in *some respects* (a good athlete or organizer) he must also be excellent in *all others*. Seeing that even conscientious instructors are liable to such inaccuracy, what are we to expect of social observers? In many cases a word of caution is sufficient to prevent further errors in this regard. An instructor, for instance, will do well to correct papers without knowing the names of the persons. It has happened that the mere image in the instructor's mind of the amiability and attractiveness of a student have resulted in an undeserved score. Objective tests are supposed to aid in overcoming this subjectivity in scoring success in schoolwork.

The life or case history method is of special utility in studying the childhood growth of faulty or troublesome social habits. This method is the only substitute for rigidly controlled experiment. One can study an individual at different times and keep a complete report of the changes from day to day. In this way, for example, a nurse or a mother can ascertain whether a child comes up to the level of the average child in such social abilities as speaking, accepting responsibilities, cooperating with others, and avoiding emotional disturbances.

Clinical psychologists, of course, need to collect all available information about a given person before attempting to give him any helpful suggestions. Today, as never before, persons who suffer from emotional difficulties, or who are a cause of trouble in the home or school environment owing to their stubbornness and irritability, are appealing for help to the clinicians. Since an accurately written life history is seldom to be had in these cases, recourse must be had to batteries of tests and to the written reports of parents, teachers, and social agencies. Care must be taken to discover the presence of physical disabilities which might predispose to problem behavior, and tests are available covering most human abilities from intelligence through mechanical skills to aptitudes and interests. In addition, accurate reports will be made by social workers on home conditions, parent-child relations, and group reactions among the children themselves. All of these reports demand great accuracy which often comes only after years spent in the laboratory, lecture room, and guidance center. The final interpretation of all these data, and the use which is made of them in recommending a change in behavior, require the services of many persons. These persons must be trained not only in the sound principles of experimental social and clinical psychology, but must also and especially have a philosophy of life which is based upon a recognition of the rational nature of man.

THE INTERVIEW AND THE QUESTIONNAIRE. As an aid to clinicians and personnel workers, standardized forms for interviews have been devised. The interviewer is expected to fill in the answers accurately after securing the data from the subject. A skilled interviewer will, however, get a deeper insight into the needs of his client if he uses the printed form only as a guide to his questioning, and then proceeds to converse quite informally on various topics. He must, unless his memory is prodigious and the interview is short, make written notes throughout the talk, for the blank forms merely supply a plan of reminders as to the essential questions to be asked. Most clinical subjects require prudent and delicate treatment in order that their real needs may be detected and suitable advice may be given them. The interviewer for vocational guidance requires, in addition, a keen insight into the motives, interests, and character of the client. He must also be well informed on the kinds of occupations available at a particular time and place.

Closely allied to the questionnaire is the self-inventory as a means of studying social personality. It has been used most extensively and successfully in personality studies and in some investigations of attitudes. The Woodworth Personal Data Sheet was designed during the last war and has been subsequently perfected and standardized. In the hands of competent psychologists, this and other personality inventories can prognosticate with high probability whether or not a prospective soldier will come through the emotional hazards of war unscathed. Inventories are useful when a large number of raters or interviewers cannot be readily secured.

The above devices are convenient tools for collecting material quickly, but great caution must be observed in interpreting the material thus gathered. After all, we cannot assume that every person is always truthful to the highest degree in filling out a form, especially if he fears that he has something to lose in so doing. Also, he may be mistaken about certain facts and is thus incapable of giving accurate information. Many persons are apt to take a "none-of-your-business" attitude toward the agencies which send out questionnaires and may fill them out fictitiously, to the great chagrin of the investigator. Both case histories and self-inventories should, whenever possible, be checked for truthfulness by reference to independent sources. When there is question of personality traits, the subject may not be altogether certain about his own inner self. He may have deceived himself into thinking that he is popular, peculiar, etc. In these cases there seems to be no way of making test items reliable.

Inventories do tend, in spite of all these limitations, to get below the surface of a person's habits and pretenses, perhaps because they make him think seriously about himself for the first time. They tend to reveal the deeper intricacies of his attitudes and desires. Their weakness lies chiefly in the fact that a clever person can sometimes answer the questions in such a way that others will judge him to be what he knows they wish him to be. It has been alleged that almost the only conclusion which can be drawn from the questionnaire reports of sophisticated persons is whether and to what degree they are sophisticated. We think this is an overstatement, for persons who really desire assistance from a personnel worker or clinician because of some actual need will reveal in their answers how they actually think, feel, and would like to act in certain situations.

RATING SCALES. These are the most commonly used modern tools for investigating personality and attitudes. They may be employed by others to evaluate one's personal traits, such as generosity, friendliness, or popularity; they may be used by the person himself, and then they are called self-rating scales. The principle of the rating scale is the same as that of the grade sheet or report card. Instead of scoring pupils from 0–100 per cent, the rater evaluates a given individual in respect to a certain quality. Today industrial managers often wish to have ratings of the prospective employees made by their college superiors. The various instructors and directors who were well acquainted with the person are asked to rate him. From several independent ratings a fairly accurate estimate may be made. Of course, the raters must all understand the terms of the scale in the same sense, otherwise the data will be worthless. Obviously, too, the results cannot be relied upon if the set of raters do not agree among themselves at all. An extensively used scale of this type is here reproduced with modifications.[11] It forms part of H. Fletcher's Personality Rating Sheet for Freshmen.

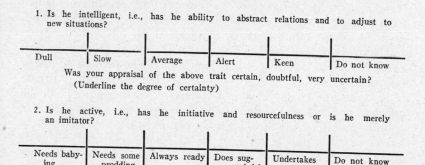

1. Is he intelligent, i.e., has he ability to abstract relations and to adjust to new situations?

Dull	Slow	Average	Alert	Keen	Do not know

Was your appraisal of the above trait certain, doubtful, very uncertain? (Underline the degree of certainty)

2. Is he active, i.e., has he initiative and resourcefulness or is he merely an imitator?

Needs babying	Needs some prodding	Always ready	Does suggested job	Undertakes projects anew	Do not know

Was your appraisal certain, doubtful, very uncertain? (Underscore.)

3. Is he emotional, i.e., all nerves, excitable, unstable?

Irascible, moody, apathetic	Somewhat unresponsive	Well balanced	Composed generally	Always controlled	Do not know

Was your appraisal certain, doubtful, very uncertain? (Underscore.)

4. Is he a leader, i.e., does he get cooperation with prudence and energy?

Just a follower	Tries to influence others	Usually successful	Inspiring at times	Always able to organize	Do not know

Was your judgment certain, doubtful, very uncertain? (Underscore.)

The rater is simply asked to place a check mark on the appropriate horizontal line at that position which represents his evaluation of the student, and to rate himself on his convictions. From such data the student may be compared with other students or applicants and some opinion formed of his qualifications. A psychograph or psychological profile chart is a much more complete description of the subject. It gives his relative standing or percentile ranking with respect to thousands of others in regard to such traits as emotional stability, self-sufficiency, extroversion, dominance, sensory discrimination, mathematical ability, science, and social abilities.

Rating scales are easily and quickly handled, but errors creep into their application when the rater does not answer truthfully. In the long run, however, evaluations obtained by means of rating scales can hardly be considered more unreliable than those obtained from a single letter of recommendation written by a favorite friend, or from a single rating made by the dean of the school.

There are at least four or five special techniques for rating, each of which has its advantages and limitations. The method of *paired comparisons* gives the person a standing merely in reference to those in his own little group. Thus in a fraternity, each member might be asked to compare each individual with every other one in regard to popularity. If John is rated as more popular than any one else, or let us say, less unpopular, then we at least know what his little group of admirers think of him. Usually John is not asked to include himself in the list of comparisons, lest he be tempted to show too much humility or the opposite.

Then there is the *order-of-merit* method. This consists of listing all the members of a group in order, with the most approved, let us say the most congenial, at the top and the least congenial at the bottom, all the rest being placed somewhere in between. Such a method is difficult because one finds it almost impossible to keep all the individuals in mind while making the comparison. This method also gives the person a relative standing, namely, in regard to his own little group. It is one of the principal methods used in constructing attitude scales and is quite reliable in the hands of experts.

SERVICEABLE MATHEMATICAL CONCEPTS INTERPRETED

CORRELATION. Correlation in general means mutual relationship between two things. In psychology it means a relationship between two traits, skills, or behavior tendencies. In personality studies we can designate the tendency of two traits to accompany each other, that is, to go together all the time, in the same individual, by finding the degree or coefficient of correlation between them. To compute a correlation it is necessary to have *two sets of scores* for the same group of individuals. Each and every person in the group must have two scores or ranks, one in each of the traits to be correlated. And in social psychology it is possible to find the correlation not only between two skills or traits but also between any two activities or processes *which admit of being scored*. Thus we may find the correlation between body size and intelligence, or between emotional stability and vitamin content of food, or between endocrine function and sociability.

This tool has been much used by social psychologists in trying to predict human behavior or attitude trends in groups. Great caution is needed in attempting such predictions. They always presuppose knowledge of certain facts which is difficult to obtain. Prediction based upon the past or present behavior of human beings under certain specific circumstances cannot be valid unless those same specific circumstances remain unchanged. And we must also keep the following proviso in mind: that if human beings continue to act as they have acted in the past under a particular set of circumstances, then we may make safe predictions for these same conditions. This knowledge of the specific circumstances is most difficult to obtain. Yet it is necessary for a study of the uniformities in social trends.

For example, if children from rural districts make lower scores in the intelligence tests than children from urban areas, then we can be fairly certain that this will be the case in the future, provided conditions such as opportunity for self-improvement and recreation remain the same. We must assume that the children will continue to use these available means in the same way that they did in the past. But we cannot tell, by the mere fact of correlation alone, whether one of the correlated events is the cause of the other, or if so, which one is the cause and which is the effect. It follows from this that when correlations have been used in correctly predicting future behavior, there is no need to suppose that the activities thus predicted were determined in such a way as to preclude human freedom. Thus, correlation between two events, however perfect it may be, does not prove causal connection between them. On the other hand, a high correlation which is consistently observable under certain circumstances makes it possible and even advisable to look for the causes responsible for this constancy or uniformity.

Correlation is not a mysterious or profound device invented to terrorize students and so prevent further investigation. Most of the disputes that have arisen in psychology about human behavior and its prediction center around the various *interpretations* which have been placed upon correlations. Correlation, as applied to actions and traits, simply means the tendency for the *same person* to have a relatively high (or low) score in several traits measured, that is to say, high rank among all other persons who have been similarly tested for these same traits. Many persons may be rated thus in regard to physical, mental, or even moral qualities, provided we can give them all a score in each of these traits.

We can even rank persons according to the kind and number of garments which they wear. Thus it may be said that people living farther from the equator wear heavier clothing than those who live near the equator. The farther they live north or south of the equator, the heavier is their clothing. There is a high positive correlation between weight of garments and distance from the equator. No one would be justified in concluding from this correlation that the only reason why people wear clothes is because they live at a distance from the equator. The experience of cold at a distance from the equator is probably one very good reason for using clothes for protection. But the correlation alone does not imply that it is a reason, still less that it is the only reason.

This example is intended to show the usefulness and the limitations of correlations in describing trends of activity. In general it may be said that the freely cultivated habits — love of variety and styles — of certain individuals are the things which most frequently upset predictions about human behavior.

Numerical values may be attached to the degree of going-together of two traits. To take an example, suppose that all the political leaders were found to have intelligence quotients above the average for the population in general. The fact of their being in office allows us to designate them as leaders, and the inference is that they are also above the average in leadership ability. It would then be true to say that leadership and intelligence are positively correlated with each other. The same persons tend to be high in both intelligence and leadership. The two traits seem to go together in this group of persons. But suppose that just the reverse had been the case; the politicians were below the average for the general population on the intelligence tests. Then there would be negative correlation between intelligence and the leadership ability which we assume to be the same as before, namely high. An easy rule for the reader is this: when two skills or abilities are *positively* correlated, then those persons who are *high* in one quality tend to be *high* in the other; but when there is *negative* correlation, then those persons who are *high* in one skill tend to be *low* in the other skill. If the politicians had been of just average intelligence with high leadership ability, there would have been neither positive nor negative but *zero* correlation. This means that those persons who rank above the middle of their group in one trait will be evenly scattered all the way from low to high in the other trait. The decimals .01 and upward are used to indicate positive correlations, with plus 1.00 at the top for an imaginary perfect correlation. The decimals —.01 onward are used for negative correlations with —1.00 at the other extreme. The symbol "r" is universally used for these values. By means of suitable formulas they can be computed along with their probable errors. The probable error is important because it tells us how nearly a given value of "r" comes to being a thing of mere chance. Any correlation below .50 is rarely reliable in social psychology. Few traits have been found to correlate negatively.

THE MEAN AND ITS DEVIATION. The arithmetical mean of a series of scores is the average of all the individual scores in that series. The average deviation of the scores from this mean gives an indication of how well the scores cluster around the mean. It tells us how much scatter or dispersion there is among the individuals of the whole group in regard to a particular item. This latter point is important in comparing two means with each other, for the mean merely tells us the average, and unless we also know the degree of scatter we cannot discuss any two groups comparatively. Another name for the "mean" is central tendency. This term implies that the average does not remain constant from day to day. By comparing the mean score, say of a Latin class, for today with that for last month, we can ascertain whether the class is tending to make progress, without looking into the question of the individual scores.

The *mode* or the most frequently occurring score is a better indication of central tendency, and in the case of large groups, it is much easier to compute than the mean. When the distribution is normal, the mode and mean will coincide. In skewed distributions they will not coincide. Such a skewed distribution will contain a few individuals who deviate extremely from the mean. This large deviation will upset the normality of the distribution. We shall come back to this notion of normal distributions in discussing normal individuals and group differences.

The *median* is the middlemost measure in a group of scores arranged in the order of *size*. It has the fiftieth percentile score. It tells us that just as many persons have scored above this amount as have scored below it. It does not tell us anything about the average, but it is useful when there is question of small groups or of skewed distributions of scores. In both cases the few extreme deviations make the average a poor score to be taken as representative of the group. Centiles or percentile ranks are most extensively used when a relative rating is required. Thus a student who merits a percentile rank of 85 knows where he stands relatively to a certain group in a given trait. He knows that his score is the point below which 85 per cent and above which 15 per cent of the other cases fall.

The mean with its average deviation is often used in predicting events in group behavior. For instance, if all students at a given university taken as a whole were tested for contentedness, we could compare the average score with that made by other college students in a similar test. If the group we are considering ranked low in this trait, we might safely predict that the administration will take some action. We may safely assume that faculties do not habitually desire to have their students discontented. The prediction has validity because the college authorities do in fact have this particular attitude toward harmony among the student body.

But suppose one department of the school, say psychology, scored 90, and the sociology department scored 45. This difference appears great, but how can we tell when the difference is great enough to mean anything to the authorities, who aspire to 100 per cent contentedness in the whole school? We can do so by computing the average deviations of the individuals in each group from the means of their respective groups. By applying suitable formulas (cf. any textbook on statistics for the difference between two means), we learn when the differences are indicative of a condition uniformly prevalent in a group.

In order to see at once whether two means differ significantly, we need only plot the distribution of the scores for the two groups taken together. Such a graph or distribution curve shows at a glance whether there are two central tendencies at work in the group. Another name for this graph is the frequency polygon or histogram (bar graph).

When the distribution curve shows two humps, one near either end, with a deep dip toward the base line in the middle, then there are most likely two subgroups each of which has a mean score significantly different from that of the other. When no separate humps are evident, the curve may resemble the normal probability curve in shape. Since the probability curve is produced empirically by letting only one factor operate, namely, chance, we may take the probability curve as a norm for comparison. But we must remember that "chance" is not the only unitary factor which can give a normal bell-shaped distribution curve.

For Accelerated Reading

SHORT SUMMARY OF THE CHAPTER

The *origins* of social psychology in studies of hypnotism, suggestion, and mob psychology point to an interest in group effects, and lead to disputes about the relative potency of the environment versus hereditary endowments.

Anthropological-minded students stress the environment and geographic diffusion of culture; explain all social learning as an adaptation to a changing environment. Social behavior may often appear irrational but any *method of investigation* which ignores the individual contribution to the changes in institutions and customs is heavily weighted with environmentalism and group-mind fallacy.

A satisfactory method will allow for native physical traits, gradual acquisition of attitudes under the influence of the group, and individual direction of the whole learning process through rational thought and volition. The individuals constitute the social environment and express group behavior but no special entity called group mind exists to determine all their actions in advance.

Some *essential techniques* of investigation are accurate and objective accounts of events, systematically varying one factor at a time in the experiment, interviews, inventories, and personality scales.

The minimum *mathematical requirements* are an understanding of the method of correlation, or of finding what goes with what; of the notion of the mean and central tendency for comparing groups and for observing group changes in characteristics which can be scored. These two concepts show us uniformities, and challenge us to predict behavior.

Find Review Questions and Supplementary Reading at the end of the book.

CHAPTER 3

THE GROUP AND ITS BEHAVIOR

Regarding Groups in General — The Group and Group Classifications; The Exaggerated Groupists. *Typical Developmental Stages* — Statistical Groups and Expected Behavior: (I) The Infancy Stage; (II) The Childhood Level; (III) The Age of Adolescence; (IV) The Mature Age; (V) Old Age or Senescence. *Transitory Groups, Their Leader* — General Aspects of These Groups; Special Aspects: The Boom, Crazes and Epidemics, Fads, The Crowd, The Audience, The Co-active Group, The Nation, The Group Mind; The Role of the Leader.

REGARDING GROUPS IN GENERAL

THE GROUP AND GROUP CLASSIFICATIONS. By a group we mean a number of individuals interacting upon one another and manifesting some common form of behavior. Groups have been divided into *primary* or face-to-face groups such as the family, and *secondary* groups such as the race, nation, and crowd. In the secondary groups the contact between the members is less immediate, as in the nation, or less enduring, as in the casual crowd, or both together, as in the political party.

Cooley's original division of groups into primary and secondary has recently been superseded by a fourfold division into: (1) *intimate* groups, such as husband and wife, or lovers; (2) *primary* groups such as the family, the fraternity, or play group; (3) *intermediate* groups, such as clubs, denominational and professional groups; and finally (4) *secondary* groups such as races and political parties. Using this division, particular features of each type of group may be compared with those of each of the other types. Thus the frequency of contacts, the various types of sensory contact, the emotional intensity of contacts, and the degree of interdependence

35

among members may be compared. The first three kinds of groups
alone have direct perceptual contacts; the frequency of contacts
varies from almost continuous contacts in the first to very rare contacts in the last type; the emotional intensity of interrelations
varies from the deepest personal kind in division one, through in-
formal but superficial attachments in divisions two and three, to the
impersonal formal or unemotional relations of division four. This
plan of groupings is more practical than any yet devised because it
allows of a crude sort of measurement of the various interactions
present. It does not provide for the casual crowd, audience, or mob,
and hence these types of group behavior have to be subsumed under
some other arbitrary heading.

The division into primary and secondary groups does not coincide with another and earlier division into *in-groups* and *out-groups*.
This latter division was based almost entirely upon the existence of
emotional or preferential bonds among the members of one group
as opposed to other out-group members. It is still of some value in
explaining the unreasonable attitudes and prejudices which frequently arise in fraternity and denominational groupings to disturb
harmonious relations between the members. It may also be considered useful in discussing the basic factors of conflicting group sentiments. Thus a group of descendants of foreign-born parents may
feel itself not too well received either by the older group of foreigners
or by the younger group of their native-born contemporaries. They
are then likely to get together and commiserate with one another on
their misfortune. They do not feel that they belong either to the
in-group of the elders or to that of the youth and may thus form
attitudes which render them socially unhappy, if not actually rebellious against authority and convention alike. Failure to resolve this
in-group out-group conflict is said to be responsible for much of the
delinquency among the first generation of foreign-born parentage in
our country.

Strong in-group attitudes also tend to make people ethnocentric,
that is, unduly impressed with the exclusive superiority of their
own group and of all its members. This feeling of superiority may
also be noted among members of fraternities, religious professions,
and racial groups.

THE EXAGGERATED GROUPISTS. The Gestaltists (in America

represented by R. H. Wheeler and his school) and the topologists (notably K. Lewin and J. F. Brown),[1] object to attempting a division of groups either geographically or historically. On the ground that all groups are but functional organizations or total configurations of force, they argue that the structure of the group-as-such is to be made the chief object of scientific investigation. They aim at discovering the exact nature of the vector forces, or dynamic attractions and repulsions, which are active between the individuals of any group, in order finally to discover those typical responses which characterize behavior in typical situations. They hope to infer, from the situational or goal-directed responses of many individuals in a group which prescribes the goals, the universal laws of human social nature. Such laws, they maintain, will transcend the limitations of time and space and will describe the factors that are really responsible for such disturbances of equilibrium between members and the group as foster wars and crimes of all sorts.

At least one system of philosophy, that of St. Thomas, has already worked out these universal laws from a study of the essentials of human nature all over the world. Do the Gestaltists seek to revalidate these laws or only to make them appear more scientific? In fact, revalidation is quite unnecessary, for St. Thomas' analysis of the situation taken as a whole is far more fitting than that of the Gestalt topologists.[2]

Most of our moderns are apparently oblivious of the fact that human beings, in spite of being functionally organized into units of a higher order called groups, actually remain concrete individual units of a lower order, as far as size is concerned. These individual lower-order units or persons are able at times to plan goals for their own attainment, which are not contained in the sum total of the present prescribed or typical situations in the group. They then win others over to their views so that we have wholesale "new orders" threatening to come into being. The lower-order units are often much more dynamic than the higher-order group. At least some individual persons are not just passively impelled in the direction of one or more goals set up by a structuralized organizer called the group. They are dynamic agents as well as directive agents in the process of balancing or unbalancing the vector forces which are active in their environment. In spite of the subtle and verbose arguments of the Gestalt topologists, it cannot be denied that human beings have an existence as individual persons, and that sometimes, at least, they consciously select and organize situations to which others must react. Each human being can be defined in terms of himself and his own goal first, and can then be reorientated or redefined in terms of the group goals. The two goals need not inevitably conflict. Whether and to what extent they do conflict is a matter for the individual to decide.

Some recent Gestaltists are so enthused with their new hypothesis on the nature of *wholes* that they insist upon the importance of the group to the exclusion of the individual. They say that the concept *individual* has no meaning in itself.[3] This generalization from Gestalt experiment has no verification in fact. The concept *individual* has a very definite meaning in itself, even when the person is regarded as fitting into the background of the group of which he is a member.

Professor Krout wisely points out that there is a flaw somewhere in the theoretical framework of the exaggerated groupists. He reminds his readers that the individual in the group remains an organism in its own right and that although the individual cannot be studied sociologically independently of the group, the group cannot be studied at all independently of the individual (cf. Krout, *op. cit.*, p. 225). The exaggerated groupist view is based on the undemonstrable assumption that human individuals are always and everywhere absolutely determined to behave according to the requirements of situational stimulations (group goals). But in spite of their extravagant generalizations, these Gestaltists have devised more useful techniques for investigating group behavior than have the biological determinists. Moreno and his collaborators,[4] assuming that a person cannot be studied without a group, have attacked the problems of attraction and repulsion within group structures, especially among institutional inmates. They do not, however, think that universal or a-historical typical laws are possible with reference to group structure. Their work is closely related to studies on cooperation and competition, and on factors effective in attitude formation, and is very enlightening and practical for educators.

Much serviceable material has been collected on the analysis of group complexity as dependent upon age, sex, or occupation; on the closeness or intimacy of group interdependence; on the degree of group exclusiveness; on the effectiveness of authoritarian and democratic group controls; and finally on factors conducive to morale and consensus of opinion. These dynamic approaches to a study of the individual are possible without assuming that persons have no independent existence or that they react purely mechanically in adjusting themselves to new forces.

An interesting example of the detail with which sociometrists can work out group relations is had in the Dionne quintuplets. We already have sociograms depicting the lines of attraction joining these five individuals in their little social circle. In spite of their original similarity of inheritance, there is dissimilarity in attractiveness and aggressiveness in this small group of individuals all living in an identical social environment.[5] Marie was, at the age of four, definitely not recognized by her sisters as being a leader, or even as being popular. We wonder if Marie will aways remain an unaggressive, unsought-for, placid individual under the influence of a later and different group life. Much evidence points to the fact that she will have the tendency, but there are countless factors which influence her to modify this tendency so that it may scarcely be recognizable in later life. One significant factor in her development will be her own choice of companions.

TYPICAL DEVELOPMENT STAGES

STATISTICAL GROUPS AND EXPECTED BEHAVIOR. The utility of our modern methods of approaching social studies partly depends on the fact that some human behavior can be fairly well predicted, but, as Krout points out (*op. cit.*, p. 238), we cannot yet predict the behavior of the total group even though we can foresee definite trends in individual behavior. The reason for our failure to predict individual behavior lies in the very nature of human persons as such. The reason for the unpredictability of group behavior lies partly in the freedom of the various individuals, partly in the fact that normal novelty-seeking and inventive human beings go on endlessly attempting to regroup themselves. They will probably never do this to their complete satisfaction, but we cannot therefore expect them to cease their efforts in that direction. The case of mass movements of peoples mentioned in the latter part of this chapter is an instance of the direction these groupings may take.

In the remainder of this chapter we shall describe some selected groups, such as age levels, cooperating groups, audiences, and crowds, within which certain similarities have been observed. As occasion offers, we shall note tendencies which must be designated desirable as a consequence of the fact that man is by nature a social rational human being who realizes that he has some moral restrictions and obligations.

Age groups are primarily face-to-face groups although not exclusively so, and they have significance for us because of the typical social behavior trends which they normally manifest. They may consist of widely separated individuals who are capable of being studied as a group only because of certain broad similarities generally found at that age level. The principal age levels are the preschool, childhood, adolescent, maturity, and old-age levels. The childhood and adolescent levels are studied intensively in special treatises. Since social cooperativeness makes its appearance only gradually during the developmental process, we shall briefly outline the stages involved in its appearance.

THE AGE GROUPS

I) THE INFANCY STAGE. During the first year the child has begun to learn reactions to other persons as social beings, if we may take the smile as indicative of a social reaction. But he is not yet fully aware of the meaning of social interdependence and hence acts chiefly in a selfish and impulsive manner, showing no sure signs of intellectual foresight and planning. His bodily needs have to be attended to and thus he comes to form pleasure-seeking attachments to those who give him attention. He is as yet not clearly aware of his role as an individual. Before the age of three, most children have come to take an interest in the actions of other persons, and manifest a desire to gain their approval for various kinds of behavior. The earliest formative stages of extremely self-critical, dependent, and defeatist attitudes may now be observed. In other cases the contrary tendency toward self-sufficiency, independence, aggressiveness, and competition is manifest. The behavior of parents and tutors at this important age, sometimes called the spunk or spite age, is often largely responsible for the direction which these fundamental attitudes toward self-in-a-group may take in the growth process.

During late infancy, from about two through six, the child develops a few social contacts. His imagination may race ahead of his actual experience and arouse in him a lively interest in tales of ghosts and fairies. Charlotte Buehler considers this nursery rhyme stage in the child development extremely important in bringing out creative ability and self-confidence. Stories of Santa and of angels are believed by her to aid and not harm the imaginative development. The very young child is curious to know something about everything. At the same time because of his vast ignorance in comparison to adults, he may feel utterly helpless and lonely. It is probable that animal stories and fables give the child a sense of power and security by reason of the fact that he does not fully distinguish between reality and fancy.

As skill in language and appreciation of the real role played by other persons and things are gradually acquired, the child lives less in a world of fancy (the autistic phase) and begins to understand his real position in a world full of pleasant surprises and unpleasant tasks. Around the age of five or six the modern child faces his first major social problem. He must yield up his place of dignity in the home and go to school, where he is expected to become just one of a homogeneous group of listeners, conforming to routine daily order. At this time or very soon thereafter he learns the meaning of unselfishness and realizes the need of subjugating some of his own wants to the convenience of others. He then becomes noticeably more independent of the care of others and emotionally more secure. This new stability of disposition normally arises from the child's realization that he has a role in life and is able to share in the burdens as well as in the enjoyments of life. It may be that he is motivated largely by a desire to win for himself the approval of others, but he sees that others gain something from his actions also. Unless disturbed by some emotional crisis he will come to realize that there is some gratification in doing *what he knows he ought to do*. We might name this the responsible age which necessarily involves an awareness of the value of self for the self and for others.

The child's sense of responsibility shows itself in various ways, such as adjusting his wants and needs to those of others, or taking pleasure in doing small tasks which give satisfaction to others. By the time of late childhood, the average child should have learned, in an elementary way, the value and purpose of such courses of action as obedience to superiors, respect for the property of others, fairness in games, truthfulness as a means of understanding others. He will have developed some notions of the values of certain ways of acting and particularly of his own value as an individual who counts in the world but is not the sole performer. Needless to say he could never put any of these ideas into verbal expression. He lives them out in his ability to give and take and he lets others know that he has not developed them by the problems he creates for others around him.

II) THE CHILDHOOD LEVEL. From about eight through twelve years of age there are signs of intensified group activity. At this period, which is called the gang age, what the child seems to desire and enjoy most of all is the companionship of other children of the same sex and age as himself. The child has become group minded, or group conscious, and seems hardly able to remain alone or out of a group for any considerable length of time. His interest seems suddenly to shift from things that have to do with self to those which can be accomplished with others. He is collectivistic rather than individualistic in all his inclinations and desires. At this period in particular, great care and devotion is required on the part of those in charge of the child, to prevent the formation of undesirable social habits. The tendency of like sexes to cluster together and to be loyal to one another and secretive in behavior is one which may readily be misdirected. Criminologists and sociologists have learned to deal with these manifestations quite successfully.

We should note here that the gang spirit in itself is not to be condemned or eradicated. It can readily be utilized for the attainment of very desirable goals. The chief benefits to be derived from this youthful collectivism are a spirit of unselfishness, an interest in and devotion to projects that are shared in common, an attitude of working with instead of against others, and finally a healthy group spirit or morale.[6]

III) THE AGE OF ADOLESCENCE. As prepubertal self-consciousness and clumsiness diminish, the individual begins to see himself as a responsible member of society, which demands much of its members. During the period of adolescence the attitude demanded is that of accepting the true role of the sexes in society. Related to this is the gradual realization that each individual of either sex has duties to perform if he or she is to become capable of earning a living and providing against the time of separation from the family circle. Thus during this age plans are to be made for the future. The youth is expected to round out that sense of personal responsibility which has already reached a certain stage of development but must be supplemented by a fuller knowledge of the meaning of life before it can fit a person for adult society. The adolescent becomes noticeably reflective and serious minded, because he or she is forming serious judgments about the real role of adults in life. While there appears to be less of that group mindedness which is characteristic of an earlier age, the adolescent should not go to the opposite extreme, and develop a habit of evaluating his opportunities for advancement egotistically. He must learn the true meaning and relationship of things and nicely balance the tendency to seek personal advantages with the disposition to share comforts and responsibilities with others. It is especially desirable to cultivate interests and friendships outside as well as inside the family circle, otherwise the person may suffer both social and economic setbacks in later life.

Should an individual refuse to recognize and accept his role in the group, fostering attitudes of sullenness and vindictiveness when confronted with the task of adjusting himself to life's bigger problems, his attitude may need correction later on. Because of the doubts which spontaneously arise during adolescence — deep philosophical doubts about the real value of things, the intentions of elders, the correctness of moral standards — there is need of the helpful advice and sympathetic understanding of a trusted friend. Without this assistance many young people become so confused in their thinking about the problems of life that they lose their poise, and even indulge in morbid unsociable behavior that is apt to be harmful. Some have been known to develop oversensitivity and suspicions so that they try to shirk all responsibilities as unjust, and then justify their own attitude on the score that all the world is wrong and they alone are right. This naturally makes them feel that they are uniquely different from others, and it may easily lead to daydreaming and escape reactions of various sorts which pave the way for a career of dissipation, delinquency, and even mental disorder.

IV) THE PERIOD OF MATURITY. After they have reached maturity, we find men engaged in such a variety of occupations and possessing such a multitude of different interests and attitudes that it is difficult to study them in groups. Some of their more common tendencies and characteristic attitudes will be mentioned later in Chapter 10.

V) OLD AGE OR SENESCENCE. This age level is often neglected because habits are generally supposed to be such at this time that little may be done to change them. It will help to prepare ahead of time against certain social inconveniences arising from the relative inflexibility of old age. Degeneration of the various bodily organs and tissues along with gradual deceleration of all the bodily and mental processes are the characteristics of the old-age period. The curves for human efficiency at the different ages gives us some impression of the actual accomplishments of persons. But the writer thinks it would be unwise to retire or pension all workers at 40 because the curves show a tendency for efficiency to drop after that age. Good authority can be cited to show that the quality of work done by persons in the 50–70 age bracket is often superior to that of the overactive 21–35 group.[7]

The sophisticated attitudes of the oncoming generation are apt to come in conflict with the old-fashioned views of the senescent. The latter, when he can no longer succeed in stemming the tide of changing social customs or maintain his position of leadership, should dispose himself to accept new conventions. Otherwise he may become a chronic grumbler and universal fault finder in regard to innovations which are actually not so very reprehensible. A much more wholesome attitude would be one of meekness and understanding in a society which is becoming less and less considerate of the merits of its aged members. In any case it will benefit all of us to begin preparing in advance for this period of possible neglect and inactivity. The best preparation would be to develop an active interest in live topics of the moment, such as social welfare or Catholic action. If these activities do not appeal to us we can at least cultivate useful hobbies which will keep us from being burdensome to ourselves and others. One often admires the youthful and happy outlook of those elderly persons who can relate the latest standing of athletic stars as well as the latest fads in popular personality magazines.

Hollingworth[8] is of the opinion that we can, by our own conscious efforts, actually compensate for the slowing down of our bodily processes and the miseries which sometimes result from it. Some delightful old persons seem to succeed in avoiding that childishness of behavior and feeling toward which they often tend by broadening their interests and keeping themselves busy. It is possible that some of them might be able to share the burden of caring for the new generation of children, not only with benefit to their own mentality, but also to the relief of those busy young parents who claim they are too preoccupied to look after their offspring properly.

TRANSITORY GROUPS, THEIR LEADER

GENERAL ASPECTS OF THESE GROUPS. As distinguished from the true group, the phenomena of crowds and fads are ephemeral. They lack the basic unity of a real group and the uniformity of the age group. Yet certain broad features characterize all kinds of crowds, whether they be of the angry riotous, the joyful celebrating, or the fearful panicky type. In all of these types we find temporary manifestations of low-level or infantile reactions. An instance of such reactions is the emotional and uncritical behavior of the angry mob, which is often called, by way of hyperbole, irrational or abnormal behavior. The irrationality, if it can be styled so, usually consists either in frenzied demonstrations or in giving free vent to destructive tendencies. We should rather call such behavior uncontrolled, since the best psychologists nowadays admit the possibility of subjecting emotional behavior to reason, at least to some extent. When such behavior becomes habitual, we admit, the reasons for it may no longer be present in consciousness at the time of its execution. Instances of a mild sort of uncontrolled behavior similar to that of a crowd are the phenomena known as fads, booms, and crazes. Although good or plausible reasons for such behavior seem lacking, most persons who find themselves following a fad or becoming involved in a boom would very likely try to justify their behavior somehow later on.

SPECIAL ASPECTS OF THESE GROUPS

THE BOOM. This term refers to such long-time deviations from usual social behavior as the stock-market boom of the 1920's or the gold rush of the past century. The boom ordinarily builds itself up gradually, catches many individuals in its sweep, and then collapses suddenly. The following actual case is sufficiently typical to be illustrative. The proprietor of a lumber and contracting business in a midwestern town hoped to get rich quick by buying timber land cheap in Florida during the first decades of this century, with a view to shipping the low-priced lumber north later on. He is still land poor because the timber land turned out, on inspection, to be mostly a swamp, although he did manage to build a house or two near Miami in which to spend his declining years meditating on the follies of his youth.

CRAZES AND EPIDEMICS. These are similar to booms except that their progress is much more sudden. They are usually more stupid than either fads or fashions, but may persist in the form of fashions at times. Epidemics of fear usually following boom times may reach a culminating point followed by wholesale collapse of morale. President Roosevelt is said to have prevented such a panic or epidemic by his now famous Bank Holiday Technique. Some popular crazes of the recent past were walkathons, chain letters, flagpole and tree-house dwelling, shoestring cutting, zoot suits, etc. In the year 1938, the writer had occasion to witness an epidemic of superstitions which swept the whole of Germany and was only checked by the outbreak of the long-anticipated war. Daily newspapers had been suppressed and as a result of the existing tension a substitute for news soon developed in the form of rumors and prophecies of all sorts. These were whispered about surreptitiously but could always be more freely discussed than could local politics. Eventually this type of gossip mongering aroused the indignation of the Party, and University Professors were requisitioned to deliver popular lectures on the dangers of rumors and prophecies for the morale of the people.

FADS. Fads are very similar to fashions. The difference seems to be that when a fad persists over a long time it may become a fashion, and Emily Post may condescend to prescribe for it. A fad is some trifling modification of an accepted form of behavior, which is usually meant to be humorous, or at least to divert attention from more serious thoughts and actions. Slack suits are modern fads in dress, especially among the young. Knee pants, usually of leather, for the Workers' Party in Germany probably were used in ancient times, then were revived, and now are an approved article of apparel for young and old. Chinese checkers, "mahjong," and "monopoly" have probably had their day, whereas chess and contract bridge remain the fashion for the entertainment of the upper classes. Some very short-lived fads among the young have been such slang expressions as "knock-knock" and "oh y-e-a-h," clothes like bell pants, zippered fastenings, etc. Some of these may persist as fashions, provided economic factors, such as shortage of essential materials, do not intervene. The simultaneous handling of knife and fork while conveying food to the mouth is an accepted fashion in England, but in America it is considered impolite.

When we reflect upon the quick succession of fads and fashions, we may be provoked to laughter, for they hardly ever become sources of real social problems, although they account for a large percentage of the expenditure of our daily incomes. The "upper classes" likely feel more cosmopolitan when they adopt fads, and the ordinary man probably feels more important in doing so.

THE CROWD. Under this head we include all loosely organized gatherings for the purpose of celebrating, or of demonstrating disapproval. The outstanding features of crowd behavior are the following: stupid imitation of the actions of others; community of motive and drive; intense emotional thrills and apprehension; low level of active reasoning and critical power; heightened suggestibility; lowered sense of responsibility; delusions of power, grandeur, and self-righteousness; uncontrollability by a leader. Regardless of what theory one holds about crowd behavior, the fact remains that human beings often fail to conduct themselves as rational beings when under the influence of crowds or panics. Basic selfishness is the chief characteristic of the crowd. The techniques for escaping, momentarily at least, from the restrictions and duties of human society are as numerous and as varied as human ingenuity can make them. Anyone who realizes the importance of order and stability in a society will be inclined to prevent the occurrence of riotous crowds, and will certainly refrain from being the cause of, or contributing to, mobs, panics, and epidemics.

There is such a thing as being unwillingly caught up and carried away by the mob spirit which prevails at a given moment. Another American and the writer had the opportunity of studying the reactions of "celebrating" crowds in Vienna before the Annexation, and also at the triumphal entrance of the Fuehrer into his home country in March, 1938. The Ring Strasse on this historic Sunday afternoon was packed to the limit with eager spectators. The crowd extended for miles around the gaudily decorated inner Ring of the city. A subdued silence weighed down upon all, and we "foreigners" could perceive that something similar to religious awe was depicted on the faces of all, especially of the women and children. As the hours wore on — public figures know better than to arrive promptly — after the children had sung their hymns of respect for their beloved and welcome liberator, we compared notes on the complexity of our emotions. Just then a deafening cry was raised and the parade was on. A woman near by, more than sixty years of age, stood with arms uplifted as if in veneration, and kept mumbling incessantly "Isn't he wonderful!" Had it not been for this incident we Americans also might have been carried away with the fervor and ecstasy of the moment, for we were both conscious of the force of mob psychology at that time.

Connected with the nonrational tendencies just described are war fevers, beliefs in augury and astrology, and revolutionary discontents. We may even find in an otherwise calm and peaceful people wholesale tendencies toward fear and disorganized behavior, which are often so powerful that thousands of absolutely normal individuals will flock out into the streets and dash off in frenzied flight from some fictitious superman who is thought to be invading our earth from the planet Mars. If suppression of human freedom alone were the cause of the feelings of insecurity and the apprehensions of calamity which lead to epidemics and panics, then we Americans should have been the last to be deceived by the radio drama of Orson Welles in the autumn of 1938. It was said by Europeans at that time that only excitable Americans could have made the Orson Welles panic an actuality. The truth is that the excitabilities of different peoples are much the same, and a superior attitude toward people of another country is most likely an attempt to compensate for the irrational behavior of one's own compatriots.[9]

The rules which help to avoid local panics such as might occur during an air raid or a fire are simply to break up the crowd into smaller units if possible, and to keep them busily occupied with something to distract their minds from the danger which is imminent. Preparation in advance should consist in warning the public that they will act automatically during the first moments after a shock, and that their past habits of courage and attitudes of calm and security will be of great service in any new emergency. In discussing fear we shall show that new energy is actually supplied for the organism during emergencies, and that it can be directed toward useful ends if the person has cultivated the proper habits.

THE AUDIENCE. This type of gathering should properly be studied in classes of rhetoric. Since political orators and dictators in general mingle much mob psychology with their oratory, we may here consider the so-called "rally" type of audience. The successful rally orator must be above all a salesman, and if possible also a logical thinker and a persuasive speaker. He hardly ever fails to make use of certain propaganda measures, in the sense that he makes his own cause appear to be the only desirable one under the circumstances. He aims chiefly at making his audience hang on his words as if spellbound; they must never for a moment suspect that they are not hearing just what they would like to hear. This compelling effect of oratory is sometimes called the polarizing effect on the audience. We can discern a great similarity between this effect and the processes of suggestion and hypnotism which we shall discuss later. The trick of compelling attention by an appeal to spontaneous preferences produces unity among the members of an audience. The minds of the listeners are not directed toward one another or toward an extraneous object but solely toward the speaker. The listeners become of one mind with one another by sharing the mind of the speaker. They might almost be said to possess a group mind.

THE CO-ACTIVE GROUP. The term co-active must not be confused with coactive. It means acting together without any implication of compulsory activity, and is a technical term met everywhere today in the literature. Persons may act together in an intellectual manner, as during a round-table discussion or such games as anagrams. Again, they may act together physically, as when many persons working on the assembly line turn out a Ford. They may also act in both capacities at the same time, as when scientists or engineers work together in their laboratories. The advantages of group intellectual activity are clear, since individual errors or oversights may be brought to light through group discussion. Most persons, however, prefer solitude as the best environment for solving difficult and complicated problems.

Discussion alone cannot be an adequate substitute for diligent study and investigation of all the relevant facts in a case. Hence it would be unwise to conclude that, just because our "committee" has weighed the matter carefully, nothing further remains to be said on the subject in question, whether it be the appointing of an executive or the formulation of a scientific definition. During a group discussion held in a University class, for instance, the participants decided that the most essential property of a leader was his ability to become unobtrusive and not to antagonize others by authoritative manners. This would indicate that the students had not considered all the pertinent facts and were not experienced enough to appreciate all sides of the question. Perhaps they were also somewhat influenced by an emotional bias against a certain type of odious leader whom they had known. Professor S. H. Britt has shown very clearly that prejudices against minority groups such as Jews and Negroes can be deliberately fostered, and that they can be effectively weakened if proper leadership and discussion groups are provided.[10] Consequently a combination of individual study and group discussion seems to be the ideal state of affairs. In all cases of calm and deliberate group activity, the total accomplishment is greater than the sum of the accomplishments of the separate persons acting alone. This fact stands in striking contrast to the mob effects mentioned above. The difference seems to be due to the absence of emotional disturbance in the co-active group as compared with the frenzied mass movements of people in a panic.

We may now comment on some group effects which various investigators have tried to measure.[11] The mere presence of other persons often tends to speed up an individual's work, but may at the same time make it less accurate. We call this result of parallel activity the reinforcing or facilitating effect of the group. It may be present even when the associates are actually separated from one another, if only they know that all are engaged in a similar task. It may also be present when the workers are deliberately trying not to compete with one another and think that they are not influenced by a spirit of rivalry. In general, most persons in a group are more inclined toward making a show than when they are not acting collectively. But in such intellectual group activities as intelligence tests, the very opposite effect may be observed. In these cases some seem to be facilitated by the presence of a group, others blocked or inhibited.

Moreover, if we study the action of one person working alone, then bring him to realize that the whole group will be judged by the grade of his performance, it seems possible that he may rise to the occasion and make as good a score alone as when working in the group. The real basis for social facilitation, then, may be found rather in the attitudes and motivating factors of the various individuals, than in the group factors of imitation or of active competition. We often notice, for instance, that many workers in industry will loiter around and kill time when the foreman is absent, but will *apparently* vie with one another to make the best possible impression when a superior is watching them.

THE NATION. Here we may seem to be invading the domain of sociology or of political theory. But the question of the difference between a race and a nation is a cultural and psychological question as well as a sociological or political one. At the present stage of history, it seems absolutely impossible for any biologically pure racial stock to designate itself a nation solely because of its racial unity. There is race mixture in almost every known nation, manifest in physical as well as mental traits. Even in Germany and as late as 1939, reliable statisticians have pointed out that no certain criterion exists for setting any one race in western Europe apart from any other, much less *above all others in all respects*. There is too much overlap between them even in cases where a supposedly unitary trait, such as intelligence, has been measured.

If this is true in the relatively homogeneous countries of Europe, it must be all the more true with respect to the American people. It is a well-known fact that in America racial characteristics, however one may wish to define the term, are completely shot through and transformed by cultural patterns of various sorts. The instrument which is said to effect the change or fusion of traits is the so-called "melting pot." Apparent differences in intelligence quotients among Americans have been one of the chief arguments for racial superiority of the Nordics. But these differences can be explained on a basis of the language factor which enters into the tests. It is a known fact that children of English-speaking parents show a greater language facility from their earliest years than do children from homes where some other language is also spoken. And there is no test which can dispense with the language factor entirely in measuring intelligence. This fact also gives evidence of the great influence which early family training may have on speech as well as the measurable aspects of intelligence.

Individual differences in language ability, together with the similarity which languages of the same family have to one another, may be largely responsible for the rankings given in tests to the various nationalities in America. An example of such rankings computed from the results of the army Alpha and Beta tests of foreign-born draftees in World War I is the following: English, Dutch, Danish, Scotch, German, Swedish, Canadian, Belgian, Norwegian, Austrian, Irish, Turkish, Greek, Russian, Italian, and Polish. If the immigrants from the northern countries were actually superior in intelligence, then this superiority should be noticeable when we administer tests to those people in their own native countries. But this is definitely not the case. In fact there is found to be a greater difference between rural and urban residents in Germany alone or in Italy alone, than there is between residents of these two countries, whether we take rural or urban populations for our comparison.[12]

But are there not temperamental differences between the various stocks, at least in Europe? This would seem to be the case, but they are of relatively small importance as regards the general good of the nation. Hurwicz[13] says that the English are individualistic, conservative, and unsociable. Other authorities claim that they are muddlers, commercial minded, haughty, and unphilosophical. Hurwicz also says that the French are rationalistic, that is, inclined toward a priori deductions, and that socially they are very chummy. Others say that they are passionate and demonstrative, and materialistic in their philosophy. Again, according to Hurwicz, the Germans are introverted, patient, diligent, and have metaphysical as well as scientific ability of a high rank. But others describe the Germans as emotional, submissive, irritable, gullible, and backward in the sciences of government and empirical philosophy. These various appraisals have something in common with each other but the total impression made on the mind of the reader regarding a given people is apt to be very conflicting. For example, one would scarcely arrive at the notion of gullibility or of emotionality as characteristic of the Germans from the neutral observer Hurwicz's account of them. It is often necessary to know the cultural background and preferences of a writer before we read his report and we must surely know how he defines his terms.[14] There is too often a tendency to apply stereotyped notions of racial differences to other people, with perhaps the secret wish that they were true. At any rate, the characterizations just given are not based on purity of racial origin, but rather on cultures, and hence the differences mentioned may also be largely culturally developed.

The following pair of characterizations of Americans may serve as a final example. J. Froebes, an internationally known European psychologist, thinks that Americans are commercial minded, that they incline to restlessness of manner, that there is a noticeable shifting toward an Indian body type due to the influence of the environment.[15] The late Mr. McDougall of Duke University, quite famous in social psychology, says that Americans are optimistic, self-determined, cosmopolitan, and confident of rising by their own individual efforts to the highest position in the land.

This is not the place to discuss the varying contributions of heredity and environment to national traits. A nation, nowadays at least, is merely a collection of persons with common customs and traditions, who are united in a single political system. The efforts of race psychologists to identify race with nation at this stage of our civilization can only result in political and social confusion. The race hypothesis or Nordic myth, according to some investigators, is but the outcome of wishful thinking on the part of biologically minded reformers who are compensating for their own feelings of inferiority. Yet how many of us tend to form an opinion about the persons we meet daily, as soon as we hear their family name, at once attributing to them some stereotype of racial characteristics. Individual differences within a race are of far greater importance socially than the so-called temperamental differences which fiction and fable have attached to various peoples and which habit continues to perpetuate in the minds of many persons.

We agree, finally, with the conclusion of Gurnee when he says that the psychological conditions which make for national strength are the habits and attitudes which a people possess. He fails, however, to point out that all these habits should be such as to furnish a measure of security for the citizens of earth so that they may more effectively aim at a happiness and security which are not of this earth, and which take no account either of racial or of national distinctions.[16] Can any social reformer seriously hope to bring contentedness and security to all by urging them to compete for unlimited possession of material goods and to conquer the whole world? Some attitudes which will surely further the material prosperity of a people, without fostering avaricious practices or disruptive tendencies, are habits of industry, enthusiasm for scientific research, respect for law and order, devotion to the ideals of liberty, equality, and justice, and group spirit provided it is not national exclusiveness.

THE GROUP MIND. We have already mentioned the group-mind theory which holds that the crowd or society is not a mere sum or average of its component individuals but a new transcendental entity of some sort. Spencer, the evolutionist, also wrote frequently about the "Social Organism." Our description of crowd behavior shows that the separate individuals behave quite differently when in a crowd than when alone or when working calmly in a group. But do these facts prove that the separate individuals are always acting as a group when they conform to customs, or that they cease to be individuals in the crowd? Do they prove that a new special entity called the "group mind" has emerged from nowhere only to disappear again when the crowd is dispersed? Such is not the case. For the individual, whoever he may be, retains his personal identity no matter how primitive or emotional he may have been *when he yielded himself* up to the frenzy of the mob.

Modern writers, even in our own country, are not always clear in giving the individual his proper place in the social organism. Perhaps they are only reacting against the exaggerated rugged individualism of an earlier era. They will perhaps begin to reflect seriously upon the consequences of their theorizing when they learn that foreign psychologists make use of just this concept of the group mind to prove that the *common good* is the only important thing in society. These authorities appeal to the experiments in Gestalt psychology in support of their claims. They apply the "principle of primacy of the whole" in order to take away individual rights of whatever sort, such as the right to worship God, or to dispose of property. They mean that the separate person has no rights to yield, because he has no kind of independent existence. Thus, owing to an exaggerated and distorted notion of the totality of the group, they provided an incentive for the social-experimenters. We wonder how many of them could explain the fundamental experiments in Gestalt psychology which they so often quote in support of the assumption that the individual has no separate or independent existence.[17]

THE ROLE OF THE LEADER. In a frenzied mob, such as a street riot or a revolution, the leader is often paradoxically compelled to follow the mob, over which he has lost all control or leadership. In a sane human society, the leader's personal traits make him respected and revered by his followers. In a divinely instituted society, the authorized leader possesses authority to command obedience and submission. The ideal leader inspires the followers with a love of righteousness of his cause. He sets them an example of sacrifice and labor, and appeals to their generosity to excel one another in attempting to do things which are worth while: to alleviate the sufferings of the afflicted, to right the injustices of the wicked, and to eradicate the hatreds, jealousies, and conspiracies which tear human hearts asunder and destroy the peace. He tries to foster attitudes which are just the opposite of rebellious, because he knows that strife never brings permanent peace to anyone. With this concept of leadership in mind, let us glance at some recent attempts to catalogue the qualities which a true leader must possess.

Over sixty students of social psychology were asked by the present writer to list the qualities which they thought an efficient executive leader ought to possess. The answer most frequently given was this: "He must be able to get things done, that is, he must help others to attain their desired end." The answer which was second in frequency was that the leader "must be popular or well liked for some reason or other." From these answers we may conjecture that college students, prior to any formal courses in social psychology, have some definite views on the question of leadership which, incidentally, are very similar to the views of modern authors. Britt, for instance, says that although leaders in science and religion will probably possess qualities different from those in the field of business or politics, both types of leaders are influential only so far as they try gradually to change the existing attitudes and ways of thinking and acting of those who are led. In fact he defines leadership as the activity of influencing people to cooperate toward some goal which they come to find desirable.[18]

None of the writers on social psychology, including Britt himself, is explicit in describing exactly what goals are to be deemed desirable. This is only to be expected, because they rely exclusively on the empirical method in making their investigations. For them the leader who actually accomplishes something, whether it be to excite a rebellion or to quell the same, must be considered objectively. Such an objective procedure emphasizes some important facts, especially the fact that leaders need specific qualifications for each specific kind of leadership situation in which they may find themselves. Thus, for instance, a leader in a religious institution needs skill in carrying on religious activities; a leader of a group of armed forces will require other kinds of skills. We also need reminding that no individual is ever a leader in all possible kinds of activity. A leader in industrial techniques is not necessarily equipped to prescribe child guidance measures. In other words, each leader is in some respect also a follower. Both army officers and religious leaders are subject to the authority of their legitimate superiors, and in relation to them they are followers.

There are some traits, however, which seem to be common to all types of leaders, such as excellence in some one ability, some degree of honesty and fair play, trustworthiness, and sociability or social personality. In order to discover and acquire the traits needed for specific kinds of situations, we can do no better than observe the behavior of successful leaders, and then try to incorporate these behavior patterns into our own lives by means of practice.

There is a related question which is often overlooked in studies of leadership: the question why human beings in society need any leaders at all. Student answers to this question are chiefly of two kinds. Some maintain that we do not always need a leader and that we have too many aggressive persons seeking to gain power over others. Others answer that leaders are necessary simply because of the differences which exist in human personalities. Owing to these dissimilarities, one person could be of service to others in that matter in which he was especially endowed, by helping to direct their efforts along useful and efficient lines.

The first answer, it seems, is partly due to a prejudice against that type of self-appointed admonitor who tries to foist himself upon others when there is no real need of his advice or assistance. The second answer indicates the actual basis for all kinds of leadership, namely, our need for mutual assistance and organization if we are to get the best results out of our efforts. This point should emerge clearly from our chapter on personality (Chapter 11). Youthful students of leadership are not slow to realize that the position of a superior of any kind has duties as well as privileges attached to it. Inexperienced leaders or superiors are apt to be very zealous in carrying out their duties at first and to disregard the privileges and honors, although they evidently receive some satisfaction from the latter. It is to be regretted that certain types of leaders tend, as Thorndike points out,[19] to become jealous of their authority and somewhat dictatorial. Ways and means of cultivating firm habits of responsibility must be studied just as intensively as techniques for securing the desired goals of the group. The haughty, domineering, crafty type of leader is generally not very acceptable to the followers, nor is he efficient in the long run. The authoritarian or dictatorial type is often described somewhat in the following manner: he tries to make his followers feel their weakness and inferiority (to himself), he appeals to some grudge or ancient grievance in order to arouse uniform sentiments of hatred for all outside groups, and then, by exercising his full power and authority, makes the followers willing to rely upon the strong man who alone can liberate them from their miseries. The opposite type, referred to in some books as the democratic leader, tries to make the subjects feel important and strong, appeals to their own individual self-interests and sympathies in order to gain their support, and uses suggestion instead of propaganda as a means of controlling public opinion along preconceived lines.

The followers of dictatorial leaders are all too prone to be deceived into a false security by the alluring promises of their leaders, who, as a matter of fact, often have no other way of commanding respect from their followers than by using threats or promises. These leaders also frequently fail to respect the inalienable rights and privileges of their subjects, generally because they fail to recognize the source of all authority and power, a supreme Ruler of the universe. Have democratic leaders always been faultless in this regard, it might be asked. Experiments and observations regarding children in nurseries may be useful in showing what types of leadership spontaneously develop in such groups, and may tell us much about the reactions of subjects to various types of leaders, but they can hardly help us to answer the question, toward what end should a leader guide his subjects, and what means may he legitimately use in doing so.

Both types of leadership here described fall short of the ideal type of leader, as judged by Christian and true humanitarian standards. A truly effective leader of men must appeal to the unselfishness and cooperativeness of his followers and not merely to their selfish desires for power and aggression and competition. He will not use deceit as a means of propagandizing but, in appealing to their sympathies and emotions, he will show them the reasons why unity of purpose is desirable. Thus, inflamed by a common zeal and united by a common cause, the leader and the followers will manifest in their lives the dignity and perfection which befits all rational beings, the dignity of the children of God.

FOR ACCELERATED READING

SHORT SUMMARY OF THE CHAPTER

Classification of groups is possible into primary and secondary, in groups and out groups (we group and you group). Feelings of unity characterize most groups; the conception of social forces and fields of force is applicable at times. Individuals often select their own groups, regroup themselves without warning.

Groups considered statistically, that is, on the basis of common traits without actual contact, are the Age Groups. The impulsive infancy level, the socially conscious childhood, the reflective adolescent, and the stable senescent levels are portrayed briefly.

Some transitory groupings such as booms, epidemics, and mobs are described. Fads, crazes, and fashions typify conforming but rather variable modes of behavior. Audience groups and co-active groups, when calm, do not confirm the belief in group facilitation. The total group effect in any situation depends upon the attitude and preparation of the individuals.

Racial and national groups are considered and the possibility of proving racial superiority in all respects is denied. The group-mind effect is noticeable in *esprit de corps* but calmly cooperating groups have qualities opposed to those of mobs and excitable concourses of people.

The *leader* is one who co-ordinates activity toward a preconceived goal. If no two persons in any society are identical in all respects, then someone will be able to help others in their efforts. The requirements for each type of leadership differ for specific situations but each type needs some trait of excellence or outstandingness. The ideal leader will direct men toward worthy goals, and use techniques of influencing others in accordance with moral principles and the rights of rational human beings. Since society is an organization toward a hierarchy of goals, all persons will be followers in some respect and some must lead.

Find Review Questions and Supplementary Reading at the end of the book.

Chapter 4

SOCIAL LEARNING

Motives and Mechanisms of Learning — Preliminary Remarks; Learning in the Child; Mental Learning and Mental Sets; Conditioning in the Case of Human Beings; The Experiments; Conclusions; Effects of Change of Attitude Upon Perception. *Other Methods of Learning* — Learning by Trial and Error; Learning by Imitation; Circular Reflexes; Learning by Insight and Reflection.

MOTIVES AND MECHANISMS OF LEARNING

Preliminary Remarks. We must now consider the process called social learning, that process by which a person acquires the habits which we call social. Needless to say, most social habits as such are acquired, not inherited in the strict sense. The accident of birth in a given place and at a given time confers upon each individual a unique opportunity of copying the habits of the other human beings who are present at that time and in that place. The term "Social Tradition" is used to designate the process of transmitting customs and conventions from one generation to another. The term "Tradition" often refers also to the body of knowledge and customs thus transmitted.

We cannot help acquiring many customs and habits from our immediate ancestors, owing to the helpless condition of our tender years. This acquisition need not accrue to our disadvantage. Generally the habits and manners which we acquire in childhood fit us better for our particular mode of adult life than any other habits would, although they might not be so suitable for adult life in some other culture. It is important to remember, in studying the process of social learning, that although all of us have acquired many habits automatically and with no clearly formulated purpose, still each has been able to select at least some of his habits on a basis of conscious purpose. For instance, a child sometimes does the approved thing in order not to be regarded as singular or peculiar. In so doing, he may be consciously trying to gain the approval of others for himself. In gaining the respect of others he may also be gaining self-respect, in so far as he has already learned to approve that kind of behavior in himself which others desire to find in him. This shows that a large variety of motives may influence the formation of even the simplest sort of social habit or custom. We all had to learn the language of our parents in order to make ourselves understood by them. We tried to acquire pleasing manners in order not to offend the sensitivities of others. We tried and may still be trying to acquire new skills in order to prepare ourselves for a profession. Perhaps a desire to please others is always a partial motive in our actions, but the motive of self-preservation can hardly be said to be lacking at any time. And in some cases a person will make a long series of great sacrifices in order to be of service to others, or will devote his whole life to the cause of the social and moral uplift of his fellow man. The number and kinds of possible motives which actually influence a given person during his life cannot easily be estimated, yet they are admittedly of prime importance in all social study.

The fact that customs and traditions are uniformly transmitted and often uncritically accepted has so impressed many writers that they incline to see in the process of learning only one side of man's nature.[1, 2] They like to consider him as a sort of stage actor or professional impersonator, who takes on the ways of behaving and the habits of thinking of those around him by chance or necessity, or at least as a result of impulse, suggestion, imitation, or sympathy.[3] Some of them seem to assume that man is a mere stimulus-response reagent, directed only by the motive of selfish pleasure, when not actually mechanically determined to this or that kind of behavior.[4] In other words they assume and apply a mechanistic and hedonistic philosophy to their study of human behavior without any attempt at verifying their philosophical assumptions.

Many other unproved assumptions regarding the process of learning creep into the literature, and are apt to deceive the uncritical reader. It is easy to accept the suggestion of the theorists that men in general merely put on a mask of behavior which turns out to be a stereotyped form of social response prevalent in a given group. The reader, especially if he is suggestible, may conclude that his sole personal motive in thus behaving is to avoid conflicts with the group. He may feel that he is accepting social standards merely because they give him the satisfaction of conforming to customs, and that whenever he dares to violate the conventions, or to institute a reform, he must needs be motivated by a desire to gain more social recognition or prestige for himself. These broad generalizations of the theorists, then, need careful and critical consideration, particularly the so-called scientific accounts of the laws of social learning and social incentives.

A preliminary comment on the views of most experimentalists is pertinent here. It is perhaps true that, as they say, children learn rather uncritically and mechanically. But when they grow up they do sometimes acquire a different technique in learning. They become less selfish, uncooperative, impulsive, and attention seeking than they were as infants, and so become more independent and feel more secure in the world of strife. It is too much to say that they are utterly unconscious of their motives during all this time. On the contrary they need constant and conscious stimulation in order not to form the habit of unduly pitying themselves, or of lauding themselves for the possession of imaginary traits and ultimately giving way to self-deceit and pretense. In other words, unless human beings develop, by conscious purpose and effort, the qualities which make them recognized as intelligent and reasoning individuals, their companions are likely to characterize them as being emotionally immature, or as having regressed to the infantile level. It seems possible that the scientists have drawn their examples of human behavior from this class of undeveloped persons, spoken of today as the class of selfish, emotionally insecure, maladjusted individuals.

One cannot fail to observe the great emphasis placed by the social psychologist today upon the emotional and irrational aspects of human behavior.[5] A careful reader will recognize that this emphasis is exaggerated. There is at least a possibility that some of the social psychologists are themselves victims of a mild sort of maladjustment, in trying to gain prestige and attention for themselves by their proposed sweeping measures of social reform. They should consider this possibility very seriously, because, according to current theory, we are all somewhat maladjusted; only selected individuals here and there are boldly critical enough to find fault with existing norms, and to inaugurate reform measures.[6]

Common sense tells us that we are motivated by all kinds of desires, selfish and unselfish, cooperative and competitive, during childhood as well as when we reach maturity. We acquire these motives by a process of training and learning. Most of us in adult life still learn and think uncritically in various situations. Yet in other situations we may be immoderately critical. At least we do not always imitate in parrot fashion everything that is suggested to us by others, no matter how learned they may be. And we do not always act under the influence of uncontrollable emotional drives. Naturally enough, children are different from adults in many respects. They need to acquire rational appreciations of the purposes of things. But it is most unscientific to infer irrationality in adults from experiments performed on child or adolescent learning. A consideration of the various ways in which human beings come to acquire social habits will bring to light the errors of those who generalize, not only beyond their own data, but also contrary to the readily observed facts of introspection. They derive a few laws of learning from their studies of controlled situations, and then extend these laws to the whole human race in all situations. Some typical statements garnered from the literature are the following: all learning is explained by conditioned reflexes, simple or configural; all thinking is a chain of connected responses; all willing is a restoration of disturbed equilibrium between inner and outer stresses.[7, 8] That these assertions are by no means well founded may be seen from the following section.

LEARNING IN THE CHILD. The child uses its five senses, as they mature and become integrated with bodily movements, in discovering how to obtain various advantages from his surroundings. In order to react efficiently, he must come to interpret the meaning of various happenings, and must learn to use impressions derived from the experiences of the past. He will probably be reacting purposively to his surroundings long before any fully formed ideas are present. He has innate tendencies to guide him in the absence of fully developed intelligence. When he suits certain actions to the attainment of definite goals, we say that he can co-ordinate his movements. At the age of six months the infant can see an object dangling in front of it, reach forward to grasp that object, and succeed in doing so. This is a new acquisition or an adaptation of his behavior. We call it an adaptation because the child has modified his previous random behavior so that he now appears to obtain what he wants by the activity he manifests. If he does not get some of the things which he seeks after there will be discontent and irritation. When he is allowed to satisfy his wants by collecting toys or by winning caresses from others, he is learning to act with a purpose, often enough for a purpose which seems desirable to others, not necessarily to himself. He may at this early age often strive toward dangerous objects and have to be prevented from handling things which are injurious. By submitting to the corrections thus imposed on him by persons who have more knowledge, the child gradually builds up his own system of knowledge and values.

Before he reaches the age of six months, the child has modified his original reflexes in numerous ways that are adaptive or serviceable. He manages to explore bigger and better objects and learns their uses. The process whereby the child associates new experiences with previous ones may be called *conditioning*. Thus sucking reactions may at first be elicited in the child by the sight of a bottle. Later the same reactions may be elicited by the rattle of dishes. At an early date the child responds agreeably to the sound of his mother's voice. Still later, unless he has been unduly alarmed, he may show signs of appreciating the heavier voice of the father. In forming these early associations, which are usually related in some way to feeling states of pleasantness or unpleasantness, he appears to behave in a manner which is very similar to that of domestic animals. He seeks pleasant sensations and attention; he avoids pain and cannot tolerate utter neglect. A comparison of this early type of human learning with that of the infra-human species is not altogether useless, provided we keep in mind the future career that is in store for the child. In a complete study of human behavior, we must carefully investigate how this process of conditioning works, not only with children who cannot tell us their mental states, but also with adults who can. Perhaps we shall find that much older persons sometimes acquire habits in the unintentional, mechanical fashion which we call being conditioned.

Mental Learning and Mental Sets. We have already remarked that social responses are of two chief kinds: external or overt responses, and internal or mental reactions. In most cases of either adult or childhood learning, although there may be overt and externally observable response to the situation, there will certainly be mental reaction which, for want of a better name we call an *attitudinal* or *preparatory response*. Thus, when a child's hand has been struck after an attempt to seize his mother's hair or spectacles, the child is at once disposed to avoid reaching wildly in the future. His tendency to snatch at things indiscriminately has been curbed, perhaps by the infliction of pain. Just what goes on in the child's mind is not known, but it appears that the child learns to take the right mental attitude toward bodily movements because it is more pleasant to do so than not to do so. He learns to direct random gestures and expressions of his needs along the lines laid down for him by others. But the child himself is constantly making mental gestures or inner responses to the new situations, for which the classical name in modern literature is *attitude-formation*.

Mental attitudes or preparatory sets are continually being established in the mind of the child, especially as regards other human beings. Adults also possess many such inner attitudes or tendencies, but they are modifying them incessantly. They can learn, under sufficient motivation, to change some of their attitudes at a moment's notice. Of course, they usually do not change them without first realizing their existence, and often enough the necessity of changing an attitude is our first indication of its presence within us. A meddlesome person, for example, may feel urged to investigate the workings of a radio or of an electric clock, and may believe that his desire is due solely to scientific interest. After experiencing an electric shock he may realize for the first time that there is a deficiency in his knowledge as well as in his habitual method of approaching problems. He has been too hasty in attempting tasks beyond his abilities, and if his attitude is not changed as a result of this incident, it may at least become consciously adverted to. So, too, an adult may find it more convenient to observe the prescriptions of politeness and etiquette only after he has overheard a friend criticizing his boorish manners. Mental sets or attitudes influence behavior and direct its course. The attitudes themselves go through a process of change which is partly dependent upon the present intentions of the person himself and partly upon unknown factors.

Most of our attitudes prepare us to react efficiently to our social environment. It matters little whether or not they have been developed indeliberately and by way of response to unpleasant situations; the crucial question for social psychology is to discover what can be done about them. For once these attitudes have been formed, various factors in the environment become signals for calling out this or that kind of reaction, and the whole process may be quite uniform and spontaneous as long as events run on smoothly and comfortably for ourselves and others.

Numerous external and physical criteria could be set down as indicating the presence of an attitude. All these external signs must be checked against the internal conscious experience, as reported by himself, of the person in question if we are to avoid false or doubtful accusations against him. Thus, when a pupil in a spelling contest ends his answer with a rising inflection, the instructor immediately suspects that the pupil has an uncertain frame of mind, and this suspicion will in general be confirmed by the facts. Again, a student suspected of trying to cheat in an examination may blush and begin to explain that the test was too difficult, thus indicating to the instructor quite unintentionally that the suspicion *may* be correct. Nevertheless, this student might have a habit of similarly excusing himself in all difficult situations, whether there is question of cheating or not. Hence such external signs cannot be taken as conclusive evidence of an inner attitude, the experimentalists notwithstanding. A confidential talk with the student *might* reveal the fact that he is habitually dishonest whenever possible, and, to the delight of the behaviorist and psychoanalyst, that his attitude of trying to justify himself was not clearly known to and admitted by himself. In this case the only practical rule that can be given for detecting and directing attitudes in others is to advise them to keep watch over their conscious attitudes and tendencies and then the unconscious attitudes and sets will take care of themselves.

The formation of attitudes, though an important study, is made doubly difficult by the fact that the true attitudes are often difficult to detect. Most adults believe that their own attitudes are formed, in part at least, as a result of their own conscious efforts and reasoning processes. They ought also to realize that some faulty and undesirable attitudes, as well as some approved ones, are the result of unreflecting responses to social pressure, propaganda, and emotional appeals.

A study of faulty attitudes which have moral implications properly belongs to characterology. Inefficient mental habits and attitudes are exhaustively studied in applied and educational psychology. The present treatise will merely outline the various ways in which human learning, mental and nonmental, normally proceeds.

CONDITIONING IN THE CASE OF HUMAN BEINGS. Numerous attempts have been made by experimenters to show that human beings can be trained or conditioned by stimulations in their environment in such a way that all their reactions appear to be determined and predictable. These experiments were considered by some as a proof that man's actions were merely responses to inner states, or to outer environmental situations, or to both combined.[9] Besides being vague and overgeneral, the response-to-inner-and-outer-stimuli theory is not verified in the least by the investigations which are said to prove it. These well-controlled experimental attempts do seem to show that human beings sometimes react physiologically and emotionally without being fully aware of their total reaction. But they also demonstrate another fact not generally intended or admitted by the experimenters. They show that conscious human subjects sometimes direct the course of the unconscious conditioning process by their inner attitudes of voluntary attention. They may not actually be aware of the results which are taking place, yet they change the total result by means of their control of attention. Moreover, the adult human subject is fully aware throughout the experiment of the fact that he can direct this process of attention in ways which cannot be predicted by the experimenter. He is not at all aware that inner stimulations are effecting a chain of responses which compel him to react in one way rather than another.

Some research workers seem to have rediscovered that human beings possess the power of generalizing, and that they begin at an early age to engage in reflective and attentive thinking. This power of generalizing and of abstracting enables us to arrive at the meaning of situations, to form concepts of them, to make judgments of their value, and to guide our actions accordingly. Generalization implies the extending of the meaning of one concept so as to include under it many diversified situations and events. Thus a child who begins to realize that stealing is not approved has only to discover what situations would come under the general heading of taking what belongs to another. Not until later, perhaps, will he be able to reason out the general principle that stealing is morally wrong. But this again presupposes that the child knows what it means for a thing to be wrong. Every child gradually does acquire these notions, partly through the influence of others, and partly through his own efforts. Countless other reasoning processes must be engaged in by every thinking individual at some time in his life. If we are not willing to accept the fact that human beings actually carry on secret mental operations for themselves, then we should not attempt to lay down the laws for their social behavior. If we neglect the all-important factor of conscious attention during the learning process, we are actually rejecting evidence in favor of theoretical speculations.

There is no need of an appeal to experimental findings in order to show that human beings can voluntarily direct their powers of attention to various aspects of a situation. We mention these experiments only to show that they give us no good reason at all for doubting this universally known fact. Some social psychologists profess not to deny free will, but to prescind from all such philosophical and moral questions. Such a limitation of their field is, of course, quite proper, but it does not justify their asserting that there is no room for the "free-will" concept in any of their theories. What they should say on the basis of their own findings is this: there is no certain external evidence either for or against the existence of free will, but there is positive internal awareness on the part of the subjects that they are not merely responding in a predetermined fashion to the situations in which they find themselves. Writers who maintain that simple and patterned conditioning explains all attitude and habit formation in human beings[10] have apparently not examined the actual reports of the experimenters. For these reports show clearly that the philosophical and scientific dogma of determinism is not only unverified but contradicted by experimental evidence, and is therefore a faulty theory.

THE EXPERIMENTS. K. Young describes an experiment of Krasnogorski on the conditioning of the swallowing reflex of children to various artificial stimuli such as tones and scratchings.[11] Krasnogorski found that children, like animals, showed very transitory conditioned responses unless the responses were reinforced through repetition. Candy was the unconditioned stimulus, and tones, etc., were the conditioned stimuli. He noted, however, some very divergent features. The children showed a much greater degree of individual differences than did the animals used in Pavlov's laboratory. Moreover, the range of association of the conditioned stimuli (tones) was markedly greater for children. That is to say, children became conditioned to *many* tones of nearly the same pitch, and not merely to the one tone used in the experimental situation. In view of these differences, Young observes that the human being is much more plastic (than animals), with more complex possibilities both for conditioning and for inhibition. He further remarks that the conditioning which takes place during emotional disturbance of the organism is far more lasting and effective than that which takes place in a calm and undisturbed state. After giving an account of the famous experiment in which Albert was conditioned to fear many furry objects by the use of a loud sound as the unconditioned stimulus, Young reminds us that in the case of infants and young children the differentiated conditioning is much less specific; that there is a diffusion of the association to new objects, as the more generalized response to furriness indicates; that this flexibility of human association is necessary for the rise of concepts and abstractions; and that concepts are basic assets to man's more complex life. Evidently K. Young sees more than a predetermined response in human conditioning. He admits a greater variability of response in human beings, but instead of finding the explanation of this phenomenon in the active use of the human powers of selecting and approving, he puts forward the hypothesis that the cerebral cortex produces the inhibitions and associations described in the experiment.

G. Murphy, who has a slightly different theory, admits the role of conscious attitudes. He describes Razran's famous experiment in which the salivary glands of human adults were conditioned to such stimuli as words and beats of the metronome.[12] In time the salivary glands would secrete at the sound of the word *pretzel*. But he found three radically different types of response to the conditioning situation in three types of persons. The first included those who built up conditioned responses exactly like Pavlov's dogs; the second, those who showed no increased flow of saliva even after numerous attempts at conditioning; the third, those who conditioned in the reverse direction, so as to have a decreased flow of saliva when the signal for response was given. Murphy concludes that the attitude of the subjects toward the experimenter — the desire to accept, ignore, or defeat his purposes — appears to be the chief clue to the results. Speaking of the experiments on conditioning children to fear, he admits that maturity, intelligence, and emotional factors make the results uncertain, and that higher order conditionings do occur although the range of situations under which they occur has not been defined. It is abundantly clear, he says in summarizing his views, that whether or not the specific stimulus (the element) acquires the power to control a specific response depends upon the whole situation within the organism and the whole stimulus field (the pattern) in which this element must function.

Had Murphy allowed for the effect of conscious *attentional* factors within the total condition of the organism, he would have expressed a view more in harmony with the facts of introspection. Instead, he goes on to say that the very attitude present in the mind of the subject, who does or does not become conditioned, is the result of "dominance" of cortical patterns. Now students of physiological psychology know that the theory of cortical dominance of pathways is only one of many that have been devised to explain canalization or habit formation neurologically. Freeman very wisely admits that,[13] if we insist on reducing all conscious activity to "neural processes," we must have some theories; but he adds that these theories should not be taken too seriously, since they are only bridges to fill the gaps in our knowledge, and may need to be torn down in favor of bigger and better ones.

CONCLUSIONS FROM THE ABOVE. From these few accounts it should be evident that human beings sometimes acquire habits by reason of passive reaction to the environment, and that patterns of response may be spontaneously formed in us as well as in animals. It is also clear that no amount of investigation has as yet revealed the workings of all the attitudinal and attentional factors which enter into the acquisition. This is because voluntary attention enters into the experiments to make prediction of results uncertain. It is hard to be sure that subjects will always direct their inner powers of attention to those "elements" which are presented by the experimenter, owing to distractions or perhaps secret likes and dislikes. Attention does appear to make a difference, even in the involuntary conditioning of salivary glands. Whether it be attention or attitude which differentiates the three types of men, we cannot say that their behavior is predictable before the event of their having taken such and such an attitude. The fact that there are cases of unconscious conditioning in human beings merely means that they do not become conscious of all their vegetative processes. It may on occasion be very useful for them to know more about such reflexes because they may wish some day to redirect them along the lines of co-ordinated muscular responses. Examples of undesirable reflex bodily conditions are stuttering, blinking, twitching of muscles. Persons rarely try to acquire these reflexes, but may be very much interested in trying to control them. They will be pleased to learn that through conscious and deliberate efforts even stuttering is curable.[14] In all these cases success or failure of the attempts at reconditioning seems to depend to a large degree upon the way in which the subject directs his attention voluntarily during the exercises.

THE EFFECT OF CHANGE OF ATTITUDE UPON PERCEPTUAL HABITS. Let us suppose that a person has been conditioned all his life to light stimulations in such wise that, owing to the contrast effect of one object upon other near-by objects in the field of vision, he mistakes the true brightness value of that first object. As a matter of fact this "illusion" is one to which we are all subject in varying degrees. Experiments show that each person has a rather fixed value for this contrast effect, and that there are wide individual differences. In fact, one school of psychologists attempts to use this "brightness constancy" as an indicator of a whole syndrome of personality traits. We do not acquire this perceptual habit deliberately, nor are we conscious of possessing it, although we do, of course, perceive brightness consciously.

Now we might expect that, since the attitude or mental set required for making the judgments in these experiments is such a permanent and indeliberate affair, little could be done to change a subject's attitude or the score for brightness contrast resulting from it. If, on the other hand, attentional factors can change the effects of past conditioning, then we may hope to bring about a change in a subject's scores by inducing him to take a different attitude. As a matter of fact Brunswick has produced diminutions of the "size" illusions by instructing subjects to take an isolating attitude. Woodworth[15] says that in all the perceptions of total situations, an analytical attitude will change the response values. The present writer, under the direction of K. Buehler of Vienna, worked out an experiment in which the average contrast effects for sixty subjects changed by 30 per cent in consequence of the instruction to take a part-view instead of a whole-view attitude toward the color mixers. Conscious factors of attention can change, however gradually, the most deep-seated unconsciously formed perceptual habits.[16]

We may conclude this discussion of conditioning by saying that human beings sometimes react by being unintentionally conditioned to stimulations around them. By "sometimes" we mean in some of their wide variety of bodily and mental processes. The fact that unintentional conditioning occurs does not alter the further fact that the direction and course of our conditioning processes is susceptible to change. In order to initiate a change, one must know in what direction the process is to be reconditioned. When he knows this and has the proper instruction, he can redirect habits and responses that have to do with bodily movements, perceptual patterns, judgments and decisions, in a word, he can form the kind of habits and attitudes which he deems desirable.

OTHER METHODS OF LEARNING

LEARNING BY TRIAL AND ERROR. The complete psychological account of problem solving in all situations, and of independent discovery of new solutions to old problems (inventions), has not yet been written. Hence certain theories may be allowed in discussing this topic. But in all our speculations about the learning process we should be guided by the facts of experience. We should realize that such solutions as "conditioning of reflexes," "organization of patterns of experience," and "neural traces" are merely provisional substitutes for knowledge. In the following accounts of the various methods whereby human beings come to acquire social habits, we shall take care to point out the facts as well as to evaluate the tentative theories often used to explain them.

The method of *guessing* or of random attempts is often used by human beings to deal with a task for which no clear logical solution is readily found. No amount of reasoning will enable one, for instance, to learn to find the keys on a typewriter or on a musical instrument blindfolded. Preliminary study and instruction are somewhat helpful, but the proper habits of co-ordination can be acquired only by "hit-and-miss" efforts. Similarly one may try out various means of winning popularity with his friends without reasoning very much about their efficacy. The first time school children try to read aloud, they appear to use this trial-and-error method. Gradually accents and inflections are modified, until the young reader learns to voice the thoughts of another in a manner which is approved for a given locality. Animals also use the trial-and-error method in learning to rake in food to their dens, to open puzzle boxes, and to get out of mazes. They appear to be guided by past impressions obtained in similar situations. Their motives cannot be analyzed fully but there is no clear evidence of anything more than a tendency to secure such a goal as food or some object associated with food. Many social adjustments that have to do with food have to be learned by human beings in much the same way, and the same is true of conforming to conventional social behavior in such matters as dressing, eating, writing, etc.

Sometimes trial-and-error methods may be all that is required in the way of techniques of learning. But when we attempt to acquire socially cooperative and constructive forms of behavior, some individual reasoning and planning will be required. The successful athlete has to learn to think quickly, and the skilled stage performer needs more than random efforts in learning to imitate the behavior of other actors. So, too, in such complicated tasks as managing a business, engaging in scientific research, or discussing politics, something more than random efforts is called for. Success in these activities demands real human insight and intelligence. The theory of trial-and-error learning cannot account for all the facts of human learning.

LEARNING BY IMITATION. In this matter there is probably more theorizing and inaccurate statement on the part of social scientists than in the matter of conditioning. A writer who observes the powerful forces operative in crowd and mob behavior is apt to forget the fact that human beings have the power of thinking and acting for themselves. Yet the fact remains that some men do think independently at times and that such thinking is absolutely necessary for everyone who does more than respond in a stereotyped fashion to prepared situations. Original thinking is also needed in discovering some suitable solution to problems which are new to us, whether they have been solved by others or not. We must all be discoverers or inventors in solving our own particular social and economic problems. For no two problems of social adjustment are exactly the same, and the person who can come to a decision on the basis of his own self-knowledge is the one who will be most successfully adjusted.

Tarde and the early students of social process believed that at least the uniformities in human behavior could be explained by the laws of *imitation*. But this belief is not supported by an inquiry into the motives of such imitative behavior as we find in styles, fashions, and fads. Externally there may be imitation but such a variety of motives is involved that the mere naming of the external process has little significance for social study, especially since the motives often lead to action which is anything but imitative. Thorndike's investigation of the reasons why people spend money is relevant here, although we are not at all sure that he used adequate means to discover the true reasons. According to the estimate of his group of psychologists, the spending of eight billions of dollars for clothing in 1929 is attributable to at least six or seven different motives, such as protection, approval of others, self-approval, pleasures of vision, etc. Of this total only 12½ per cent, they say, was probably spent for the purpose of winning approval from a motive of conformity or imitation.[17]

The evolutionary dogmatists alleged that the human race at one time changed from an instinctive to a reflective form of behavior, merely because human beings saw the advantages of imitating such behavior in others. On this view it was obviously impossible to explain how the first person began to reflect, except by saying that reflection in its very beginnings was an accident. This is a useless sort of explanation, in view of the fact that human beings do not simply await chance happenings but rather actively manipulate concepts until they arrive at some special solution. Woodworth insists that imitation is never a mere reflex mechanism but that it is a process in which one actually intends a goal. The anticipated satisfaction in reaching the goal directs the goal-seeking efforts.[18] Ellwood says that imitation which engenders unity in a group may be on an instinctive, an habitual, or a rational level.[19] We think that imitation on the deliberately rational level is rather the exception than the rule. As soon as imitation of the styles and attitudes of others is seen to be nothing but mimicry, the tendency is to adopt a different way of acting, or else to find some rational grounds for continuing the imitative behavior. The Murphys and Newcomb,[20] in summarizing the matter of learning by imitation, insist that the motive for imitating is far more important than the imitation itself. They hold that there are three kinds of learning: (1) learning by conditioning; (2) imitation after trial and error; and (3) deliberate imitation. The first kind, they say, occurs indeliberately, unconsciously for the most part, in men and animals. We have already indicated how action patterns could have begun in this way in the child. Learning by trial and error, they say, always implies a strong motive, such as food, by way of reward for the attempts. In the case of children we can seldom detect their actual inner motives, but we can readily observe their repeated efforts at imitating all kinds of behavior, even that of animals, when they are acquiring the all-important speech habits. Our authors hold that in human beings we find deliberate imitation because concepts enter in to guide the learner toward a desired goal. A student of oratory, for instance, may be required to do actual thinking in his efforts to imitate the quality and inflections of the teacher's voice meaningfully. But intensity differences may be reproduced quite unthinkingly.

Human learning, then, sometimes involves reasoning processes on the basis of past impressions which are somehow retained. It does so most frequently and clearly in the life of adults. Thus an auto driver may have learned to slow down in traffic by automatically using the brake pedal. It would be impossible to discover the exact manner in which he learned to do this. But the habit once acquired makes his movements appear automatic like those of ducks flying in formation. An individual changes its direction of flight whenever there is a change in the direction of the whole group. This kind of activity, which we might call falling in line, differs radically from the kind of thing required when the car fails to slow down in response to a push of the brake pedal. The driver might perhaps begin to analyze the situation, unless his mind goes completely blank, and may remember that there is a hand brake, or that hydraulic brakes can be "pumped." The quicker he can think in this instance, the more apt he is to avoid disaster. After having successfully avoided an accident, or in the very instant of danger, he has resolved to have his brakes adjusted as soon as possible. An animal could never have begun to discover any of the complex relations of cause and effect which the auto driver reflected upon in his predicament. This is precisely because he lacks the powers of foresight and reasoning. A primitive person, on the other hand, would manipulate his paddle and canoe, or plan an assault upon his neighbor with just such powers of thought and reflection as characterize human beings in general.

CIRCULAR REFLEXES. Prepotent or dominant reflexes, circular reflexes and canalized tendencies figure largely in the behaviorists' account of the learning process. Allport tries to explain all stages of human learning by means of these concepts.[21] The notion of circular reflexes, as applied to human learning, is open to very serious objections. Circular reflexes are self-stimulated movements, i.e., movements in which an initial action becomes the stimulus for a repetition of the action itself. Thus, pressing the palm of the hand with the forefinger excites tactile end organs which report the sensation to higher centers. These in turn send back impulses resulting in more pressing of the palm with the finger. Similarly the child may say "da," and on hearing it, be stimulated to do it again and we hear "da, da, da." This explanation clearly involves a vicious circle. What needs to be explained is the very first occurrence of that new kind of action which we call learning. Not much seems to be gained by saying that the action is the stimulus for itself. This might indeed explain the continuation of a particular kind of action, not the beginning or cessation of the same. Such attempts at reducing learning to unending responses or chains of reflexes are rather ingenious than informative. They do not tell us much about the way in which a person comes to learn by imitation, unless he happens quite by chance to make a right beginning.

Such phenomena as mimicry in animals and young children, stereotypy of response in adults when they keep mumbling things they hear like "an apple a day . . . " and cases of echopraxia and echolalia among psychopathic individuals, have probably suggested the above explanation. Also the fact that certain nerve cells have recently been found to have this property of self-stimulation may have influenced the views of the investigators. In echopraxia the patient keeps aping the gestures of others; in echolalia he mumbles unceasingly whatever he hears. It is difficult to see why we should extend an explanation of learning drawn from these cases to all adult endeavor, unless we hold that all persons who pass through childhood are arrested in their development at a premature level. The current view of normal development rather assumes that adults transcend the level of infants and abnormals in development of intelligence as well as of emotion. The person who fails to mature in these respects is said to be regressing toward the infantile level.

The main features of adult learning cannot be outlined without mentioning the functions of intellectual insight and reason in human behavior. Along with the processes of conditioning and imitation there goes on a mental process whereby human adults consciously motivate themselves in a multitude of different ways, sometimes to be different from others, sometimes to imitate those whom they respect. Their adjustment to their surroundings must be looked upon as a process guided by thinking and decisions, and it is actually considered in this light by those who try to explain it by means of imitation or trial-and-error learning. For they insist that each human being must direct his own course of action in accordance with the so-called sound principles of good adjustment.

LEARNING BY INSIGHT AND REFLECTION. There are some intellectual elements involved in imitation and suggestion. The function of reason in these processes will be discussed later. No theory of suggestion can neglect the role of voluntary attention if it is to fit the facts of observed behavior. When an adult voluntarily directs his attention to some one element in a situation, he is using his power of reason to guide him. It is unfortunate that reason and volition are so often misused by us under stressing circumstances. But without some use of these two powers, no kind of active seeking of a solution of new problems, no rational adjustment to society is possible. Sensory representations merely report to us previous concrete experiences, and we must use our intellect, aided by imagination, in order to combine these past experiences in a suitable way, and to make generalizations about the future upon the basis of these experiences. Only through the intellect do we acquire knowledge of possible and serviceable relationships between ourselves and our environment. Imitation of others takes place, in all probability, when sensory impressions fail to evoke the process of rational thinking. The contagious cough in an audience may be an example of this, though at the time its imitative character may escape our attention entirely. Imitation may also occur by reason of acquired habit or instinctive tendency or both, as when we feel hungry on seeing others take food. In this latter case the process involves suggestion, but in both cases the external stimulating objects evoke reactions founded on bodily conditions over which we have no need to exercise rational control all the time. When the need does arise we may find ourselves able to avoid the cough and to neglect the feeling of hunger.

True it is that human beings, though endowed at birth with potentialities for rational thought and volition, must gradually actuate these capacities under the influence of maturation and environment. These factors constantly interact with one another in varying proportion. In trifling matters and in the matter of conventions we do well to imitate. After the age of six there is apparent in every individual a process whereby he learns to evaluate the things around him in terms of personal gain and of advantage to the group. In dealing with social and economic problems, as well as with problems of personal adjustment to our immediate circle of friends, we normally rely on intellectual insight. This implies an inner understanding of the values and purposes of things and of the possible ways of utilizing them to attain preconceived goals. It also involves seeing into the distant future beyond the confines of a present total situation, and providing for many eventualities which only human beings are able to foresee. Animals can relive the past and thus learn to combine objects into patterns which enable them to attain an immediate goal. The human mind can do much more. It can bring the future before the forum of thought and submit past, present, and future to analysis, criticism, and evaluation. The human mind also thinks in terms of moral values, and does not merely apprehend what is useful for bodily needs. Human beings take an interest in their distant final goals or objectives. They modify their actions according to the moral value which they set upon the thing to be attained. They weigh motives and formulate rules for action which will insure the attainment of their desired goals. Needless to say they do not always attain these goals, but if they did not have the power to aspire to them they would not be human. If they merely drifted with the current of thought, as with a stream of traffic, and did not envisage for themselves a life which has lasting value, and did not at any time cooperate with others in striving toward deeds of real value, then they would be very similar to the animals used in many studies in social psychology.[22]

Activities which require insight and reflective thinking are — besides the general matter of self-management — such activities as discussing social problems, planning civic projects and recreation, devising punitive and preventive measures against crime, preparing for a career of service to humanity, and engaging in scientific research and invention. Research writers often pass over these items in silence when discussing social learning. Without specifically human powers, namely those of intellect and will, no discovery would be possible. For in invention and discovery a new relation, of which no one else has been aware, is conceived in the mind and brought into actuality outside the mind. The power which gives rise to this kind of mental activity is the same as that involved in discovering rational solutions to personal problems. A wrong solution is always traceable, at least in part, to the fact that we do not reason out and strive after a satisfactory relationship between ourselves and others. The definitely psychopathic individual may lose for a time the ability to solve his problems realistically, and thus he imagines relationships of antagonism and persecution which do not exist. During recovery and afterwards there is a revival of this lost power of insight. His rediscovery of himself often comes with a flash, and he cannot see why he was so prone to misjudge other persons previously. He sometimes knows better than the one who advises him that the power of rational control of social reactions is a specifically human characteristic.

Children and aboriginals, in spite of all that has been written about their lack of reason and their low level of intelligence (their identification of themselves with their surroundings), make numerous discoveries regarding adjustment of themselves and control of the forces of nature. Many of the things they learn are obviously patterns of behavior deemed useful or necessary by the group. Some individuals in each such group, however, may one day make a new discovery after using insight, planning, and experimentation. It matters little whether we are able to penetrate their minds fully and see just what happens when a discovery is made. The fact remains that they sometimes discover relationships between familiar objects which are new to themselves and others.

Thus the natives of Central Africa still lack certain means of traveling by water routes. Their neighbors to the east and west possess these means, the former having perfected seamed bark canoes, the latter the famous hollow-tree boats.[23] Someone must have planned these instruments on the basis of experience and of generalizations upon past observations. Someone had to understand the very definite relations of causality existing between various kinds of materials. Chance may have facilitated the discoveries. Interest in nature and a desire to control some of its forces must have stimulated their efforts. Insight into possible advantages or disadvantages aided them in producing useful utensils of all sorts.

Thus the Incas of South America had discovered, ages ago, the art of using pig bladders or similar objects for spraying tobacco powder into the nostrils, and some of their techniques for inducing stupor by means of alcoholic beverages were most ingenious. Any writer who claims that primitive man was altogether emotional and irrational is doing great violence to the facts.[24]

FOR ACCELERATED READING

SHORT SUMMARY OF THE CHAPTER

The *learning process* is the most useful one among all those studied for predicting later group phenomena and individual differences in behavior. The process is rather spontaneous and the human child may form fixed attitudes at a very early date. Selfishness appears to motivate infants, social prestige becomes a factor later, innumerable factors contribute to the formation and change of conscious attitudes. When impulsive and irrational behavior persists in a person despite training he may become unfit to cope with social problems. The process of conditioning can be directed through conscious attention. It is not merely an automatic response occurrence although many attitudes may be formed unknowingly.

The several *methods* whereby learning can occur are by conditioning to what is pleasant and good, establishing mental readiness or set, learning to abstract and think. Attitudes however formed are not immutable once their presence has been detected. The hit-and-miss system of learning may be employed in simpler conventional matters (fads, fashions, and customs); it is inadequate in the case of those who need to plan a complex scheme of operations leading to personal or group adjustment.

Imitation plays a role in all our learning, but it is not a powerful motive apart from the attitude taken toward the persons and operations imitated. No amount of imitation will enable an individual to solve personal problems. *Circular reflexes* may be involved in automatic behavior, especially found in animals, abnormal people, and crowds.

Learning by insight is the typically human prerogative. It implies apprehension of relations in the abstract. All individual adjustment requires such prevision of consequences and suiting means to the end desired. Irrational conformity (copying behavior without thinking of the consequences) leads to stereotypes of behavior and may make readjustment to new situations difficult for individuals and for groups.

Find Review Questions and Supplementary Reading at the end of the book.

CHAPTER 5

SOCIAL MOTIVES AND MOTIVATION

Preamble — The Problem; Meaning of Terms; The Animal Nature of Man; Why Prediction Is Often Correct; The Criteria of Instincts; The Confusion of Terms. *Classification of Drives* — Difficulty of the Division Into Drives and Incentives; Our Division: (I) Instincts or Drives: (A) Food Drives; (B) Sex Drives; (C) Maternal, i.e., Cooperative and Protective Behavior. (II) The Social Motives and Incentives: (A) Selfish Motives: (*a*) Self-Assertion; (*b*) Wish for Security (*c*) Rewards; (*d*) Rivalry. (B) Unselfish Motives: Submissive Tendency and Cooperation.

PREAMBLE

THE PROBLEM. The question of motives of behavior is considered today to be of prime importance in social psychology. Some authors claim that we cannot consider either nature or nurture, heredity or environment, as separate forces or determiners of human behavior because of the uncertainties of motivation.[1] The implication is that two persons with an identical kind and amount of inherited qualities may develop quite differently in consequence of the motives and incentives which they have for acting in a given way.

Hardly anyone, whether scientist or layman, believes that inheritance contributes nothing to the structure and behavior of a given person. We shall be quite justified, then, in considering some tendencies which are innate in the whole human race because of the fact that bodily structures may be inherited. Our emphasis will be upon *conscious* tendencies, because it is through our own personal awareness that a superstructure of higher incentives is built upon the basic bodily tendencies through the use of bodily sensations and perceptions. We shall see that some of these basic or biological tendencies are the active accompaniments of social learning especially in young children. We shall not fail to indicate that such tendencies, based on bodily needs and processes, though real and fundamental, are not the only kind of *motives* or *incentives* for human action. They may not even be the most significant ones for the guidance of human behavior although it may be true that human beings are in fact greatly influenced by them in their habitual everyday life.

We shall discuss first the meaning of the relevant terms; second, the instinctive tendencies in human individuals; and finally, the social motives and incentives.

MEANING OF TERMS. A *motive* is any kind of value or good that is recognized in any object or activity, and consequently it is that in an object which, when recognized, impels a person toward or away from that object. This is the ancient concept of motive and it is straightforward enough, provided we do not lose sight of the fact that only human beings are capable of acting according to motives in this strict sense. This is so because they alone among earthly living things are capable of reflecting upon the inherent value of a proposed way of acting and of reasoning out the final implications and goals of their actions.

But human beings are also often impelled toward or away from objects apart from a full use of their power of reflection. Very frequently they act upon impulse or habit. Hence it is necessary to say that, although men *can act* from motives strictly so called, they can also act or tend to act owing to other kinds of impelling forces. We call all such other forces or tendencies within a person the *motivating factors*. Among such other forces or factors are to be found some innate or instinctive tendencies. There are other tendencies which are acquired during the process of growth and learning, and we call these the habitual tendencies.

THE ANIMAL NATURE OF MAN. We have mentioned that, because of the uniformity manifested in certain concrete forms of human behavior, the social scientist is able to predict future reactions fairly accurately. In the case of animals these predictions are most reliable, provided we know enough about the habits of the animals in question. Thus we know that birds will build nests for rearing their young, spiders will spin webs, mammals will suckle their young, etc. On the other hand primates will acquire skills in manipulating sticks and clubs; clawed mammals like cats and racoons will perform better with strings and latches than with sticks, when confronted with a laboratory problem.[2]

Human beings also develop similar useful patterns of behavior and gradually come to manifest those abilities which we call thinking, that is, manipulating verbal concepts and abstract symbols. We are safe in predicting that this will be true of all human beings, including those peoples called primitive, as well as the so-called "feral" or wolf men. Psychologists have found that whenever these latter individuals are of normal health and are not too far advanced in years they can and do acquire some skill in the use of language if properly taught. The other ways of acting which they manifest indicate quite clearly the presence of instinctive or animal tendencies. Professor Krout gives a short account of some of these abandoned persons, and tries to prove that language ability is altogether a socially conditioned trait.[3] He does not tell us why it is that social conditioning does not produce language ability in the other primates.

It is thus clear that mere predictability of behavior is no certain sign that it is of its very nature either instinctive or habitual or rational activity. In regard to those actions of human beings which are the result of free choice, there can be no question of prevision and prediction of their actual course, on the part of someone else, unless one had perfect knowledge of all things. The social scientist who denies the existence of an all-knowing Being appears to claim for himself the possession of this divine knowledge when he asserts that he can predict all human behavior. For instance, he might try to predict whether or not I shall choose to complete the sentence which I am now in the process of writing. The attempt would presumably be based on his thorough acquaintance with my inner drives and habit tendencies (which he would call motives) in similar situations — an acquaintance obtained by observation of me and my behavior in just such situations as this. In case I should happen to choose as he had predicted, or as a hundred other persons chose under like circumstances, the scientist might flatter himself that he had discovered a law of behavior. His law might read something like this: writers trained in philosophical as well as in scientific method always elect to finish sentences that contain criticisms of science, once they are "set" upon writing treatises like this. The scientist might then be asked how he came to know that the writer would be "set" to attempt such a treatise just at this time. The answer would have to be evasive, namely, that previous inner motives or chains of responses have resulted in this particular set or determining tendency. This would be the scientist's way of expressing the simple fact of experience, that the writer of these lines had "resolved" to carry out his task. Of course, a mere guess on the part of the predicter, as to my finishing or not finishing the task, would have a fifty-fifty chance of being correct. But deterministic scientists do not admit that their hypotheses are mere guesses, especially when tested in the laboratory. They claim rather to be discovering the laws which determine behavior. Sometimes they admit, and rightly so, that they are applying general principles, which are *tacitly assumed* as true, to the particular event in question, without any possibility of testing them in the laboratory. That is the case with the "assumption" that all human choices are predetermined.

We are able to predict some forms of animal behavior by reason of the fact that animals follow uniform patterns. From the presence of these patterns we may argue to an inner cause or source of activity even though we may not be able to ask the animal what this source may be. But from the mere absence of uniformity, as in the case of animal learning, we may not argue to the presence of rational choice. Unpredictability is no more a sign of self-determination than predictability alone is of outside determinism. Unpredictability follows from human freedom because of the difficulty of penetrating the motives of human beings. Since man is free, his actions may be unpredictable, but he is not free because of this fact alone.

This point is of great importance, because some readers will always object that we cannot predict all types of animal behavior, and hence there is no difference between animal and human choices. We may fail, it is true, to predict all the possibilities for animals, but we do know, on the basis of continual observation, that animals do not give clear signs of possessing the power of reason. Also on the basis of the Kellogg experiment[4] we know that the chimpanzee developed to the limit, and we may reasonably infer that it would have manifested human reasoning powers if it possessed them. It did not manifest them, and any assumption that it was hiding some of its valuable potentialities is without foundation.[5] The experiment was called off precisely because the female chimpanzee showed no prospects whatever of future development in its human environment.

The human infant, in the above experiment, did show signs of using reflective power, as any other infant might do. When a child is old enough he can tell us that he is able to make a choice among many possible courses of action, on the basis of ideas which he possesses. We should notice that whenever the sociologist, for instance, predicts the number of suicides, etc., that will take place in a given community, he can never tell us who the acting persons will be; similarly when the psychologist, equipped with thorough knowledge of the innner motives of a person, fails to predict the time and place of his future actions, he is made very cognizant of the fact that man is a reflecting, spontaneous, self-determining agent.

WHY PREDICTION IS OFTEN CORRECT. Whenever prediction of human actions is correct, this may be due to one or more of three mutually dependent factors. In the example of the writer concluding his sentence, chance could have been a factor in making a right prediction. Habit or perseveration tendency, known to some outside observer, might also have urged the writer to complete his task, somewhat after the fashion of the chimpanzee who continued to act churlishly until she secured the attention of her master. Finally the writer might have had an innate tendency to write whenever a pencil was within reach, just as the chimpanzee was wont to scribble and manipulate small sticks endlessly and almost from birth. Which of these three factors was responsible for the writer's particular action *cannot be known* by an external observer. The writer himself would have been able to tell whether or not he was trying to exercise his will in the matter. If he were, then who else could be sure of this fact but himself! He could also have recognized the presence of some habitual tendencies, but he would have no sure way of learning that they were acquired and not innate.

The main points about human motivation may be summed up as follows: Some of the behavior of human beings is consequent upon the use of rational choice or volition, and thus all of it is difficult to predict. Competent writers today admit this fundamental fact.[6] Outside knowledge of the inner habit tendencies of a person and of their effective external stimulations permits fairly correct predictions to be made especially when the person in question is acting without much advertence and deliberation. But when we human beings reflect upon the reasons for our actions, we become conscious of yielding to or of resisting our inner urges. There can be no question of our always being deceived as to our motives, because we are the only ones who can be relied upon to state what our conscious rational motives may be at a given moment. Those who maintain that we unconsciously deceive ourselves as to our true motives and intentions are manifestly misusing the term motive. We are actually moved by *real* motives even though they are disguised and repre sented to us as only apparent goods, as, for example, the benefits of studying Freudian psychology. When Morgan contends[7] that the honest man admits personal interest in all activities, and the dishonest man denies it, he is probably referring to such disguises of motives as we find in many apparently abnormally selfish clinical patients. A selfish motive is still a motive of the will, and who but the self will be able to diagnose the true character of the same!

THE CRITERIA OF INSTINCTS. In the case of animals, instinctive drives are distinguished from acquired or learned behavior by the fact that the latter can be changed through various kinds of new contacts with the environment, whereas the former manifest themselves under all circumstances, and mature universally in every known environment, assuming, of course, that normal health is maintained. Instinctive forms of behavior are so uniform that they are fairly predictable, and they lead to useful goals, the attainment of which has been observed among animals by biologists from earliest times. The presence of intellectual insight and conceptual thinking among animals has not yet been unequivocally established in spite of persistent attempts to set up an experiment in proof of it. Krout,[8] commenting upon the reported negative results of one such experiment, says that while symbolic or algebraic thinking is impossible for the infra-human species, many humans fail to acquire it also. He apparently does not admit that conceptual language is a universal and necessary sign of conceptual thinking.

Behavior on the part of animals of a given species is called purely instinctive only when such behavior is not found to be modifiable through training or changing the environment. The Murphys[9] have collected ample evidence of the fact that animals have instincts in this sense. Behavior patterns which manifest themselves in every environment but in delayed fashion are said to be instinctive but matured. Instinctive behavior is therefore that uniform, complex, and serviceable type of behavior which is characteristic of a species independently of learning.

Human beings, as soon as they become socially active — at the age of 3 or 4 months according to the Murphys[10] — do not manifest much of purely instinctive behavior in the above sense. Yet men are all aware of the tendencies which arise universally in later life as a result of certain changes in bodily tissues. They are also aware of developing habits automatically, that is, without much reflection, in response to aspects of their environment. Finally they are aware of the ability to select types of behavior among a variety of possibilities, and to attend at will to any one of a host of attractive stimulations in their environment. Their learning processes are of two kinds, the automatic and the reflective. Hence when Ruch[11] and others attempt to apply their criterion of learned and unlearned motives to human beings they are altogether neglecting this third kind of voluntarily chosen habit formation. We know that human beings learn to modify their habits voluntarily. After a certain age they develop a capacity to do something about their environment, and to use their power of reason to guide them in regard to external stimulations.

We can therefore distinguish the innate tendencies from many individually acquired habits by appealing to the conscious testimony of human beings. Both the innate and the acquired tendencies will impel toward uniform behavior. But if a person remembers that he at some time acquired a certain habit such as lying or swearing, even though he may not remember when or why he acquired it, then he is able to begin changing the habit deliberately. Any new acquisition of habits will not (in this country) be termed instinctive behavior. Action tendencies based on bodily drives, that is, the normal functioning of the biological organism which is inherited, may be classed as instinctive tendencies. They satisfy the threefold criterion already mentioned, namely, they are universal in all men, they arise independently of individual experience or effort to change them, and they lead to uniform, serviceable, pleasurable forms of behavior.

The real difference, therefore, between animal and human instincts consists in the ability which every normal human being possesses to guide his learning processes voluntarily along preconceived lines. In thus shaping the course of his own activities, he will be directed by notions of value, by motives in the strict sense. Not all of his actions will be caused by selfish impulses toward pleasures of the senses, or by inner drives and needs. He will compare the value of different motives and distinguish, at times, between self-gratifying actions and socially cooperative or disturbing behavior.

The acts of human beings are therefore influenced by two different kinds of causes: by *motivating factors*, such as native endowment and habitual tendencies, and by *motives in the strict sense,* intellectually conceived notions of value. We shall keep this distinction of terms clear throughout our chapter. The instinctive tendencies impel men toward actions which result in self-conservation, conservation of the species, and socially cooperative and congenial forms of behavior. Organic conditions can make these tendencies conscious and then one speaks of drives or urges. Human beings tend to direct these urges and the expression of their instinctive tendencies along unforeseen lines even though the urges have their origin in biological tensions. Hence the utmost precaution must be taken in the use of the terms, otherwise the reader may overlook the important fact that imagination and reflection can modify the strength of the bodily drives.

THE CONFUSION OF TERMS. Woodworth, an outstanding exponent of dynamic psychology today, does not use the word *instinct,* but substitutes "unlearned motives" for what he formerly called instinct. He thinks we must keep this concept distinct from the concept of habit. Regularized food habits or sex habits, he maintains, are something quite different from the general tendency to seek food or sexual gratification, and the concept of instinct is one of a system of interrelated and contrasting concepts among which we find reflex, emotion, and habit. Although he sometimes substitutes "set" for "motive," it is not clear that he distinguishes rational motive from "set," unless he assumes that rational motives are "learned." The "set," according to him, is a state of the individual which disposes him toward a certain form of behavior and for seeking certain goals. He considers the organism to be equipped by nature to deal with the environment effectively. He wisely remarks that whereas learned performances occur in regard to eating and seeking sexual pleasure, the trend toward these activities is the same for all.[12]

There is no difficulty about finding new names for old facts, so long as the new name expresses these same facts. It is well to remember, however, that no amount of juggling of terms will get rid of the age-old fact of rationally directed behavior. Gurnee[13] calls mental tendencies in general by the name of desires, cravings, and impulses. He reserves the terms urges, drives, and needs for bodily conditions. This terminology implies that the bodily needs are not mental in any sense, and that they may determine behavior absolutely. Bird[14] is somewhat clearer in his terms. He speaks of mental tendencies as if they were or could be real intellectual appreciations of the values of things, real incentives, motives. He also calls bodily urges "primary drives." In our chapter the term "mental" must be taken in either one of two senses. It may mean mental sensory, as in the case of conscious but unpremeditated tendencies toward sensory objects. Or it may mean mental rational, that is, conscious volitional tendencies toward objects which can be understood to have value. Thus we, too, may dispense with the words *instinctive behavior,* but only because of the fact that all known processes of human motivation may be subsumed under the headings of conscious rational motives and motivating factors, some of which are founded upon sensory appetites.

The reason for the dispute among contemporary writers is their vagueness in the use of terms, resulting from theoretical bias in favor of a system or school of psychology. Consider the following definitions, for example. The behaviorist, since he denies consciousness as a scientific fact, calls an instinctive action a universal stereotyped form of behavior resulting from innate equipment alone. Instincts thus become practically synonymous with reflexes. The definition is too narrow in the sense that it excludes conscious tendencies altogether. For the hormic psychologist and for some functionalists, instincts provide us with primitive desires and purposes which continue to express themselves in various ways under the influence of training until they are satisfied. This view makes instinct indistinguishable from learning. It exaggerates the influence of heredity, original urges, and drives, just as the behaviorist view exaggerates the influence of environmental and developmental factors. Both views overlook the possibility of rational learning and of voluntary selection of a course of action which will change the course of human progress.

A hybrid or eclectic view which is popular today postulates innate drives or urges, and allows for unlimited variation in them during the adjustment to the social forces by means of conditioning processes. This is the view adopted in most of the newest textbooks on social psychology.

CLASSIFICATION OF DRIVES

DIFFICULTY OF THE DIVISION INTO DRIVES AND INCENTIVES. Bird gives what might appear as a satisfactory simple classification of all human motives. He lists three tendencies in man which have no known physiological basis, but which interact with one another to produce tension systems in the organism. They are play tendencies, friendship tendencies, and simple "activity" drives. Then he gives a list of those drives which have a bodily basis. His lists are very similar to those of the Murphys.[15] The latter, however, list five organic drives and three groups of nonorganic or mental drives, namely, the drive to activity, the aesthetic drives, and the emotional drives. They thus class mental tendencies with the drives. There is no indication in this classification that conscious rational processes direct the activities of men. It seems to be a plain fact that the hunger drive, for instance, is based upon bodily needs, but that the need to plan a diet or to ration a whole community requires some deliberation. An old bias against admitting anything like a rational faculty in scientific studies probably accounts for the failure of many authors to clarify their terms. The fact that introspection itself does not enable us to distinguish perfectly between our rational and our sensory tendencies may also be responsible for the confusion.

In view of what we have already stated, an instinctive tendency in man may be reacted to unreflectingly, or it may be modified by other conscious motives and intentions. Similarly, a rational motive such as love of our country and our flag may be reacted to automatically by imitating the salute of the crowd, or it may be consciously reflected upon and evaluated, and may finally lead to a deliberate act of loyalty. For this reason, all division of motivating factors (without motives) into inner bodily urges and outer incentives without bodily basis will be inadequate. The incentives listed by most authors, such as rewards and punishments, competition, success or knowledge of results, may all be but need not always be rational motives. It depends upon the individual cases. Besides, such incentives are more than concrete unevaluated physical objects *outside* the one who strives for them. When an incentive becomes capable of moving the will it is no longer merely an outside object. It is an object known and appreciated.

It is refreshing to notice that Bird is one of the few modern authors who finds fault with the conditioned-reflex theory of learning. He says that human beings manage or can manage the situations which they meet in a way which differs from that of the animal both in *kind* and in *degree*.[16] He holds that the intellect of man engages in planning and the will in choosing and guiding the course of our action tendencies of whatever kind. In the following division it must be remembered that drives may present material for rational deliberation, and that outer incentives may be reacted to by force of habit or inner tendency. In men neither process goes on entirely without guidance from reason, and neither process can take place in total isolation from bodily processes.

OUR DIVISION: THE BODILY DRIVES AND SOCIAL INCENTIVES

I) INSTINCTIVE TENDENCIES OR BODILY DRIVES.

A) Food Drives. Animals stalk about in search of food, or of other needed materials. The behavior of a satiated human individual differs from that of a hungry one. Yet, conflicting with the craving for food may be some other human desire such as for the solution of a business problem, or for a game of chess or golf. The human being, even when hungry, may lightly pass over his physiological urges and yield to the dominance of psychological or mental urges. He may then act in a queer and distracted manner and even disregard the niceties of human conventions until the psychological need is satisfied. Physiological urges, as possessed by human beings are overlaid with and complicated by conscious desires and conscious tendencies.

Examples could be multiplied to illustrate the fact that organic drives in adults become camouflaged by socialized motives. The unsophisticated infant has not yet had its native urges disturbed by very much reasoning. Nevertheless young children seem to be guided rather effectively toward what is beneficial for them. Perhaps there is too much interference with the food habits of children on the part of parents. This would certainly be the case if the investigation of Dr. Aldrich is to be relied upon.[17] He and his associates found that infants would select a sufficiently balanced diet to maintain good health when a great variety of delectable foods had been placed before them. Primitive peoples seem also directed by nature in the selection of the needed food materials. Of course, we cannot say that their selection is purely instinctive. A. Morgan[18] has investigated the food habits of primitive groups and maintains that modern scientists have artificially removed the vitamin-rich part of natural foods and then prescribed the elements removed as medicine. Obviously we have so surrounded our food habits today with customs and ceremonies that the instinctive basis is not readily apparent. A vast army of human engineers is required in a modern society to aid in satisfying the artificially created food preferences of human beings. While food seeking and food getting are native drives, food planning has become socialized and commercialized by modern rational man.

Closely related to the food drive and probably fundamental to it is the urge to *self-preservation,* with inclinations toward a reasonable self-defense. Feelings of security arise from a proper balance between these urges and the opportunities for satisfying them.

B) Sex Drives. At a certain age in the life of an individual there arises what is called sexual inclination. By the time of puberty this urge, too, has been complicated by conscious factors and acquired habits. Experiment seems to have convinced certain doubters that animals will act on the sex urge very uniformly even when all opportunity for learning sexual behavior from other animals has been precluded.

There are really two kinds of sensations which are capable of being called sexual, but which can be readily distinguished in one's own case. There are sensations arising from the external genitalia even before puberty, and there are those which are experienced only after full sexual development is reached. An understanding of these experiences may aid in dealing with many instances of childhood behavior which lead to problem cases for the clinician. Although the child lacks fully functional genital organs, it can undoubtedly experience pleasures which are localized in the region of the genitalia. Habits formed by reason of these early experiences may persist and lead to a misdirection of the normal adult behavior tendencies. They become conscious habits and cravings and they may agitate the person even when stimulations from the sex glands are absent. In other words, the imagination and recollection of an intensely pleasurable sensation can re-excite the whole neurosexual mechanism without the presence of a local stimulation. Such stored impressions may lead to dangerous symptoms and obsessions when proper guidance is lacking. By reason of the fact that human beings can recall the past and envision the future, they can plan a course of action that is in accord with right principles and with good adjustment. They must sometime or other construct desirable habit systems upon the basis of their bodily sex drives. Many children unfortunately acquire undesirable habits accidentally or through the malicious practices of adults. It is reassuring to know that such habit systems, because they have been acquired, can also be modified through the influence of training and motivation. Most children are, unhappily, less thoroughly trained in matters relating to the sex impulse than they are in such conventions as behaving politely and acting cleverly.

We have already noted that in the case of the sex drive, past experience is able to arouse a desire in the absence of direct stimulation from the sex organs themselves. This has been known to happen in the case of castrated persons as well as animals. Our knowledge of animal desires is based on analogy, but it is said to be the case that if the gonads of animals are removed before sexual maturity is reached, the mating impulse is stifled and no desire is manifested. In the case of human beings it does not seem to matter whether the gonads are removed before or after there has been sexual experience. Because of his power of understanding and of imagination, a human being can arouse conscious desires and repugnances by his own efforts, and does not have these inclinations and feelings because of mechanically aroused stimulations alone. The powers of reason and volition are therefore valuable to man in so far as they lead to behavior which is called desirable (morally good) by those scientists who have the true interests of humanity at heart.

Courses in mental hygiene include a detailed discussion of basic urges and their redirection in the case of maladjusted sexual tendencies. Our task is ended when we have called attention to the important role of motivation in the establishment of suitable sexual behavior.

C) Maternal, that is, Socially Cooperative Behavior. Under this heading we shall include all tendencies growing out of the keenly felt human need for social cooperation and congenial forms of social contact. The behavior of parents and especially of mothers is only a particular case which has occasioned some dispute among the writers on instincts. Maternal behavior occurs both in human beings and in animals, and may to some extent be influenced by hormones. But for human beings, social factors are probably much more important than glandular secretions in shaping the course of parental activity. Unless warped by mistaken notions, man has the intelligence to realize that the helpless infant is a thing of value, and that it has a right to protection from the first moment of its existence. The so-called protective instinct, which is founded on the general physical weakness of the protected party rather than upon any particular bodily function of the protector, includes a predominant element of rational activity. Undoubtedly every person also instinctively protects himself and his closest friends from evils that can be avoided, but persons learn to guide their protective behavior according to certain standards which they approve. When writers ignore this fact, they try to prove the absence of maternal instincts by recording the number of times the mother in labor complains of her sufferings, or to measure the strength of the maternal drive by the amount of fondling bestowed on the child. Humane psychologists ought to recognize the fact that questions put to expectant mothers regarding their desires for offspring are ill-advised and little to the point. As soon as her days of travail are over the ordinary mother will acknowledge that her baby is dear to her, though we admit the bonds of affection become strengthened by each succeeding contact. Mothers whose actions are guided by reason, and not by mere sentiment or remorse for past misdemeanors, admit that the very helplessness of the infant demands protective behavior on their part. They also understand that the family is a necessary institution for the rearing and education of children whose destiny is sublime and whose value is not restricted to the good of the home or of the nation. Misguided and selfish corrupters of the home would show more understanding themselves if, instead of trying to prove or disprove maternal instincts, they would help parents to a fuller realization of the social obligations and singular privileges connected with the role of parenthood.

Closely related to the parental tendencies are impulses to cooperate with others in overcoming their difficulties and in warding off dangers to personal and group safety. Feelings of weakness and inadequacy are apt to accompany unsuccessful efforts to sustain ourselves under difficult circumstances. Most energetic persons manage to find and maintain a middle course between too much insecurity and too much aggression and competition. Though we admire the energy of the experimental social psychologists in trying to detect the causes of wars and of social conflicts, they are unduly concerned about the existence or nonexistence of the fighting instinct, and seem to forget that whether or not there is such an instinct, battles do take place now and then even among small children. The Murphys treat the matter with much insight when they state: "For a full understanding of aggression in any group we need, then, to understand the cultural and situational pressures in relation to the personality make-up of individual children, and their concrete ways of finding a way out amid the conflicts presented by moral precepts, the need for self-defense, and the aggression piled up in their early contacts with big and small human beings."[19] This statement contains all the elements that go into the formation of the total social individual, including his needs, his habits, and the concrete ways of finding solutions to his problems. Compare this with the psychoanalytic view of conflicts which implies determinism either by social environment or by the drive to aggression or by both.[20]

II) THE SOCIAL MOTIVES AND INCENTIVES.

A) *Selfish Motives.* Bearing in mind our previous distinction between motives and motivating factors, we may now consider what other writers have termed nonbiological motives or external incentives. Actually all these factors may involve rational motives in the strict sense, as well as fundamental needs of the whole man. No one of these incentives may be considered as an object totally outside the thinking and acting person.

Gurnee lists the following social motives: (1) gregariousness; (2) social approval; (3) assertive tendencies; (4) submissive tendencies.[21] W. I. Thomas and many sociologists claim to have found the four fundamental wishes which are more universal than any other incentives. They are: (1) the wish for security; (2) the wish for novelty; (3) the wish for response; (4) the wish for recognition. Thomas makes no mention of submissiveness as a fundamental wish. Bird allows for the great variability of all these drives and incentives at different times and under different systems of education.[22] He lists the following: (1) play, friendship, and activity; (2) praise, blame, and knowledge of results; (3) competition; (4) cooperation. Bird's four groups agree fairly well with Gurnee's except that they are more explicit. Both these authors fail to make the wish for security a fundamental or basic one, but place submission and co-operation in their treatises. We shall make some comments on all these five groups of incentives. They all imply a certain emotional factor in the individual who possesses them, and this may be the reason for the difficulty of classification. Most people develop parallel emotional responses in connection with their social habits of all sorts. It may be said that new impulses arise because of the satisfaction which results from any action. In other words emotional reactions often give expression to new and more intense conscious impulses and desires. The child, for instance, may be emotionally insecure and at the same time ostensibly aggressive. The more emotional it becomes, the more powerful, as a rule, will the aggressive tendencies turn out to be. This means that there is continual interaction of motives and motivating factors in the total conscious experience of any individual at a given time.

Relief from emotional strain of some sort, then, is apt to be a partial aspect of all the incentives to human action. This is true because human beings remember their past difficulties and successes and try to reason out schemes for avoiding difficulties and for making sure of success. Therefore, a natural and easy classification of all motives, in theory at least, is the following: *unselfish motives,* including those goals or objectives toward which people strive in such a manner that the advantages of their actions are *intended* to be shared with others; *selfish motives,* in which cases this intention is not included, even implicitly, in the desires of a given person. The completely selfish person excludes the advantages of his fellow man from his intentions and purposes. The thoughtless person, often enough, may fail to advert to the fact that he is not concerning himself with the needs of his fellow man. Provided a person actually or habitually intends to share his advantages with others, he cannot be called a totally selfish individual. It is hard to see how any human being who realizes his true position in the scheme of things can fail to see the real need of acting from unselfish motives some of the time.

a) Self-assertiveness, Prestige-seeking, Sociability. These are types of activities in which the dominant motive may be selfishness. All of the incentives contained in these activities may be present at the same time, and they need not exclude the satisfaction and enjoyment of the other person. Thus the golf player can use his play tendency to secure new business contacts, as well as to obtain the admiration of others for his skill, and to entertain them by his remarks. If he becomes more aggressive and self-assertive as he becomes more proficient in his game, that is a matter for his own personal consideration. So long as no positive injury is intended for others, it seems that he may be said to be acting from socially desirable motives. But if his failure to secure the attention he desires from his friends should lead to compensatory irritable behavior in his home, then he is surely in need of self-examination.

When persons fail to secure any recognition whatever of their own worth, even from those whose duty it is to respect them as human beings, they need more than purely selfish motives to maintain their self-respect. We need not recount here those manifestations of irritability so well known to all of us. Some psychiatrists tell us that when men are too badly frustrated by their losses, they may lose their emotional balance and sense of social responsibility. Or again, they may take refuge in inconsolable grief and thoughts of self-condemnation and self-pity. Obviously we must all strike some middle course between seeking recognition and approval for our actions on the one hand, and learning to respect ourselves for our own merits on the other, for our own peace of mind.

It is not evident that any of the extremes of behavior mentioned by the psychiatrists in connection with loss of status and prestige follow necessarily from the faulty action of others or from some curable defect in the structure of society taken as a whole. Failure to adjust ourselves to the changing demands upon us for sociability probably proceeds more from selfish motives than from their opposite. When the social psychologist treats such maladjustments as undesirable he is often at a loss to show just why this is so. Every reasoning human being who reflects upon the social consequences of his actions knows that extremes of self-assertiveness and aggressiveness cannot be agreeable to others and motivates himself accordingly.

b) *The Wish for Security.* This desire arises in most people because of a certain fundamental respect for righteousness and order. Connected with it is the "activity" drive, or the tendency to complete tasks which were begun with the intention of completing them. Many writers now prefer the term "activity toward further activity" to the older notion of seeking a goal or purpose.[23] Common sense rightly assumes that human beings tend to engage and to persevere in useful and necessary occupations, if they are given a chance. Buehler was probably the first recent investigator who insisted, contrary to the views of Freud, that very small children act from a motive of "joy of accomplishment" and not merely from motives of praise and reward.[24, 25]

It is not difficult to find human beings who persevere in their efforts, in spite of frustrations, until some goal is reached. The goal called "security" is such a changeable one that one never seems satisfied that he has actually attained it. We think that it is more properly a feeling resulting from the attainment of those things which are deemed desirable, and when we hear persons speaking of their need for security we wonder if they could tell us just what it is that they need. Perhaps it is nothing more than health, happiness, and the opportunity to act as a human being should be allowed to act. Social reformers will aid society effectively to find security by appealing to motives of cooperation and fairness coupled with diligent planning and provision for future contingencies. In wartime most persons come to realize that the necessities of life must be rationed. They learn to make their needs such that they can be satisfied by the amount of materials available. This heightened realization of the needs of a community leads to a security in co-operative activities which could serve as a suitable goal for much of our striving. In times of stress we are brought to understand more clearly than ever that needs are sometimes actual and real, sometimes created artificially by the changes in the customs and attitudes found in a given locality.

c) *Rewards and Punishments.* Most accounts of these two motives contain data from experiments on social learning in children and adolescents. Such experiments are fruitful because habits formed at these ages are very apt to persist, and the profit-seeking motive is easily evident in adult behavior. Modern educationists are very earnest in trying to find out what effect the knowledge of the successful or unsuccessful outcome of efforts will have upon future striving. Often, however, no serious effort has been made by them to find out what attitude the experimental subjects have taken toward the thing called success, reward, or punishment. And it is admittedly impossible to determine these effects in any activity unless we also know what value the subject attaches to motives of praise, reward, success, and their contraries. In school matters, the "aspiration" level must be taken into account, otherwise we find no regularity at all in the effects of these motives upon the accomplishment of the student.

By "aspiration" level the social psychologist seems to mean "ideal" of attainment, or degree of appreciation of one's own powers. The efficacy of all human motivation seems to depend upon the value any person sets upon a particular kind of objective, that is, upon the desirability of a given incentive in regard to that particular person. We do not believe that notions of value are amenable to experimental investigation. They develop in secret ways along with intellectual insight and knowledge of principles. They cannot be instantly injected into a human being or dislodged from habits of thought very readily. We cannot decide what these value objects are from a mere description of the scores made during a test in which some persons have been promised a medal or a prize.

The Murphys[26] report that there appears to be a rather stable relationship between the level of aspiration and the permanent personality pattern of any individual. They think this pattern cannot be so very immutable because other persons have learned to be reconciled to failures, when their self-confidence was bolstered up by the consideration of possible successes in other enterprises. It seems that failure or success is always relative to some limited sphere of activity, and that no person need really consider himself a failure in all possible types of endeavor.

Some rather consistent results which have been reported in the journals of social psychology indicate the presence of certain basic tendencies in regard to human attitudes toward rewards and punishments. Both these incentives are more effective than their absence. Rewards appear to be more potent incentives than punishments. Thorndike[27] maintains that punishment is not the psychological opposite of reward, and that it is in fact not a real incentive to desirable behavior. He admits, however, that punishments would be more effective if properly administered. They must follow the offense quickly, be reasonably proportioned to the gravity of the offense; but they lose most of their efficacy if administered with a show of wrath or vengeance. Class honors seem more effective incentives for pupils in the lower grades, whereas mastery of a field or of a profession are stronger motives for older persons. Husband, in opposition to Thorndike, asserts that both rewards and punishments are effective incentives to action in most instances.[28]

d) Competition and Rivalry. We class these with the selfish motives and although they are often active without being recognized as signs of selfishness, there is no good reason for calling them instincts. If a person tends to seek satisfaction by methods which of their very nature deprive others of similar satisfactions, we speak of a competitive motive. Both competition and rivalry indicate the presence of habitual attitudes, and these are, in turn, consequent upon value judgments regarding ourselves, others, and human pursuits in general.

The developing child normally passes through stages in his attitude development. At first he seems rather selfish and aggressively acquisitive, later he strives for status and seeks competition, but if he is to be well adjusted he sooner or later becomes somewhat socially cooperative. He must form some kind of an opinion and attitude toward those who happen to be his competitors. His degree of competitiveness will depend largely upon his desires for the objects sought and his lack of concern about his actual competitors. Conflicts of attitudes may, as the Murphys claim,[29] have been fostered as a result of the child's being taught apparently contradictory doctrines, such as, that a great and good man politely allows others to take precedence over himself, but that he must ambition wealth, power, and prestige in order to be a success. How to prevent some individuals from eventually developing undesirable competitive attitudes against others, whom perhaps they do not even know, is a problem which Christianity can do much to solve, aided by the cooperative efforts of social scientists.

We do not believe that the competitive tendency is necessarily fostered by cultural factors which place men in a predicament between seeking selfish gain and preventing the competitor's loss; nor that the success of competitive enterprises such as wars or business projects depends solely or even largely upon inhibiting fellow feeling by keeping oneself blind to the individual competitor as a human being. The interested reader should by all means read Dr. Allers' excellent account of the conflict between the will to power and the will to community.[30]

It is perhaps not beside the point to recall that the mere presence of other human beings tends to modify in some way our prevailing attitudes toward ourselves and our task. Just because we are social human beings, we are often more intent upon displaying our good points or our imagined superiorities to the world than we are willing to admit. Because we are reasonable social agents, we need not necessarily be moved to compete with other human beings, just because they happen to possess something which we ourselves desire.

B) Unselfish Motives: Submissive Tendency and Cooperation. Cooperation is the opposite of competition. It involves a tendency to share our advantages with others who have similar needs. Cooperativeness, along with self-submissiveness which it always implies, constitutes the great altruistic motive. The cooperative individual must submit his actions to the needs and purposes of the group. He need not avoid all consideration of advantages accruing to himself as well as others. A discussion of this motive can hardly be separated from a study of the great theological virtue of charity or love of our neighbor, but since this study is properly a matter of ethics, it must here be omitted. We may remark, however, that the humanitarians and exponents of the altruistic creed could inspire greater enthusiasm for their antiegotistical campaigns if they realized the true nature and destiny of man and the role of the supernatural in attaining this destiny.

LaPiere and Farnsworth[31] are singular among social scientists in calling attention to the neglect of the cooperative motive in social psychology. Perhaps utilitarian motives impel many authors to discuss the glaring defects in social structure and the breakdown of functional relations between economic classes resulting in conflicts and struggle for security. Whatever their motives may be, the cooperative motive must be recognized as one which is deeply rooted in human nature. It is also much more apt to bring about a cessation of conflicts than its opposite, if it is adequately inculcated in the system of values of the members of any society.

FOR ACCELERATED READING
SHORT SUMMARY OF THE CHAPTER

Great caution is needed in the use of the terms *motive* and *drive*. Because of the animal nature of man certain inherited traits make their appearance. The term *instinctive tendency* is used to designate those useful tendencies which occur uniformly in a species without the need of learning. Acquired habits should not be called instinctive. Voluntarily directed processes involve conscious rational motives in the strict sense; conscious motives may not be strictly divided into internal drives and external incentives because all evaluated motives become internal.

The action patterns based on bodily drives (motivating factors) in men are all shot through with conventionally accepted and rationally or irrationally approved motives. In particular, food drives may be complicated by psychological needs of various sorts. Feelings of security depend on adjustment of real needs to opportunities for satisfying them. Sex drives develop slowly and hence are modified by social pressure and the imagination and thinking of the individual who is being trained in the accepted forms of behavior. Maternal behavior manifests the protective and cooperative tendency. The helplessness of the infant is the basis for this need of protection and cooperation. The defensive and aggressive tendencies grow out of feelings of inadequacy in satisfying needs of various sorts.

The actions proceeding from the social motives require a thorough personal study in order to discover their origin. The selfishly directed motives involve exclusion of the needs of others, but they are complicated by other factors so that they are seldom totally selfish. In self-assertion and prestige seeking, a nice balance between respect for others and self-satisfaction is desirable. In the wish for security, the activity drive and joy of accomplishment are factors influencing one to seek satisfaction in gainful occupations. Rewards and punishments derive much efficacy from the attitude and ideals of the one who strives for success. Competition and rivalry may be motives without direct intent to harm the competitor. The great altruistic motives are cooperation and submissiveness since they diminish tendencies toward aggressiveness.

Find Review Questions and Supplementary Reading at the end of the book.

CHAPTER 6

AFFECTIVE SOCIAL LIFE — THE EMOTIONS

General Notions — Not All Action Emotional; Any Nonethical Treatment Inadequate; Characteristics of Emotion; Physiological Basis for Emotions. *Kinds of Emotions* — I) The Primitive or Crude Emotions: (A) Fear; (B) Anger and Rage; (C) Like and Dislikes. II) Human Emotions and Sentiments: (A) Sympathy; (B) Love; (C) Enthusiasm; (D) Morale. *Emotional Habits* — Acquiring and Breaking Emotional Habits. Emotional Learning Contrasted With Rational Learning.

GENERAL NOTIONS

NOT ALL ACTION EMOTIONAL. The study of the emotional or affective aspects of human adjustment properly belongs to courses in mental hygiene. The relationship of the emotions, sentiments and passions to the exercise of free will is important in a study of ethics. In the present course the reader must understand clearly what is meant by the term emotion in social psychology. In order to verify our descriptions and divisions of the emotions he must appeal to his own conscious experience. His own consciousness will also have to bear witness to the fact that there is a distinction between calm and undisturbed mental activity, and the disorganized, diffuse, excited mental states. We do not here assume, as many writers do, that every action of every human being is emotionally disturbed in some way. Feelings of pleasantness or unpleasantness accompany most of our conscious states, but these differ from emotions in not causing such internal excitement that a person may lose full awareness of the consequences of his actions. Once the reader has verified the fact of emotional tendencies in his own life, he will then be able to evaluate those theories according to which emotional factors are the sole determiners of all social reactions, and the glands and nervous sys-

105

tem are the sole determiners of the emotions. He may also understand why so much stress is laid, in most recent discussions of individual and group conflicts and of abnormal adjustment to the group, upon the attainment of emotional stability.

NONETHICAL TREATMENT INADEQUATE. Emotions are conscious states of excitement, brought about by the recognition of a stimulating situation, and accompanied by disturbed conditions of the whole bodily mechanism. All recent writers agree that emotional states as such are diffuse disturbances of the whole human being, which means that our mind and our body, our thinking and willing may be quite profoundly affected in some of their activities. It is agreed, also, that many emotional disturbances can supply new energy for action. Some of them, on the other hand, can cause a depression or lack of available energy for certain actions. Finally, in extremely disturbed emotional states, there may be disorganized and purposeless behavior which is undesirable and harmful by any standards. The degree of harm or injury is in proportion to the degree of emotional intensity. Such intense excitements cause suffering to the person who experiences them, and also to other persons around him. The reactions of mobs and panic-stricken multitudes, as well as the violent outbursts and vicious temper tantrums of unstable individuals, are instances of disorganized behavior. Such examples, not to mention others of a similar nature, show how important is the subject of emotional equilibrium in a study of social reactions.

The emotions are specifically human types of behavior in so far as they can and should develop under the guidance of reason. That is to say there must and will be exercised in every individual some particular kind of self-control. Any human being, at some time or other in his life, comes to experience excitement in the presence of certain objects which seem to him harmful, or of others which seem agreeable and desirable. The degree of difficulty, either real or imaginary, connected with obtaining the one and avoiding the other, will largely determine the intensity of these excited states. But since intelligence is required in order to know whether an object is truly desirable or not, and hence whether it *ought* to be loved or hated, a complete account of the human emotions must involve the normative science of ethics.

Our present treatment will differ from the so-called modern treatises in the following way. The moderns seem to think that they can study and control emotions without any reference to a moral law which would dictate the true value of the objects of desire. This does not mean, however, that such a law does not exist, or that it is unimportant for social life. In our treatise we shall prescind from the moral law and proceed in a purely scientific way to investigate the practical value of the emotions. We shall consider the usefulness of certain reactions in maintaining health and in winning social approval. We can thus speak of appropriate emotional responses to certain situations without investigating the ethical implications of such responses. There is no way of settling disputes about the real desirability of certain reactions such as anger and fear unless we appeal to ethical norms. Many scientists refuse to recognize such fixed norms as philosophy can establish, and incline toward relativity of morals. Having denied that human reason is superior to the intelligence of brutes, they cannot logically appeal to this same reason as a guide to human emotional tendencies. Although we maintain and are prepared to prove that conscience and the moral law can supply these guiding norms, we must also admit that men do not always follow them because they are free. We shall consider the conventional value which attaches to emotional reactions whether they have been formed through the use of reason or as a consequence of acting unreflectingly according to mere custom and convention.

Modern psychiatrists, at least, would like to bring back the notion of rational guidance into their treatises on emotional development. They even advise patients to aim at re-establising the proper balance between their rational and their emotional life.[1] They agree fully with our view that emotions are forces which can and must be directed along proper channels. If thus directed, the emotions become energizing forces for greater accomplishment. When misdirected or undirected they often lead to maladjustment or unadjustment. As typical instances of misdirection we might mention persons who, through groundless fears of being neglected and persecuted by others, set up attitudes of resistance toward them, or develop prejudices and hatreds which make themselves and others very miserable. They may seek to escape their imagined persecutors by complete withdrawal from society, or they may try to attack them outright. LaPiere and Farnsworth[2] summarize the two chief types of emotional reaction formation somewhat as follows: There are those who psychologically fill in a felt inadequacy in social reality by reactions of withdrawal and daydreaming; and there are those who try to evade some reality which they cannot tolerate by shifting the blame to others. The authors term the latter type of adjustment escape mechanisms and the former type compensations. They are not at all convinced that either of these forms of behavior is totally undesirable until it reaches an extreme form requiring institutionalization.

Emotional prejudices and antipathies, when deeply rooted in the mental organization of a person, become powerful but dangerous factors in his behavior and thus react upon the whole group. They have received much attention from social psychologists and we shall deal with them in a later chapter.

CHARACTERISTICS OF EMOTION. Since emotions are disturbances of the whole individual an account of them will include two fairly distinct classes which are important socially. To the first class belong such reactions as human beings possess in common with animals, the so-called primitive emotions. To the second class belong reactions which must be called specifically human. Animals should strictly be said to possess analogous emotions, since intellectual knowledge is required to grasp the real value as such of the stimulus object. By reason of estimative power, however, an animal can probably size up certain situations as dangerous or difficult and thus show signs of being violently disturbed by certain objects in its environment. Much experimental work on emotions has been performed with animal subjects, and some useful facts about bodily reactions under the influence of drugs and surgical treatment have been brought to light. We may not apply these findings to human beings without considering the additional influence of human reflective power upon the responses of the whole person. Due to the formation of habitual attitudes some of which are emotional, human beings will be able to organize and reorganize their habits from time to time. They will also form changing attitudes toward their bodily needs and toward the value of various socially approved forms of behavior. When we discuss animal anger, fear, hunger, and love reactions we must realize the important fact that attitudes of value are lacking in the animals.

Human beings manifest their judgments of value at a very early age. Throughout life they also display, at times, the cruder forms of emotional excitement, whenever they do not reason out and reflect upon the consequences of their actions.

PHYSIOLOGICAL BASIS FOR EMOTIONS. It is not possible to make a clear-cut division of all the emotions as such on the basis of their physiological accompaniments. The physiologist may, however, consider the bodily processes as having been depressed or enlivened during the experience of an emotion. In actual life, one and the same emotional state of mind may have a depressing or a reinforcing effect upon the organism, because of the interaction of mental factors upon one another. Thus a state of anger may depress certain vital processes and reinforce others, since it can scarcely occur without being accompanied by other complex mental states. Similarly fear may inhibit some processes and facilitate others. The attempt to classify all emotions as either depressing or stimulating is based upon the notion that bodily resonance is the salient feature of an emotion. Moreover the division makes it impossible to explain why conscious states are effective in modifying bodily resonance. The theories of Cannon and his collaborators, while based upon investigations of the balance between various parts of the nervous system, allow for conscious control of the centers which regulate this balance. Although these research workers can tell what is happening in the nervous system when some one emotion is dominant, they do not even attempt to predict, on a physiological basis alone, when that conscious dominant emotion will be present.

The study of the disturbed equilibrium of the nervous system which accompanies certain emotions is serviceable because it tells us what conscious states are favorable to the healthiest kind of bodily resonance. Although it seems possible for a person to be in a very depressed mental condition for a time, and then to shift to a very elated mental state, such depressions and elations are looked on as exceptional; while they last, the general efficiency of the whole organism is lowered. Most persons do not wish to be so completely dominated by any emotion that they lose control of themselves. They try to find reasons for arousing gladness in regard to some objects and a moderate calm or placidity in regard to others. When they have been told that prolonged cheerfulness and hopeful attitudes are conducive toward a better state of health, they usually find themselves interested in controlling these fluctuating states. They try to find practical means for directing their emotional states when they learn that exaggerated moroseness and despondency are the signals of approaching mental disorders.

We may not assume, then, that the bodily mechanisms control the full course of emotional life independently of conscious factors. Such bodily states can make control of emotion difficult, and medical attention to the glandular functions is sometimes necessary. Whenever the disorganized bodily functions have been occasioned by an unhealthy mental outlook, some relief can be afforded the sufferer by remedying the bodily functions first. But the remedy will not be enduring unless the sufferer also tries to cultivate healthier mental habits.

It seems also to be a fact that the increased physical energy which results from properly organized emotions can be used to reinforce all our strivings, and therefore that emotional reinforcement need not be a hindrance to normal activity. There is no general rule which says that all depressing emotions are harmful and all reinforcing ones beneficial. Emotions are of themselves indifferent, and their usefulness depends upon the direction in which our energies flow, the goal toward which bodily and mental tendencies are directed. An intact nervous system is needed for adequate direction, but it is not sufficient. Appropriate emotional habits are not automatically instilled into a person by giving him glandular extracts or electrical shocks, any more than logical ideas are produced in him by measuring brain waves. Direction and control of emotions must be cultivated even after the emotional blocks have presumably been removed by the operation known as lobotomy. No one knows this better than the confidential advisers of persons who have received the various forms of medical treatment for emotional disorders. We shall now briefly discuss the two classes of socially important emotional tendencies, the cruder and the finer human emotions.

KINDS OF EMOTIONS

I) THE PRIMITIVE OR CRUDE EMOTIONS

A) Fear. An experimentalist's description of the fear situation might be the following: Any change which requires a sudden adjustment that the individual is not prepared to make results in a series of responses which we call "fear."[3] This description of the whole situation tells us little about the conscious states of a person who is unprepared for a change in the stimulation, and it seems to imply that fears are the natural accompaniment of our precarious state of existence. The experimenter obviously tries to isolate the one factor of unpreparedness and to study it intensively in its external reactions.

Allied with fear is the tendency to withdraw from an object which seems dangerous or difficult of attainment. Introspectively considered, fears are states of mental stress traceable to the thought of an inescapable or threatening evil. There is experienced a conscious movement of the whole person away from this evil, real or imagined, just as in boldness or courage there may be an initial impulse towards aggressive attack on the obstacle. The habit of fearing difficult and dangerous situations, as well as those which are not really dangerous, may develop in human beings through the use of a vivid imagination. Animals show little evidence of this variety and complexity of emotional life and apparently do not worry much about possible dangers.

Normally reasonable fears are protective, and increase our power of resistance to a threatening situation. Stage fright, panics, and fears caused by violent scenes and accidents, may induce disorganized forms of behavior unless the public is prepared in advance. Methods of preparing them are suggested by the advice given on air raid precautions, and on how to become an efficient leader in emergencies. Morbid and irrational fears are a common symptom of a lack of self-confidence and fortitude, and they are not healthy. We must all learn to acquire calmness and courage while trying to avoid obstacles and attain security. Many conflicts and much frustration have to be expected owing to the multiplicity and variety of desirable and undesirable goals presented to us in every walk of life. Despondency would dampen our efforts, whereas confidence founded on a normal self-respect, if not on any higher motives, would relieve us of much unnecessary strain in the matter of adjusting ourselves to difficult situations. What we need is a system of values or motives which is adequate to bring our emotional life into agreement with the requirements of good health — not to speak of good morals. This double aspect, namely the aspect of mere utility or serviceability, and that of moral propriety, must be kept in mind during all our discussions of emotions. This is because emotions are forces inherent in human beings which depend upon the power of reason for their direction.

B) *Anger and Rage.* A description of anger in terms of situational and behavior manifestations is the following: Anger responses involve active though inadequate participation in the situation; they occur in childlife when the child is somehow blocked in the activity in which he is engaged or about to be engaged.[4] Introspectively, anger is caused by an awareness of some dissatisfaction or present annoyance because a disliked evil has actually come upon us. There may be spontaneous movements of our conscious tendencies toward getting some other desirable thing to replace this evil. Such movements probably account for the active manifestations as well as the apparent blocking of activity mentioned by the experimenters. No adult is readily deceived by a child's efforts to hide his anger. But an older person who sulks and inwardly harbors a grudge, may utterly deceive his best friends in regard to his actual emotions. Such negative reactions are called inadequate participations in the situation by the objective psychologists.

The ancients called the emotions "passions," and reminded their readers that emotional disturbances of anger and rage follow upon interferences with their accustomed ways of acting, their dominant tendencies, their irascibility. Today we speak of frustration of wants and privation of needs and are eager to investigate all the causes of the annoyances which disturb the harmonious behavior of infants. We are told that as infants we tended to fly into a rage when our freedom of action was impeded, and that as adults we are more easily angered when our self-love is wounded. An honest effort at reflection reveals that this description is only partially complete. Whether as children or as adults, we tend to be disturbed when a distasteful burden is placed upon us or when we are slighted or insulted. Apart from the moral implications of this question, we may note that feelings of anger can add new energy to our efforts toward a desired goal, such as social uplift or crime prevention. This will be especially true if righteousness of purpose enlivens our hopes of success. Uncontrolled temper tantrums, on the other hand, are always put down as socially undesirable, because they tend to hinder the attainment of any useful goals by their disorganizing effects upon behavior. They may lead to violent disturbances of right order in society and hence are considered important by students of social reform.

Much time and energy has been spent in proving that people must experience some annoyances in everyday life. Each individual knows very well what some of his grievances are, although not everyone is ready to admit the extent to which his own selfishness is the cause of them. Many realize the need of keeping calm and dispassionate for purely hygienic reasons despite the irritations which surround them. The question of avoiding frustrations and conflicts is stressed so much today, perhaps, because we think civilized man is too enlightened and advanced to deserve such afflictions. Some prominent humanitarians become emotionally upset at the thought of so much suffering and strife. A more successful way of dealing with conflicts and frustrations would be dispassionately to inculcate adequate motives in human beings for making them more tolerant of the rights of others, more brave in suffering trials, and more energetic in their efforts not to offend others.

Much dispute has arisen as to whether there is a fighting instinct in man. It appears to be a fact that men acquire strong likes and dislikes for other persons. Men are not only habitually selfish but also deliberately aggressive and competitive at times, either by nature or by acquisition. To play upon their suggestibility by telling them that they must avoid frustrations and strive after more pleasure is to encourage selfishness to some degree. It would benefit humanity much more if we were to propose measures for the control of selfishness and hate. Irritations will hardly be removed and appropriate emotional responses will hardly be created by merely informing men that somebody ought to remove all their annoyances and, as Dr. Brown advises,[5] redirect their aggressiveness into more desirable channels.

C) *Likes and Dislikes, Attraction and Aversion.* Every human being has either a liking or a dislike for almost every object which he encounters in reality or in thought. The attraction may be strong or weak, but it involves cognition in some way in that the object has been recognized as capable of giving pleasure or pain. Philosophers from time immemorial have referred to these habitual inclinations as *appetites*. They called attention to the fact that human beings possess sensual appetites as well as rational appetites. We are concerned here chiefly with the sensual appetites and with sensual pleasures. The normal exercise of any human power results in felt gratification, whereas excessive activity or excessive restraint results in unpleasant experience. Displeasure, reflectively considered, seems to occur also as a result of any opposition between the tendencies toward activity and those toward calm or quiet.[6] The unpleasantness of tedium and idleness seems to involve such an opposition. Buehler is probably referring to the pleasantness of activity when he speaks of the "joy of accomplishment" found in small children. Since many people testify that drugs, narcotics, and alcoholic drinks were distasteful to them when they were first sampled, it is clear that training and custom have much to do with the development of likes and dislikes in regard to food and drink. One who always avoids what is unpleasant and always seeks what is pleasant to his senses will scarcely be able to meet and deal with the real problems of life effectively. He must act on the "reality" principle and not on the "pleasure" principle if his tastes, preferences, and aversions are to be suitable for a healthy adjustment. Regardless of what the Freudians mean by these two principles, it is patent that pleasures and pains will actually be experienced by everyone and that some importance will be attached to both these experiences. The kind of importance which a person will attach to them depends upon his system of evaluation and his habitual attitudes.

We shall discuss attitudes at length later on, but it should be remarked here that a system of values includes more than what the Murphys call "habitual sets toward attaining objects which satisfy a future need."[7] This physiological notion of values implies that the process of value formation is one involving nothing more than fixation or canalization of dominant central tendencies. Such a notion of values does not enable the person who has them to distinguish between set cravings of his sensory appetites and the rational appreciation of certain objects whose value is understood and desired. Whatever his dominant or habitual tendencies may be at a given moment, it remains true that his other tendencies and appreciations will influence his choices. The craving for an object which gives sensory pleasure and is accompanied by the "set toward getting the object" is surely not identical with the intellectual approval or disapproval of that object.

II) Human Emotions and Sentiments

The specifically human emotions are of much greater interest to students of society than are the cruder emotions, and they can be very effective in regulating the social reactions of other human beings. They are closely related to the sentiments, such as devotion, awe, respect, and submission. Whereas emotional outbursts may be sporadic and variable, sentiments deeply imprinted in the heart of man are more constant and enduring with regard to the same object. McDougall regards as sentiments all complex emotions which are organized around a value. Though they are properly affective manifestations, the cognitive ability or the idea has become functionally linked in them with a native propensity. This "hormic" notion of sentiments will be found quite widely accepted in social psychology today.

Since we cannot enumerate our native propensities accurately, but can readily identify our ideas of value, a better way of classifying emotions and sentiments is to study the process whereby such ideas as virtue or valor become valuable to a thinking human being. It may be descriptively helpful to remember that sentiments are clustered around only a few very strongly evaluated objects such as institutions or persons, and that it is the appreciated value of these things which attracts or repels us. Sentiments and attitudes are closely interrelated since both involve the appreciation of a value. Sentiments, then, may be somewhat narrower in scope than human emotions, because they are restricted to fewer objects. We may have the emotion of love for all humanity but we may be devotedly sympathetic to only a few persons. We have enthusiasm and joy in regard to many things, but we usually have sentiments of awe, respect, and admiration for the beautiful, the great, the good. The question of value seems to be the same for both sentiments and emotions.

McDougall and his followers thought that in discovering the laws of imitation, suggestion, and sympathetic reaction they could scientifically explain all social phenomena.[8] Allport attempts to interpret the same processes in terms of "prepotent reflexes" established through canalization.[9] Human emotions are so complicated that a rigid scientific experimental method such as Allport's cannot deal with them effectively. Some useful results have been obtained especially with regard to suggestion and sympathy. Many students are devoted to the task of tracing the progress of the child's sympathetic and cooperative reactions to other persons. But not enough stress has hitherto been laid upon determining what kind of emotions the child should possess when he is fully developed. This is properly an ethical question, but the scientists can be of assistance in finding out how such and such a particular kind of emotion can be best produced.

An exhaustive account of all the emotions is out of place here. Nor can the social psychologist deal adequately with such exalted sentiments as those centering about religion, though he ought not deny that such sentiments are of great value to all of us. The following discussion of *sympathy, love, enthusiasm,* and *morale* aims chiefly at pointing out the rational element that makes these human experiences distinguishable from mere sensory feelings.

A) Sympathy. According to the root meaning of the term, sympathy means "feeling with" another person. It means to share with another his conscious discomfort or sorrow over some calamity. When we are sad at the sight of a bereaved person, or feel afraid in the company of others who are apprehensive, we may be said to react sympathetically. When a psychiatrist who is intent upon a complete understanding of the symptoms of his patient comes to feel the sufferings of the patient as his own, he has reacted sympathetically, in the broadest meaning of the term. The spontaneity of his reactions may be such that he, without realizing it, begins to imitate some of the patients' idiosyncracies. The process appears to be one of passive imitation or resonance, but human beings need not always take on the ways of others in this passive indeliberate manner. Imitating the emotional state of another may presuppose that the imitator knows what the state is and desires to put himself in the same state. We can and often do actually understand the reasons for the sufferings of others and then deliberately aim at manifesting similar emotions ourselves.

The reason why the experimental social psychologists tend to overlook this phenomenon of deliberate transfer of emotions is to be sought in the nature of their recent discoveries about emotions. They agree that we cannot tell what the real conscious emotion of another person is by simply studying his picture or his bodily reactions. But when we meet and deal with our friends every day, we can do much better than the experimenters. We can know what their actual inner emotions are in given situations. In more recent years the view of the experimenters is being modified to allow for this fact, namely that we can learn to appraise emotional expression accurately by a study of the total situation in which it occurs. It has never been denied that we can detect the extremely complex and conflicting emotions which actors on the stage are trying to express. And in real life situations such as the home or the school, we often rightly interpret emotional expression and react accordingly. Errors in interpretation have been known to occasion disputes and quarrels, and hence we normally assume that we can avoid these errors sometimes at least.

We can reproduce in our own life the emotions which we find in our neighbors by instantly realizing what their true character is and by appreciating the desirability of expressing the same emotion. When we congratulate others or condole with them, we put ourselves in their position and experience their own inner realization of the sorrow or joy. Thus we sympathize with the mother who has just received news of the death of her son, and we become elated at the sight of a mother whose son receives some high honor or decoration for bravery. We do not wish to be called mere pretenders when we express our sympathy and congratulate others. Yet we would have to be so considered if we were merely passively imitating their behavior without any understanding of its true meaning.

Often enough, no doubt, we release habitual and conventional reaction patterns in a mechanical way, and mumble meaningless expressions which may or may not conform to our true inner sentiments, but this state of affairs is by no means ideal, even in the eyes of the very persons who habitually behave thus. Real sincere human sympathy will often give rise to a better understanding among human sufferers, provided it goes beyond the imitation and pretense stage and leads to actions which alleviate pain and suffering. This can happen only when we try to understand the motives and causes of the suffering and are willing to do more than pity the sufferer or congratulate ourselves on having avoided a similar misfortune. Sympathy is not always an indication of altruism, nor does it always aid in bringing about social justice, as Allport points out. But it will have this good effect if it is accompanied by that great human sentiment of devotion to the wants and needs of others. Sympathy is fostered by love and increases kindness to others only when it is cultivated in response to strictly human motivation and is not allowed to degenerate into childish mimicry.

B) *Love*. This emotion has been so much abused at the hands of the Freudians that it would take a separate volume to disentangle their confusion of terms and ideas. We need not delay here on their fantastical speculations about the sexual nature of all libido, of all striving and inclination, because the facts of conscious experience are contrary to their purely theoretical views. Introspection tells us that animal passion is something different from human affection. In passion one seeks gratification through the use of natural functions, from a consciously dominant motive of self-satisfaction. In human affection or love one lets some consideration for the pleasure and satisfaction of another enter into and direct his course of action. For this reason he has a right to expect others to reciprocate his affections. No amount of self-interest, however enlightened, seems likely to result in a state of affairs in which each person respects the rights of the other to life, liberty, and the pursuit of happiness. Each person must learn to regard the rights and dignity of the other person unless he wishes to develop into the egotistic, attention seeking, self-centered neurotic individual described by the psychiatrist.

The societal manifestations of this great human emotion entail a sharing of the good things of life with some one else. Basic to all real altruistic love is the conviction of a common destiny for all. Persons possessed of this conviction have devotion to a common cause, enthusiasm for its success, and show energy in the pursuit of a common goal. Gurnee claims that real emotions of love in this sense are very rare because one can apparently love very few people out of the whole human race.[10] Here he is speaking as a scientist who must be content with describing what is actually the case without suggesting what ought to be the case. He admits that love is biologically serviceable in preserving the human family and in strengthening it to resist the difficult stresses and disruptive forces of modern life. A true psychology of human emotion cannot ignore the fact that all men belong to one great family, and that love must in some degree at least extend beyond the family circle. Social psychologists agree that much conflict and maladjustment arise in the life of adults when their affections have been cramped and their interests narrowed within the confines of their immediate families. Family exclusiveness is one of the chief factors which fosters prejudices and hostile social attitudes.

C) Enthusiasm. The social importance of this quality probably depends on the fact that it is contagious. Sympathy and enthusiasm together can move men as a group either to the celebration of glorious deeds or to gross demonstrations of hatred and dissatisfaction with the existing order. In the former case we have festive celebrations; in the latter, riotous outbursts, strikes, and destructive mobs. We all tend to support a cause which is popular, or a leader who has a following. We share the wholehearted enthusiasm of the leader and followers alike, whereas we do not readily yield to a leader who is apathetic or indifferent to his own cause. This potent human emotion or sentiment has been much abused at the hands of propagandists, yet it seems to be an indispensable asset for any effort.

Related to enthusiasm is *joy* or heightened contentment at the attainment of some desired object. An emotional state often identified with joy is that of thrill and excitement accompanied by laughter.

Laughter has been defined as a method of getting release from tension when every other method fails. We do not intend to discuss theories of humor or of laughter but both are specifically human emotions no matter what one holds with regard to their nature and causes. If an animal relishes a bone we say that it likes it. If a human being reacts to an artistic musical performance or to a clever and comical use of words by smiling or laughing, we are safe in thinking that he appreciates it. When his reactions to jokes and humor go beyond the mere stage of mimicry, we may expect some typically human manifestations. Were we to neglect this true human appreciation of the incongruous or unusual or ludicrous in a situation, we might be inclined to look on laughter as just another of those conditioned responses, or as a mechanism for release of emotional tension which could not otherwise be appropriately released. Such a behavioristic notion of humor ignores the fact that the laughter which is provoked by certain types of wit and humor ought scarcely be called an appropriate release from tension. Again we see how difficult it is to separate the true meaning of propriety in human behavior from what is just approved or tolerated by custom and convention.

The number and kinds of possible motives for adult laughter and joy are unlimited and this fact cannot be contradicted by the research investigations which attempt to discover what jokes are considered the funniest by college students. In those cases in which the students reported that objects associated with sex were the most capable of evoking laughter, the fact remains that intelligence was needed to grasp the meaning. An interesting problem for research might be to discover whether the persons with lowest I. Q.'s were also the ones who responded most frequently to suggestive bits of humor. The problem could hardly be solved scientifically unless each person were tested separately, for in actual life laughter is contagious and often reflexly imitated.

When habit has brought it about that cheerful and joyful states predominate over their contraries, the whole level of efficiency of the organism is raised. Let us observe again that the first response of the human child indicative of his participation in social life is the smile. *Incipe, parve puer, risu cognoscere matrem.* We can see that the smile is a sign of social communication of some sort, because its first appearance is usually associated with the recognition of some other human being. Thus both the smile and the laugh are human acquisitions calculated to facilitate social interactions. Conventional *college* humor is a typical adult accomplishment, for the most popular college joke does not evoke even a smile in the preadolescent. Yet humor is not restricted to adults or to our civilized nations. In the matter of humor, more clearly than in any other, we find a demonstration of the unity of the whole human family, from cliff dweller and cave man to the inhabitants of modern sky scrapers and trailer houses.

D) Morale. Morale is an intellectual-emotional attitude which is most conducive to unity and group strength. It involves the emotions of wholehearted sympathy and devotion to our fellow man, and a reasonable enthusiasm for a common cause. Obviously unity of purpose and confidence in a leader are the essentials of *group morale*. When these emotions are fanned to white heat, then cooperative efforts are at a maximum, for every one sets himself up as the person responsible for the attainment of a common purpose. The more each one identifies himself with the other, and the more all act as one, the more impossible it becomes for anyone to act in a way that is not approved and still escape detection.

Leaders often succeed in maintaining enthusiastic morale at this intense level by various propaganda techniques. Part of their technique is constantly to din into the ears of the public, by means of the radio, the press, and public oratory, the inestimable advantages of united effort to attain the desired end. In war time there are special techniques for strengthening national morale. Each nation tries to win other nations over to its own cause, and seeks to demoralize the civilians, the military and political leaders of the enemy. Each nation may also attempt to instil hatred of the enemy and of all that the enemy stands for in the hearts of its own citizens.

We must here omit the emotions of *jealousy, envy, prejudice,* and *superstition,* if these can really be called emotions. The social implications of these undesirable habit tendencies will be considered under attitudes. Although infant jealousy has attracted much attention among child psychologists, little agreement is found in their writings, except that this tendency is undesirable, since it leads to behavior of the aggressive or competitive sort. The Murphys, reviewing the literature on this subject,[11] conclude that jealousy in the early years is definitely correlated with maladjustment in the home. In homes where there was continual quarreling, faultfinding, indifference or jealousy between parents, as well as emotional tension in the parent-child relationship, and oversolicitude probably arising from economic and social difficulties, there was found a high percentage of jealous children. Parents need to be informed of these dangers, otherwise they may unconsciously be producing habits of insecurity and worry in their children.

Adult emotional habits, when associated with deep-seated attitudes of jealousy and prejudice, may be very difficult to eradicate. Perhaps this is often due to the fact that the persons possessing these attitudes have failed to notice them for a long time.

EMOTIONAL HABITS

ACQUIRING AND BREAKING EMOTIONAL HABITS. The eradication of emotional habits and complexes which are undesirable both to ourselves and to others is no small task. The full discussion of the various means and methods to be used belongs to courses in mental hygiene. In spite of the experiments on reconditioning fears, it is now admitted that social training and instruction at any time, even in later life, are effective in changing the course of emotional development. During the plastic years of childhood the habits are more easily broken, for adults often refuse to admit that they have undesirable habits. Husband, reporting on the work of Jersild and Holmes,[12] tells us that since undesirable fears and angers are the result of learning, they can be corrected if suitable measures are taken. The author does not call these undesirable habits bad, but seems to realize that they are not good, and also appears quite convinced that they may be the result of consciously directed mental habits. He says that even adults can control their emotional expressions, in particular of anger and grouchiness, by their own will power.[13]

EMOTIONAL LEARNING CONTRASTED WITH RATIONAL LEARNING. It should be noted that our learning processes are of two different kinds, and as soon as we notice this it is easy to select instances of the two kinds of learning from our own lives. Emotional habits can often be acquired suddenly and inadvertently, whereas the so-called intellectual skills are seldom obtainable without deliberate effort. We may also at any time use our power of reason to redirect the course of spontaneous emotional tendencies. Emotional habits may disappear quite suddenly even though a long time was required in their formation. This suddenness of disappearance is also noticeable in the case of intellectual habits at a time of strong emotional stress. The disappearance of such a habit need not be permanent. Witness the example of a person who has mastered a foreign language, and in the presence of a person whom he fears or respects, seems to have lost the skill entirely. Usually he will find himself in possession of it again after the emotional strain is over. Perhaps some emotional habits which seem to disappear suddenly, actually leave their traces deeply rooted in the personality. At any rate, some emotional habits are more permanent than others; but as long as the forgotten traces remain forgotten, little can be done with them in the way of conscious control. All these facts taken together indicate that much is as yet unknown about the deeper factors involved in emotional as well as in intellectual learning.

FOR ACCELERATED READING

SHORT SUMMARY OF THE CHAPTER

The significance of transitory emotional states lies in the fact that they sometimes disorganize behavior, sometimes result in conflicts. Since they yield new energy when properly directed, the role of reason in *emotions* must not be neglected. Reason must also be appealed to in order to evaluate the various emotions ethically. The physiological treatment of emotions fails to pay enough attention to the role of conscious control, but it is of use in evaluating the bodily accompaniments of emotional life.

There are *primitive emotions* which are socially important because they involve some reactions of which society disapproves. In particular, *fear* needs to be moderated lest it lead to despondency or panic. *Anger* requires guidance otherwise it will lead to aggression and strife. Many *dislikes* and *prejudices* are so rooted in the life of feelings and emotion that they engender undesirable social attitudes.

The specifically *human emotions* make for nicer harmony in the group. *Sympathy,* when not mere pity, unites a group in a community of kindly sentiments. *Love,* when not totally self-seeking, leads to mutual cooperation. *Enthusiasm* supplies energy and joyful celebrations afford release from tension. *Morale* cements a group in a unity of purpose under a common leadership, and requires the elimination of petty jealousies and prejudices.

Emotional habits are more easily modified in childhood than in adult life. At any time they can be consciously redirected. They are sometimes acquired more suddenly and unintentionally than intellectual skills, and they seem to leave rather permanent effects upon the total organization of the person.

Find Review Questions and Selected Reading at the end of the book.

CHAPTER 7

THE SOCIAL TEMPERAMENT AND SOCIAL DISPOSITION

Definitions and Explanations — Personality; Character; Temperament; The Notion of Trait and of Type. *The Testing Program* — Tests of Type; Emotionality Tests; Perception of Temperament Traits; Recourse to Dominant Characteristics.

DEFINITIONS AND EXPLANATIONS

During the process of socializing the individual many factors are active. Among these should be mentioned the biological inheritance of the individual. In addition to the instincts common to all human beings, there are inherited specific kinds of organic qualities which, from the biological standpoint, are capable of being used to classify different personalities. A familiar classification of persons, from the physical and biological aspect, is that of Kretchmer, and of the constitutionalists as they are called. That Kretchmer's two (or three) types of body-build can be found among human beings is obvious enough, but the mental constitutions which are said to accompany such body types — the long, thin, hour-glass-shaped bodies and the short, thick, barrel-shaped bodies — are not so easily defined.[1]

In this chapter we shall consider those special aspects of the individual which are said to constitute *temperament, disposition,* or *biological personality.* Only human beings are rightly called persons. This is true because all and only those beings which possess the power of reason can rightly be said to have personality. This is the traditional connotation of the term, and there is no good reason for altering it. The total individual living rational human being is the person or the SELF. That which differentiates him from less perfect created beings is his spiritual power of reason and free choice. We

124

call this aspect his rationality, and it is the *specific* feature of all human personalities in the strict sense. Each person, moreover, exists as an individual and is capable of performing external actions for which he is responsible. There are thus observable individual differences between persons in regard to all of the various properties which they manifest.

Some scientific psychologists have denied that man has a soul and a faculty of reason superior to bodily activities and powers. That they have no sound basis for their denial seems evident from their continued attempts to prove that animals have intelligence and that some particular part of the human body is the seat or organ of the thought processes. In actual practice they now attach a new meaning to the old word "personality" and their use of the new meaning along with the old one leads to great confusion. In the new definitions which have been evolved, the concept of singularity or outstandingness has become predominant. Today "personality" may mean that feature of a man (or an animal) which makes him stand out as an individual easily distinguishable from all others.

Obviously the mentalities of various individuals differ considerably, and one of the ways in which they differ notably is in the outstanding quality of their emotionality, the unification and organization of their dynamic powers manifested in action and action tendencies. Hence most modern writers in social psychology devote much attention to the irrational aspects of human behavior,[2] and make emotionality along with unconscious factors of behavior the principal aspect of the total social personality. If they do not reduce these irrational features to mere bodily behavior, they at least consider external qualities such as attractability, stability, or adaptability the aspects worth investigating in society. They may even imply without explicitly stating it, that observable features of the personality are more significant than the intrinsic moral character or value of a human individual. Unquestionably a person's emotional stability is an important feature of his whole make-up. But it is also evident that proper guidance and control of the emotions and of the irrational tendencies is valuable for an efficient adjustment of any individual. And this guidance is made possible for human beings by reason of the fact that they possess the power of understanding what is really desirable and attractive in men.

There are still a few writers who maintain that emotionality is a constitutional trait fully determined by the laws of biological inheritance. Those who cannot be satisfied with this view, even as a working hypothesis, sometimes modify it to allow for the effects of the environment, social and physical, upon the developing individual. Yet none of them will explicitly admit that each individual can and does change the course of his own development by the use of unbiased reason. They prefer to look upon the processes of adjustment as strictly biological affairs which take their course in human beings in a very automatic manner.[3] It is difficult to see how these writers can overlook the contradiction involved in their views. It sounds most inconsistent when they say that a well-adjusted personality must develop to maturity by acquiring desirable adjustments and then go on to relate that all our adjustments are merely the result of environmentally determined behavior patterns. While advising us to avoid emotional immaturity by growing out of the autistic (phantastic-irrational) phase of childhood, they leave us no alternative but to grow into those ways of reacting which society forces upon us.

Having called attention to the theoretical bias of many writers on human personality and social adjustments, we must now attempt in a positive way to designate clearly the roles of emotion, temperament, character, and personality in the behavior of a social human being. It is especially important to distinguish personality from temperament. Writers like Gurnee ignore this distinction, and all who look upon personality as social prestige or social stimulus value evidently include in the term many bodily factors which should be separately analyzed. It is also evident to one who reads much about personality today that those writers who consider the external and conventional aspects of personality as most important will neglect or even deny the role of will and character in this connection. They will then treat personality as if it meant mere popularity, efficiency, fame, or "appeal" — in a word, any feature of the whole man which sets him above his fellows and makes them envy him his qualities or wish to imitate him. Unfortunately, such writers do not designate for emulation those distinguishing features of a person which make him really righteous, truly unselfish, morally upright and attractive. Of course, a scientist will have some difficulty in selecting those features if he ignores or denies the existence of any enduring standard of value or goodness; and hence he can do little more than stress the desirability of becoming well-adjusted, of resolving conflicts, of winning friends and influencing people.

PERSONALITY. This can be partially distinguished from both temperament and character without, at the same time, destroying the total unity of the human individual. The character, temperament, and personality of an individual may enter into the execution of one and the same particular action, but not to the same degree. When and if a person is confronted with the task of removing an unexploded bomb from his doorstep, his nervousness or lack of nervousness may be a matter of emotional temperament. His character will be a factor in his decision to carry out the task and, in all his reactions, the cause of praise or blame for his decision. The action itself will involve his total personality. But if a person were confronted with the task of calculating the probabilities that a given locality would be subjected to bombing, little of emotion but much intelligence and perseverance would be required. From a psychological point of view, then, we may define personality as that dynamic organization of all the various powers of man — his tendencies, impulses, and habits — which under the influence of intellect and will, characterizes his particular adjustment to his environment here and now. All the various aspects of the individual are here included, his native as well as his acquired traits. But the use of the intellect and will is here given its proper perspective, since these are the normal guiding forces in the life of every individual. Because of them especially, the personality is pliable or plastic. It becomes attuned or adjusted to this or that situation in particular ways, and therefore the circumstances of a man's training have a decided influence upon his total personality. As an individual or person he will never lose his identity, but his total mental organization around certain central values or ideals may change from day to day, and under the guidance of these ideals will manifest individuality, singularity, and adjustment in various degrees. The degree or quality of a person's particular active integration may then be studied without calling into question the existence of other differentiating features or of the basic unity of body and soul in one person.[4]

CHARACTER. By this term we mean a disposition to act according to regulative principles. The character of a man is manifested in the degree to which his life is dominated by principles, especially those which lead him to his final end. Obviously character cannot be studied adequately apart from the conscious convictions, the moral values, and the habitual attitudes which a person possesses. Some writers incline to the view that not even personality can be studied profitably apart from a consideration of moral values. It is admittedly very difficult to take a wholly nonmoral view of the thing called personality. Most persons tend to evaluate the qualities manifested by other persons. They tend to measure the good contained in certain actions, according to norms arising within their own consciousness. This spontaneously developing sense of moral values has been rediscovered by Piaget who claims to have observed it in very small children.[5] As scientists we can, however, prescind from the moral aspects of personality qualities and discuss them from the standpoint of their conventionality and mere utility.

The extent to which one allows his habits to be guided by his appreciation of what is morally good or evil determines what we call moral character. The term taken in this sense is clear and intelligible, and has been in use so long that the scientists and the semanticists will find it hard to eliminate it from psychology. The character quality of a person is not readily susceptible to accurate measurement by any available techniques.

TEMPERAMENT. We have given the above explanations in order to avoid misunderstanding in regard to this last aspect of the human person. Temperament has always meant either bodily characteristics alone, or mental traits in so far as they are subject to limitation by bodily traits. Since emotions have a way of becoming attached to certain bodily functions, and of becoming ingrained deeply in the total organization, they may be regarded as factors which modify the original temperament. The whole physiology of the organism is liable to be disturbed, and very radically, by prolonged states of intense emotion. On the other hand disturbed glandular functions can make the emotional life rather irregular. Hence, although one's basic temperament is inherited, emotional habits will generally be superimposed upon the original temperament as a result of individual experience. Character as well as personality in the above sense is developed through the conscious efforts of a person to achieve definite goals. Thus all kinds of habits may from very early childhood so completely camouflage the original temperament that it may be unrecognizable even to its possessor.

This may be the reason why recent objective studies of the total personality organization are so popular today. The experimental investigators can often help the individual to gain a clearer knowledge of the impression he makes on others. Everyone who has been a subject in these investigations knows, nevertheless, that his own willfully acquired habits of thought and his conscious attitudes toward moral values are as important to himself personally as his externally observable personality traits. He also knows that his fundamental temperamental qualities have been subject to constant modification because of his ability to understand what is really desirable and good. One's whole personality is subject to modification by reason of conscious efforts to adjust oneself to new situations, and while the moral aspects of these adjustments will manifest character qualities, his strictly temperamental features will not be observable in their true form save perhaps during the early days of childhood.

We all approve and spontaneously seek out the companionship of one who has a congenial, affable, sociable, attractive disposition as judged by our own customary standards. Most of us also respect and revere, even though we do not actually imitate, the qualities of the person of strong and solid moral character, the self-effacing, kind, cooperative, and honest person whenever we succeed in finding him.

It will be worth while to mention here the attempts that have been made to catalogue various types of temperament, without referring to the changes which may have been brought about by conscious rational factors. Many of the traits here enumerated have been called either temperament or personality traits indiscriminately by writers on social psychology. Though these traits have not been predetermined by the bodily constitution of a person alone, or merely by automatic responses to the environment, certain of them appear as predominant qualifications of the externally visible organism taken as a whole.

THE NOTION OF TRAIT AND OF TYPE. A *trait* is a distinctive mode of behavior. In studying the actions of others we are likely to attribute them to the existence of special traits. Only the thinking conscious individual really knows what his conscious inner behavior tendencies are. Hence the study of mental traits in others is sure to involve much guesswork. Yet we all undoubtedly possess both mental and physical traits which are desirable or undesirable according to our own standards or those of others. Professor Morgan warns the student that in no experiment designed to measure traits have all the variables been controlled or measured.[6] He then enumerates the various attempts that have been made to measure traits and adjustment qualities by the self-rating and by the test-situation methods. It is obvious enough that human beings differ from one another and that we can sometimes indicate the way in which they differ. To designate the differentiating features we naturally use the term trait, and then try to determine how much of a given trait one person has in comparison with another. Thus some say that Americans possess more of the trait called independence than do Europeans. Some say that Catholics are more pacifistic and conservative than members of other religious denominations. In attempting to measure the attitudes of various persons to their respective religions, we are trying to describe as accurately as possible a trait whereby one individual differs from another in a given group.

But let us suppose that one half of a whole community possesses one trait in a high degree, and the other half manifests a different trait very strikingly. We could then say that the two traits typify the members of the two groups respectively. Each member of the first group would belong to one *type,* each member of the other would be of another type. This reasoning is plain enough but in practice it is not very easy to find groups so clearly separated from one another. Perhaps the difficulty arises from the fact that traits themselves are hard to describe precisely.

THE TESTING PROGRAM

TESTS OF TYPE. Psychologists have tried, though without much success, to divide all men into mutually exclusive types on the basis of some one trait. The notion of "type" here does not necessarily indicate either desirable or undesirable traits but simply denotes the presence of some dominant distinguishing feature or other. At one time it was thought that the trait of introversion or exaggerated introspectiveness would enable us to divide people into two equal and mutually exclusive classes. The way to check the truth of this assumption was to devise reliable and valid tests of introversion and then to plot the scores of large groups of persons taken at random. If the frequency distribution of those scores had been noticeably two-humped or bimodal, the assumption would have been verified.

Numerous other attempts have been made to divide human beings into two groups on the basis of the so-called temperamental traits, but these attempts, too, have been failures when large enough samples of the population have been taken. There have been tests for perseveration tendency, nervousness, self-confidence, submissiveness, inferiority, and sociability, and it is not likely that we have seen the end. There seems to be a fundamental wish on the part of psychologists to discover dichotomies, that is, mutually opposed kinds of people, in the general population. Probably this wish has its origin in the common sense observation that there are two extremes of high and low in almost every conceivable activity of the human organism. There are the highly emotional and their contraries, the greatly efficient, etc. Common sense has not been altogether in error in assuming that there is also a smooth gradation over from the high to the low, with the vast majority of humanity falling somewhere in the middle of the distribution.

The efforts to devise tests have not yet ceased because in many instances the tests have not yielded the same scores when given to the same persons at different times. In other words the tests have not been considered reliable. Of course, when we make this admission we are also tacitly assuming that the trait which we are testing actually exists in the persons for a sufficient length of time to enable us to make a retest. It will always be difficult to determine whether the lack of correlation between test and retest is due to the unreliability of the test or to the change of the trait which is being tested. The total person seems to be too complex on the emotional side, or too variable on the mental side, or both together, to allow of any rigid classification in one or other disjunctive category.[7, 8]

What we have said about humanity in general does not apply to small isolated groups, in cases where the tests measure or are assumed to measure something tangible and real. There are definite groups of schizothymes and of cyclothymes, split personalities and cycloid types, in our institutions for mentally disordered persons. There are the highly emotional and unemotional types both inside and outside the institutions, and there are the introvert-pensive as well as the extrovert-sociable persons everywhere. It is, however, chiefly from the institutions for the disordered that the type psychologists have derived most of the notions for classification. Their intention has been praiseworthy, no doubt, for they have tried to detect dangerous tendencies in the normal persons in order to warn them of possible future developments.

It is a truism to say that a group of gangsters would appear more extroverted than a group of contemplatives living in a monastery. On the basis of a now discarded test of introversion, a certain tester published the startling conclusion that Catholic seminarians are chosen for their priestly work because of their high degree of introvertedness. A closer examination of the test and of the whole situation shows that the students gave truthful answers to questions which were interpreted differently by the testers and by the students.[9]

Most students of history know that contemplatives lead a life which demands much introspection, and that all higher religious training requires long periods of silence and meditation. One might say of seminarians that they have made themselves introverts for Christ; but in thus preparing themselves for His work they will not make themselves unsociable or unapproachable by others.

Even though the attempt to find mutually exclusive types has ended in failure, the question remains whether or not the specific or single trait tests of emotionality and temperament have been found fruitful. This question we shall now consider.

THE EMOTIONALITY TESTS. Since the time of Hippocrates students of temperament have tried to find some bodily characteristic which would account for the fact that there are different types of persons. Such time-honored expressions as the choleric-sanguine temperament are easily understood to refer to variations in anger, fear, and hope. It is quite true today, as it was in the time of Hippocrates, that some persons are more inclined to anger than others, and that some persons are much more inclined to be depressed or gloomy than others. It is also true that we shall all learn to get along better with such people after we have tried to understand their dispositions better.

In Hippocrates' division, although he and the ancients believed that four kinds of body fluids were responsible for the temperaments, there were really two chief types, characterized by extremes of external emotional reactions such as anger and cheerfulness on the one hand, and by slowness, depression, and indifference on the other. There is a renewed tendency today to make certain bodily secretions largely responsible for the emotional temperament. Endocrinologists maintain that a deficiency in secretion of all the endocrine glands, save possibly the anterior pituitary, is accompanied by lethargy, sluggishness, and irritability; whereas excessive activity of the endocrines goes with aggressiveness, restlessness, and chronic excitability.[10] If we look upon lethargy and sluggishness as related to phlegmatic melancholia, and upon aggressiveness with restlessness as associated with choleric sanguinity, we have remaining only irritability and chronic excitability which are common to both excessive and defective secretions of the endocrine glands. It is highly probable that there are daily variations in the secretions of these glands, and these changes might well be a basis for the normal irritability and excitability manifested by all of us. Actually, from early childhood, entirely normal persons manifest tendencies toward emotional excitements of various sorts, and out of a rather undifferentiated matrix, as it were, of emotions, they come to manifest the great variety of responses described in Chapter 6.[11]

The development of emotional temperament is a matter of directing the basic emotionality or excitability of the infant into channels which prepare the individual for a wholesome set of reactions in his particular social environment. In the course of the process, body and mind will both need to be regulated, so that neither may become a hindrance to the total development of a healthy and integrated personality. It now seems just as probable that defective glandular secretions can bring on undesirable emotions, as that unhealthy mental attitudes can interfere with normal glandular secretions.[12] Any individual who feels himself either excessively sluggish or excessively restless should consult a physician who can prudently deal with his glandular secretions. The skillful physician will rarely, if ever, attempt to relieve the suffering person and to bring back a normal state of glandular secretions without first establishing healthy conscious emotional attitudes on the part of the patient. It is quite generally recognized today that emotional temperament can be modified by one's conscious states, even though the exercise of volitional control of emotions may be hampered at times by defective organic conditions.. Clinicians today have learned to treat the total psychophysical personality, because they know that all functions must be co-ordinated in the one whole active agent whom we call a person.

PERCEPTION OF TEMPERAMENT TRAITS. Years of research have not done much to modify the ancient view that the only person who can identify your temperament is yourself, and yet you yourself may be mistaken. There is no known correlation between emotionality as judged by competent outside observers and emotionality as measured by physical instruments which indicate physiological processes.[13] Nor is there a reliable correlation between judgments of temperament based on other external bodily characteristics or on general body type, and those based on testable mental characteristics.[14] Such correlations have been unsuccessfully sought in regard to bodily features like the shape of the head and hands, the color of the hair, the complexion, etc.[15]

All these attempts manifest a desire on the part of psychologists to read the minds of others from their external behavior and physiognomy. And indeed we all tend to form similar judgments about temperamental traits on the basis of such external signs as the speed of reactions and the persistence of the same over a period of time. Since the conclusions drawn from the lack of correlation between physical measurements and mental traits depend upon the assumed validity of the tests, it is possible that the everyday observer can judge emotionality more accurately without these tests. Persons whom we meet every day and with whom we are quite familiar usually manifest the emotional reactions which we expect them to manifest. We are usually correct in supposing that someone whom we know well will manifest impatience when corrected, will act resentfully at times, or take on airs and become aggressive. The rule which we follow in making these judgments is something like the following: The choleric person reacts quickly and persists in his moods; the sanguine person is easily and quickly annoyed but does not persist in his mood; the melancholic person reacts slowly and remains sad, angry, or depressed for a long time; the phlegmatic person has few fears or hatreds, and in fact seems hardly to react at all, certainly not quickly and persistently. We expect that the choleric person can be relied upon to keep his promises, and we spot him by his resolute and energetic manner. We fear that the sanguine person will not keep his word, and we single him out by reason of his sprightliness, friendliness, and carelessness. We think we have discovered the melancholic person because of his slow and troubled appearance, and know that he needs kind treatment. The phlegmatic person appears as weak and devoid of expression, as he seems to lack energy and may even be judged slothful. We do not have to study human beings very long to discover that no person can be placed into one of the above categories absolutely and with certainty. Most of us have some or all of these temperamental traits in various proportions. And our judgments of our acquaintances are correct only in so far as we possess an understanding of the inner life of desire and aspirations of these persons. We have an advantage over the mere testers because we have observed our friends in all sorts of situations, even when they least suspected that they were being observed and appraised. But we also realize that very grave harm has been done others by a hasty or false appraisal of their habitual traits and tendencies.

Questionnaires and self-rating scales are often useful, as we have seen, but only when the person himself who is using the scale wishes to be helped by the information which it supplies regarding himself. He does so wish to be helped when he believes himself to be other than he would like to be, or different from what is expected of him in his present walk in life. In these instances he will often fill out the questionnaires truthfully and thus manifest his most secret desires and tendencies. Even if the testees do not always deceive themselves as to their desires and aspirations, we find as a result of using these scales that many persons are more selfish and conceited in their minds than they care to admit publicly.

RECOURSE TO DOMINANT CHARACTERISTICS. In view of the fact that it is difficult to classify types of temperament and to ascertain what all the significant traits may be, the scientific discussion of temperament is conventionally limited to a discussion of the dominant trends of any given person at a given time. We shall consider some of the desirable and undesirable traits in Chapter 11. Such a discussion is profitable because each one of us, rightly or wrongly, prefers certain forms of behavior to others. No one seems to like a lazy, deceitful, spiteful, or utterly selfish person. And most of us spontaneously incline to associate with the cheerful, humorous, sociable, and kind individual. At the same time, no matter what our actual preferences may be, each person realizes that there is a moral aspect to each of these traits, and strives to live his life according to his ethical evaluation of such qualities as selfishness, truthfulness, and honesty. It is not true that we strive to do only what others want us to do, or what custom approves, or what impulse and habit impel us to desire as good.

Some dominant characteristics are classifiable because whole groups of persons manifest them under particular circumstances. The knowledge of these situational tendencies is helpful to a student of social psychology. There are situations in which suggestibility is especially operative. (These will be studied in the next chapter.) There are the ordinary life situations in which long time preferences and prejudices may be manifested. We shall study some of these situations and attitudes in later chapters. Finally there are emergency situations which disturb the peace of many individuals because of the avalanche of unbridled emotions that is released very spontaneously. These phenomena have already been enlarged upon. In all these situations many latent tendencies are apt to break forth into the action which is undesirable, unless there is some direction of the energies of men toward preconceived goals. Each person must learn for himself to direct his habits and tendencies. One who fails to acknowledge that he has a goal, or who never knows what he is seeking and striving for, will find himself at the mercy of propagandists, tricksters, and proselytizers. Perhaps he will learn too late that he ought to have had some workable system of values and ideals.

There are other general tendencies which operate independently of special situations because they are universal and founded on human weakness. They are not strictly temperamental traits, nor are they necessarily the dominant traits of any particular group of persons. They are probably rooted so deeply in human nature that authors who refer to them as "adjustment traits" can include under this heading almost all the well-known failings and imperfections of human beings. Morgan states that it is unwholesome for a person to use any one adjustment trend excessively,[16] and he notes that most persons actually use various combinations of types of adjustment. The types listed are: playing upon the sympathy of others, rationalizing, blaming others, exploiting the good nature of others, acting rebelliously, compromising, worrying and living in the past, escaping reality, procrastinating, and seeking self-destruction. This catalogue of faults might be paraphrased by saying that we too often mimic others when we know we ought to be different, that we build up petty habits of exclusiveness, selfishness, and jealousy, that we become slothful and indifferent when we ought to be active, that we pretend to be better than we are, and imagine others to be worse than they are, etc.

The writer wonders how many practicing psychologists are able to treat all these reactions in a nonethical way. Of course, it is possible to confine oneself to describing the behavior manifestations accurately and to relating which types are socially approved or conventional or normal. Perhaps some persons may obtain a better knowledge of their own failings by discovering how much they deviate from the normal, and how introverted they can become without danger to health and happiness; but one wonders whether this information alone will be enough to bring about a change for the better. It is definitely not sufficient motivation for a person to discover that he has been using compensatory devices or escape mechanisms in order to bolster up his pride.[17] He needs and desires to know whether these devices have been used by him in a reasonable way to overcome pride, and in order to know this he also needs to have recourse to some moral principles.

Another type of dominant trait which has been much stressed lately is emotional immaturity. Persons possessing this trait are said to fall far short of the norms or standards set by the psychologists for healthy adjustment. Some characteristics of this immaturity, or this regression to the infantile level, are the following: demanding too much attention from others, insisting upon being praised, failing to get along, never trying to make others happy, overlooking one's own defects, always wanting to get things and never to give, demanding and never sharing, claiming to be misunderstood and never understanding. When we finish reading this list of maladjustments[18] very little remains for us to do but to strike our breasts and make a firm purpose of amendment. We hope that the increased self-knowledge gained by the study of maladjustments will be of some service in keeping our resolutions in the future.

We welcome the efforts of the social psychologists to enlighten men on their defects and we hope that our instructors will go on setting us a good example in all respects. The average person will recognize the proud and selfish man of the world in a movie performance like Orson Welles's "Citizen Kane," even though he may fail to grasp the psychological significance of all the incidents which contributed to the hero's childhood complexes. The subsequent behavior of the spectator will be governed by his own motives and intentions, in spite of the sad example of maladjustment portrayed on the screen.

We must all recognize the fact that we possess desirable as well as undesirable personality traits. Whether or not these traits are rooted in our total personality, and hence understandable only in terms of the total organization of our character and personality, is a moot question. The Murphys and Newcomb observe that it might be more important to know whether a trait is worth while and valuable, than just to know how it is radicated in the total personality.[19] They think that theoretical differences spring not so much from disagreement as to what is true about persons, as from divergent beliefs as to what it is important to know about them. In our final chapter we shall outline those features which we believe to be important in this connection.

FOR ACCELERATED READING

SHORT SUMMARY OF THE CHAPTER

Some working definitions of personality, character, and temperament are given. Human beings are persons, that is, rational individuals possessing the same composite sensory-rational nature. Because one person may be more outstanding than another in any number of respects, the note of singularity or popularity has become prevalent in modern personality studies. By *personality* psychologists mean the dynamic organization of man's powers around some central unifying principle. Personality may be studied from the aspect of man's active use of all his powers and hence individual differences in adjustment become important. It is recognized that this notion makes the norm of comparison for practical purposes a relative one; that the conventional aspects of behavior are artificially abstracted from all others. *Temperament* may be a feature which makes a person singular or outstanding. It is conventionally thought of as implying hereditary factors with emotional traits superimposed upon it. *Character* means life dominated by principles. It must be studied in relation to man's highest good.

Distinctive qualities of individuals are called *traits*. Purely mental traits are difficult to isolate and measure. *Tests of type* show overlap and hence no significantly different groups are found among the population taken as a whole. Basic irritability seems to develop gradually into all the known mixed types of temperament which we meet.

We perceive traits inaccurately at first, can improve our skill in discovering them, and may be assisted by the formal tests which give percentile rankings. Long time acquaintance enables us to point out persons who are more temperamental than others. Emergency situations bring out dominant tendencies. Introspection reveals characteristics common to all persons. They are traits, but not of temperament alone nor of adjustment and maturity alone. There are some desirable traits of personality besides popularity, prestige, and fame.

Find Review Questions and Selected Reading at the end of the book.

CHAPTER 8

SUGGESTIBILITY, GESTURES, AND LANGUAGE

Language Functions. Human Language Development. Gestures and Pantomime. Meaning of Suggestion. Essential Conditions of Suggestion. Some Variable Factors in Suggestion. The Supposed Unitary Trait of Suggestibility. Some Conclusions for Social Interaction. Hypnotism and Suggestion. Concluding Remarks.

LANGUAGE FUNCTIONS

We are all born into some sort of human society, and because of the fact that it happens to be some one particular kind of society, we become inducted into its membership and acquire its ways automatically and unintentionally in the beginning. Even before we are able to speak we are learning to act in ways which others specify for us. After we have reached adulthood, we may continue to live according to the conventions, customs, and mores of our group because of our association with it. But throughout the life of the individual, *human language* is the outstanding element in any culture whereby people are brought into social contact.

By means of spoken and written forms of communication the social heritage of the past is transmitted from one generation to the next. An educative process is going on continually between old and young, between leaders and followers, and human language is its chief instrument. Language has made it possible for the treasures of ancestral knowledge and traditions to be accumulated; moral codes and social conventions usually become formulated in verbal expressions. Again, progress in science, invention, commercial enterprise, and all social intercourse between groups and persons requires and is facilitated by an intelligent use of language.

Language, whether written or spoken, is a system of symbols or external signs expressive of those conscious processes which are commonly called thoughts. Language represents ideas, judgments, reasons, and feelings of an infinite variety. It is the task of the historian of culture and of the ethnologist to investigate the story of human relations and traditions. Psychologists try to describe the connection which exists between language in general and the human reactions which are called social.

Various motives may impel us to express our ideas in words. Such motives might be, for example, to clarify our ideas, to narrate them to others, to command others, to proclaim a wish, and to give vent to our emotional states. Often enough none of these motives is clearly formulated in our minds when we use words. Language becomes automatic and often somewhat meaningless, but the true purpose of language cannot escape our attention unless we allow ourselves to wander off into speculations about its evolution or the unconscious meaning — if there is such a thing — attaching to various expressions.

The accounts of Gurnee and of Allport fail to take all the simple facts of conscious experience into consideration and hence their speculations about the possible origin of language seem very absurd.[1, 2] Both of these authors seem to disregard the fact that human language serves to express and communicate ideas of rational human beings, and that no human being of any period or culture has been demonstrably and totally without any sort of conceptual language. Allport's treatment also tacitly assumes that the behaviorist explanation of learning by means of circular conditioned responses will fully account for a person's understanding of the meaning of an expression. Behaviorists try to reduce all thinking to movements of bodily organs and muscles, sensists to material images. Since neither of these doctrines has met with universal acceptance among experimental psychologists, we need not discuss them any further.[3, 4]

HUMAN LANGUAGE DEVELOPMENT

There is a sense in which language evolves in the lifetime of every human individual. Language is a human sign of human intelligence; and since the new-born babe has no language facility at all but only the noise-making faculty, this specifically human function of language must be developed gradually. It will be so developed in human society if the child in his efforts to speak is aided by the presence and stimulation of other human beings. But all the biological and evolutionistic explanations of the origin of language do violence to the plain fact that understanding arises independently of actual language ability. We have all had the experience of comprehending a certain meaning without being able to express it. Moreover, accurate observations carried on by the Vienna child psychologists bear out the fact that the child understands meanings before he can give adequate expression to his ideas. This experience of the child is similar to that of an adult who tries to speak a foreign language, save that in the latter case the ideas have already been developed in some other linguistic connection.

Buehler outlines the various steps in the process whereby the child acquires full-fledged language ability.[5] From birth on the child emits cries and makes gestures which resemble those of brute animals. These secure attention for the child and help him to satisfy his several needs. This is the *instinctive-emotional stage* of development and yet the reactions of the child will often reproduce emotional states of other human beings. The very small child can be made to laugh or cry or to show anger merely by having the nurse simulate these various emotional expressions.

Throughout the first year of life, but noticeably after the sixth month, there appears what Buehler calls the *"lall" stage* of language. This stage does not develop directly out of the previous one; Buehler thinks that the ability to "lall" has an instinctive basis in the whole human race. His argument is based upon the fact that a very small child of any nationality does not manifest "lall" expressions that would differentiate him from children of any other nationality. He tells us to analyze phonetically the sounds which different children emit spontaneously and we shall find that they contain the greatest proportion of all sounds used in every known language, and a few more besides. He reminds us that whereas simple cries and gestures serve to bring the child's needs to the attention of others, the earliest "lall" sounds are rather meaningless and seem to occur more for the purpose of amusement, yet they can come to convey all possible meanings and to persons of any nationality. He also points out that these "lall" sounds may be found in deaf-mutes and can be made the basis for teaching them to speak without the aid of hearing their own voice.

A one-year-old baby's incessant repetitions indicate the fact that he gets pleasure out of this meaningless jargon. After a little more practice the child will be able to imitate definite sounds and to suit the sounds to definite meanings, thus beginning to share his thoughts with other human beings.

The *third stage* follows quickly upon the second and is characterized by a dawning realization that certain sounds belong to and are always associated with very special meanings. Thus the child of 14 or 15 months may be heard to say "bye-bye" or "go-go" under appropriate situations. Though the sounds emitted in the first stage served to attract attention to the needs of the child himself, those of the third stage serve to obtain a definite kind of response from other human beings. Probably sensory association is sufficient to account for the connections formed in the child's mind between vocal or behavioral expression and the ability to secure action in others. Allport's description of the language function seems to imply that human beings never get much beyond this stage of learning to control other human beings by their use of language.

The fourth and last stage, according to Buehler and all competent observers, is called the *representative stage*. It follows quickly upon the third, and at this level the child gives indications that he wants to know the names of everything. The parent or nurse, during this time, will find that this curiosity about the names of things can be satisfied only by supplying the names for the things which the child happens to notice. Tutors cannot fail to observe the intense glee and keen joy which the child experiences when he succeeds in repeating the names of things. But it is likely that the child will begin by using too few names or terms; consequently, his language is not yet very intelligible. He may call all animals "dogs" or all men "daddy." His notions are too general for his vocabulary. His class concepts are too vague. He will have to devote much attention to correcting these errors so that his terms may become understandable to others. But throughout all this time the child has given his own names to all things and hence he must have been representing them abstractly without being able to find the proper words. In spite of the many mistakes which he makes in narrowing down his concepts, he seems convinced that everything must have a proper symbol and so he perseveres in the task of learning for years to come. This representative function of language cannot be explained in terms of mere association because it involves a process or a phenomenon which is abstractly general. Thus it is significant that the first categories in the child's thinking comprise what the philosophers call substance and action. He designates any unknown thing as "ting" and any action as "do" or "go."

The average child shows the results of his efforts by the speedy progress which he makes in the early years. We rightly infer that he can understand before he can speak because of the way in which he carries out the instructions of others. Our scores for the language ability of a child are based, not on his understanding, but on his actual use of certain words. This is because we have no way of discerning just when the idea or understanding is present unless the child shows some sign. Gurnee summarizes the figures, compiled from the Iowa Studies in Child Welfare.[6] At the age of 1½ years the average vocabulary of a child is 22 words. At the age of 2 years it has increased by 252 words. At the age of 3 there is an increase of 620, making a total of 890 words. These words consist mostly of nouns and verbs. The fact that the child understands the applicability of one term to *any number of objects* of a class shows that he possesses truly representative or conceptual language.

In order to complete the child's development of abstract notions, he must think out the meaning of such concepts as "being alive," or "being active," or "being good." In doing so he uses word symbols to stand for and represent general or abstract things, and he soon learns to manipulate ideas to suit himself. He seeks to discover whether all people are friendly, all toys interesting, all people given to work and play, all actions approved, and other very useful generalities. He must undoubtedly bring his vocal mechanisms into correspondence with conventional usage, otherwise he will never be understood. These accessory processes are really accidental to the ideas and thoughts themselves, yet they are very important accidentals. The precise expression of thoughts is often no less useful to us than the actual thoughts.

Since the capacity of the human mind for elaborating newer and less obvious conceptual relations between the objects of thought is virtually unlimited, no person can acquire during his lifetime the full meaning of all possible words and expressions. He usually retains only a small fraction of those which he has so laboriously acquired. The few thousand expressions needed for the average person in our civilization serve quite well to signify the properties and relationships of objects in everyday life. In advanced civilizations, at least among the more privileged classes, oral speech has been committed to written symbols which carry a rather fixed meaning, such as is found in dictionaries. The written form of language usually indicates that the persons who use it are erudite, but we can scarcely argue that illiterate and ignorant persons lack human intelligence.

Perhaps modern languages have become too complex for the functions which they were originally intended to serve. It is questionable whether a return to basic English, or to an international Esperanto would solve all the problems concerning human relations. At the same time, there is much merit in the attempts of the semanticists who are bent upon purifying language so that it may serve its function of conveying true meanings. We shall never expect to bring about a better understanding among men as long as we assume that only the elite and educated of our higher civilizations are endowed with a mentality which puts them above the brutes and so enables them to dictate, in an aristocratic manner, all human codes of values and morality. Many writers on the functions of language and on human progress seem to be doing this very thing. They ought to be reminded that the doctrine which takes the only function of language to be the control of our social environment implies the existence of this presumed superiority of those who write the books and dictate the norms of behavior. Fundamentally it is the allegiance of such writers to the evolutionary dogmas which directs their thinking along these lines.

Allport explicitly states that the control of others was the *drive* behind the original acquisition of language.[7] He makes no attempt to prove this assertion but goes on to say that a secondary drive was developed later, namely, the control of the nonsocial environment. Gurnee claims to be describing the evolution of language but he also seems to presuppose the evolution of intelligence.[8] He says that at some time or other man *had* the intelligence, not only to discover the effectiveness of shouts in gaining attention, but also to separate or abstract his vocalizations and gestures from their emotional context, and to use them for gaining other effects. These authors seem to think that civilized peoples have the best possible control over their physical and social environment just because they can invent more machines than can the more primitive peoples. They also forget that human beings have other needs and desires besides those drives which impel them to control their environment. Rational human beings can and often do direct their actions to some higher end, and they sometimes wish to communicate their desires and ambitions to other rational creatures who are willing to put aside false notions about the nature of man.

GESTURES AND PANTOMIME

We cannot touch upon such interesting topics as speech defects and their correction, or on the topic of sign language. Gestures and facial expressions may be used as substitutes for language, and are so used by young children and even by adults. In all these cases some ideas have to be present in the mind before they can be brought to verbal or gestural expression. Adults normally use pantomime very much in expressing their emotions and desires, and human beings easily learn to interpret these external signs and suggestions. There is in most languages a host of interjections and exclamations which bear some resemblance to gestures and pantomimic expressions. They are, nevertheless, real expressions of actual states of mind, and supply our deficiency of adequate words for expressing emotional tone. The fact that the emotional vocabulary of most persons is rather jejune seems to indicate that their emotional life differs radically from the intellectual. Words express ideas, but signs and exclamations often portray feelings-states of a person, of which he may or may not have a very clear idea.

It should be noted that the mere attempt to clarify emotional states and to express them verbally can be of assistance in controlling them. Most of the extreme emotional disturbances are so vaguely realized that precise description in the form of language is impossible. Perhaps this fact has suggested the array of theories on the evolution of language from meaningless sounds and gestures.[9] The above explanation of the precise functions of language will enable us to present a coherent account of the facts of suggestion and suggestibility.

MEANING OF SUGGESTION

As used in social psychology, *suggestion* has a rather technical meaning. Unfortunately this meaning does not always exclude animal manifestations akin to passive imitation and mere reflex behavior. Our use of the term will be restricted to human beings because they alone can understand meanings in the strict sense. Suggestion as used here usually requires an intelligent use of language on the part of the suggester, and it utilizes language skills on the part of other human beings. Language may be used to control the actions of other persons, but that is not its chief or only function.

True it is, the person who responds to suggestion may be quite unaware that it is being used upon him. He may fail to use rational insight and judgment but react mechanically as a result of strongly formed feelings and associations carried over from his past habits of speaking and acting. The term *suggestion,* then, is here arbitrarily limited to that function of language which serves to get action from others without violence and still without complete self-determination on the part of the other person.

Suggestion ought not to be confused with *instruction.* Teaching or instructing other persons consists in imparting knowledge, skills, and convictions to others; but their actions are presumed to be self-determined and not passive reactions to the thoughts of the instructor. Since the instructor may have a right to expect certain actions from those whom he instructs, his ministrations are often hard to distinguish from suggestion in this new sense. And since in our everyday relations with people we may never know whether the speaker intends to get action from us or merely to inform us, our distinction will not be easy to apply in actual practice. But it has some theoretical value in connection with the question of propaganda.

Propaganda differs from suggestion qualitatively in that the propagandist aims to get action from others by the selective use of either truth or falsehood, as occasion offers.[10] We see that it goes a step beyond suggestion in that it implies that an action may result automatically from the presentation of falsehood or a half-truth. Both suggestion and propaganda in the modern sense aim at getting action from persons who will react without complete knowledge of the consequences of their action, without full self-determination, and often enough, as a result of latent habits and emotional tendencies. They both differ from the traditional thing called instruction, which aims at imparting the truth so that another person can come to realize his own responsibility and direct his actions accordingly.

LaPiere and Farnsworth[11] are of the opinion that social psychologists use the term propaganda very subjectively today because there is no real objective criterion for distinguishing the process of instruction from that called suggestion. They say, for instance, that objectively there is no way to distinguish between the training which a mother gives her child in good behavior, and the coaching which an editor gives his staff in the art of distorting facts. When they say that the person who uses the two terms does so because he approves of the one kind of pressure (education) and disapproves of the other (propaganda), they show that they are trying not to introduce moral concepts into their scientific treatises. They can, however, observe that from a purely scientific standpoint, the intention to impart the truth to other persons is a different process from that other intention to get action by whatever means expediency may suggest. No writer who is really interested in the real motives and values of social agents would be content to define propaganda as a technique whereby a minority seeks to convert a majority to its approved norms, and to represent education as an attempt by a majority to convert and control a minority. He should be interested in the fact that propagandists are often untrustworthy because they try to veil the truth from others.

Modern propaganda makers actually use all sorts of devices including suggestion, instruction, and persuasion. They utilize all the tricks contained in modern psychological treatises on advertising. Thus inanimate perceptive aids, such as billboards, leaflets, and books, may be called *suggesters* in so far as they presuppose that only human beings will be able to understand them. As we might expect, direct personal contact with other persons and firsthand experience of their wants and attitudes aid the suggester in securing his desired effects. Thus direct conversation appears to be more efficacious than either the movies, the radio, or the printed document.

We all tend to be suggestible to advertisements, fads, fashions, and symbolic conventions. Those who originate these devices are sometimes called suggesters by reason of the fact that they have utilized our imitative capacity to their own advantage. They will not find it necessary to employ deliberate deceit so long as the suggestees continue to labor under the conviction that only novelties and fads will satisfy their wants.

Successful suggesters often appeal, by way of preparing the soil for their efforts, to deep-seated needs and tendencies of the persons concerned. When the Church equips her shrines of worship with artistically decorated altars and statuary, and accompanies her services with ritual, song, and symbolic drama, she is appealing to universally felt needs for these things. Because of the fact that men realize the need of worshiping a supreme being growing out of their essential dependence upon their Creator, such suggestions — if we wish so to designate them — will be effective. But when a ruler and his subordinates try to start a new religion by plagiarizing the older forms of worship, they are likely to fail because they do not appeal to fundamental convictions of mankind. They may prescribe new rituals or public salutations and songs, and try to revive an interest in the pagan gods of fertility and strength by inaugurating festal parades and celebrations, but they learn that this is not enough to get action. Hence they engage in propaganda in the modern sense.

Britt enumerates the salient features of some recent propaganda methods,[12] and in most of them we see a subtle attempt to withhold information from the persons who are being propagandized. The freedom of the press must be curtailed; there must be a scapegoat upon whom to lay the blame for all evils; there must be an outlet for feelings of inferiority in the form of arguments for race superiority; there must be promises of new weapons in order to give relief from anxiety; and everyone must learn to rationalize all actions on the home front on the plea that no other course of action was possible. We shall not attempt to discuss all the intricacies of the various types of propaganda, but the intelligent public ought to become acquainted with the methods which are used by unscrupulous individuals to influence their actions and even to take away their precious power of self-determination.

ESSENTIAL CONDITIONS OF SUGGESTION

There are some general rules for securing effective suggestion. First, the action which is suggested should be presented through the channels of the external senses and in an attractive or alluring manner. Second, the suggestee must pay attention or be made to take notice of the suggestion without reflection and in an uncritical manner. Third, persons are more susceptible to suggestion if they have a natural inclination toward the action suggested, especially when they are not fully conscious of the existence of their tendency. Finally, a person may often change his attitude toward certain things because of suggestion although the attitude will not show itself in action until some time later.

All of these facts about suggestion have a very practical bearing upon our actions in everyday life. They show how very susceptible we are to the influence of other persons even when they do not intend to sway our opinions, and when we do not advert to any change in our attitudes. If someone accuses you of being behind the times and of accepting medieval and unscientific attitudes passively, you are very liable to feel uncomfortable and to seek to change yourself somewhat. The person who makes the accusation will often enough not be able to tell you just how you should change, but he may nevertheless have initiated the process; this is especially true if you respect his judgment and authority. When a friend accuses you of being disloyal, or merely suggests "You would not want to be a slacker, would you?" there is initiated a change of mind in the direction of greater loyalty and generosity.

In many instances the associations aroused by environment alone bring out certain suggestible tendencies. Thus a person who is very susceptible to seasickness may become nauseated near water or even when sitting inside a stationary liner or airplane. Students often report that the act of buying an examination bluebook makes them nervous and excitable. Thus the spontaneously aroused inner habits and tendencies play an important part in almost all the instances where suggestion is operative.

SOME VARIABLE FACTORS IN SUGGESTION

Since suggestion must operate via the external senses, especially through sight and hearing, any conditions affecting the use of these senses will play a part in producing suggestion. Spiritistic performers know this rule and hence they make use of two important modifiers of perceptive attention, namely, expectation and imagination, in staging a séance. Since the subject of suggestion ought preferably to be in a relaxed or even an exhausted condition, he is rendered passive and receptive by means of suggestive words, a dim light, a dramatic setting, etc. All of these factors predispose him to illusory perceptions of all sorts. Practically all of the experimental tests of suggestibility introduce these same factors, with the possible exception of the state of relaxation and exhaustion. Hypnotists, as we shall see, make extensive use of the latter two factors also.

Suggestion is also very effective in regard to those senses which are little used by us or at least not utilized advertently or effectively much of the time. Thus a college professor, especially if he is renowned for his chemical discoveries, can often perform the atomizer suggestion on a group of trusting students. He fills an atomizer with plain water slightly colored, tells the students that it contains his new perfume, warns them to be very alert lest the fine odor escape them, and urges them to test their olfactory acuity by raising their hands as soon as they detect the perfume in the air. The water is then sprayed through the air, and hands are raised, near the front of the room first and later in the back, until finally most of the students claim that they can detect the odor. This experiment on group suggestion is very successful with small children, less so with adults unless the experimenter is adept at creating a false impression. Imagination, expectation, and some imitation are undoubtedly factors in creating the total effect.

Other much-used experimental tests of suggestibility make use of the progressive-line suggestion, imaginary electric shock, apparent motion, *unheated* heater coils, etc. The percentage of persons yielding to these deceptive suggestions varies with the age, past skill, and experience of the suggestees, and with their present attitude toward the experimenter. The results show quite clearly that some very significant factors in suggestion are the skill (presumed) of the experimenter, his manner, and his prestige, often created by means of his momentary eloquence.

Human memory depends largely upon perception; hence an error in the perception itself is apt to induce a series of distortions in the subsequent memory process. Emotional imbalance sometimes makes our most ordinary perceptions unreliable, unless we are aware of this danger. For instance, a skilled interrogator may make us distort the truth by his clever use of suggestive and emotionally toned words. Unfortunately much of the experimental work on suggestion has dealt with situations under which the subjects were obliged to grasp the meaning of a situation hastily and under distraction. Since they were generally uncertain of what they actually did see, they were inclined to make inaccurate reports rather than to admit frankly that they were deceived or distracted. In other words social pressure was brought to bear upon them, and hence, though the experiments have some validity as studies in distraction, they tell us little about suggestibility as such. The results show quite clearly, however, that all persons are more inclined toward inaccuracy of report about a given event, if the quiz questions are themselves suggestive of the answer. Such questions seem to stimulate the subject to guess at the answer when he would probably have to admit ignorance if he did not guess. For example, on seeing a picture flashed on the screen for 1/10 of a second, the subject might be asked: "Was the man's necktie red or green?" when in reality it was blue; or "Did he have a beard or moustache?" when in reality he had both. A rising inflection of voice on the part of the questioner, or a form of question expecting the answer yes or no, will also heighten the suggestibility of most persons, as when you are told, "You are not very suggestible, are you?"

It seems that all tests of suggestibility in perception involve the factor of the peculiar attitude of mind of the subjects toward the experimenter. He, in turn, more frequently than our friends and acquaintances, of course, deliberately makes use of deceit or ambiguity, in order to exploit the suggestibility of the subjects. It would be interesting to perform an experiment that would discover the correlation between the subjects' attitudes of *expecting* truthful statements and their degree of suggestibility. This might throw some light on the traits which really make suggestion effective. It is definitely clear from the experimental work that the prestige of the suggester, and his power to command respect and attention from others, aid him in making his suggestions effective. This means that the subjects must have some sort of confidence in him or reliance upon him because of the qualities which he is presumed to possess. This point is of great importance for all those who aspire to become leaders of men, and it shows the followers how cautious they must be in examining the credentials upon which the authority of their leaders is based.

We shall now examine the evidence as to the existence of a unitary trait such as *suggestibility* or gullibility in the general population. From the considerations given thus far, it would appear that suggestibility is a complex affair depending upon certain emotional relationships between the suggester and the suggestee. Such relationships involve the attitudes of confidence, submission, respect, and their opposites.

THE SUPPOSED UNITARY TRAIT OF SUGGESTIBILITY

The tool that has been used to discover this trait is correlation. This tool, of course, is of limited applicability, because we are not sure that the tests themselves are valid, that they really measure what they are supposed to measure. Taking them as we find them, we see that no two sets of scores correlate reliably with each other, and that none of them correlates reliably with intelligence as measured by intelligence tests. It had been previously suspected that persons of low intelligence were highly suggestible. It seems to be a fact that mentally defective persons are more suggestible than normal people, if they can be made to attend to the experimenter long enough to get a score for them. This result is in conformity with the known fact that defectives can be more easily exploited by their fellows and made to bear the responsibilities for their misdeeds. The fact that children from the ages of five to nine are more suggestible than adults may be due to their naïve and trusting attitude, or to their ignorance of the tricks employed in the tests. Gurnee finds that boys are less suggestible than girls in some situations, that the reverse is true in others.[13] Other authors point out that girls are more suggestible when a man is performing the experiment, but that few persons respond to the suggestions of those of their own age. There is evidently some such factor as prestige or sympathy which enters into the situation and affects the scores. Although it has not been tried, to the best of our knowledge, it is not very likely that adults would respond to the suggestions of infants or of youths. We normally expect that age gives prestige of a sort, and we seem to react accordingly during the time required for developing knowledge and wisdom.

SOME CONCLUSIONS FOR SOCIAL INTERACTION

It is very important for social psychologists to recognize the fact that the effective suggester must have prestige and superiority, either real or apparent, in order to get those reactions from others which we call suggestible. They may profitably recall this fact also, namely, that persons who respect others as their superiors are suggestible to the latter in some degree. One who respects another, say as a leader or as an instructor, seems to have that attitude of mind which predisposes him to follow the leader and to engage in activities which the leader suggests. This attitude of submission on the part of the follower may enable him to engage in many suggested activities whose full purpose and ultimate consequences he may not clearly realize.

Again, most persons react in a suggestible manner more readily when some sort of subjective experience, such as illness or emotional tension, has been suggested to them. This fact ought to be borne in mind when we investigate the reasons for the success of propaganda. Many people are very suggestible in matters relating to their own needs, tastes, and desires. They adopt attitudes of discontent created by propaganda and suggestion and do not always stop to ask themselves whether or not they really desire or need a certain commodity which is suggested to them as needed. They have artificially created needs and in time these become real and actual.

Finally, suggestibility depends upon some deliberately formed as well as upon many indeliberately formed attitudes and appreciations. It involves some imitation and passive conditioning to our surroundings, but the voluntary attention of a person at the moment he receives the suggestion may affect the whole course of his subsequent action. The Murphys and Newcomb may be consulted for a fuller account of the chief subjective factors which modify one's suggestibility.[14]

The totally passive and unreflecting individual often yields to suggestions and regrets it afterwards. When a person is active and critical, he accepts only those suggestions which he chooses. When he sees clearly that a given course of action is reasonable, he may even employ the device known as autosuggestion, in order to change an attitude or gain a desired good.

Persons who are emotionally unstable and excitable are more suggestible than others, because their critical ability is often impaired and their emotions are easily swayed by outside forces. The only safe course for the emotionally unstable person consists in learning to know himself better and striving to become master of his own desires and convictions. For if he cannot direct any of his own attitudes by his own volition, he will become an easy victim of any trickster or radical reformer who comes along. This tendency for people to remain so susceptible to the influence of outside suggestion, so incapable of forming rational attitudes and convictions of their own, may have given cause for the modern psychological doctrine of social determinism.

HYPNOTISM AND SUGGESTION

We introduce the question of hypnosis here because of the charge often made by agnostics[15] that all the effects of religion and the supernatural are to be explained in terms of mass hypnotism and suggestion. The charge contains the implied assumption that grace and the free will of man have nothing to do with leading a good life and experiencing religious conversion.

Modern psychologists agree that *hypnotism* is merely an extreme case of suggestibility.[16] Controlled experiments confirm this view, and the textbooks on social psychology today usually contain a detailed account of the manner in which hypnotism may be produced. There is agreement on the fact that the habitual attitudes of the subjects and their willingness or unwillingness to cooperate with the experimenter can influence their behavior even during the trance. If self-determined habits of thought can put a limitation upon the efficacy of suggestion during hypnotic trance, then it surely is possible for any individual to plan a course of action and adhere to it even against the pressure of social forces. In the first place the subject must voluntarily submit himself to the directions of the hypnotist, otherwise the trance cannot be induced in him. On one occasion the author knew that a fellow student was intending to hypnotize some boys. One of the boys was warned that the success of the hypnotist depended entirely upon the subject's attitude of attention. This boy kept thinking of the warning he had received while the student began his gesticulations and monotonous suggestions. The boy could not be hypnotized because, as the student friend explained, he was continually in a state of distraction.

There seems to be no subtle skill required of the hypnotist other than the ability to talk glibly and gain the *attention* of the subjects, while he *directs it to strange objects and sensations* long enough to induce fatigue. The hypnotist must next watch the subject closely so that he feels the effects of this new concentration of attention and the accompanying lethargy without falling into an actual state of sleep. An incessant flow of language gradually allows the attention of the subject to shift from one object to another so that eventually, if the subject is cooperative, he falls into a trance. In this state he can be made to react quite mechanically, just as a sleeping person may be made to speak and react automatically when proper techniques are used. We must note again that the hypnotic subject cannot be induced to enter the trance unless he himself allows this or is taken unawares by the suggestions and tricks of the hypnotist. The same three factors are required for inducing hypnotic trance as for effective suggestion, namely, the prestige of the suggester, the attitudes of the subjects toward him, and the general effect on the subject of the whole situation at the time.

As for the actual state of trance, which in many respects is more like a waking state than like sleep, there seems to be almost complete lack of self-control on the part of the subject. Yet during the trance the subject cannot be induced to attempt impossible feats, nor to act contrary to his predominant character trends. He can be induced to talk, bark, crawl, dance, or wave his arms, forget unpleasant experiences, become insensitive to certain stimulations. Here, as in the cases of hand rigidity and levitation suggestions, or in cases of automatic writing, the subject seems to lose partial control of his ordinary conscious processes. He reacts on the basis of past experiences and the suggestions of the hypnotist.

There is some difference of opinion among the experimenters as to whether or not the subject can make a resolution before the trance and adhere to it during the trance. Valentine gives accounts of two experiments performed independently by Young and Wells, in the attempt to settle this question.[17] When Young finds that the subjects, who really chose the task which they refused to carry out during the trance, actually did not respond to the suggestion when under the trance, Wells objects that the trance was not deep enough. Then Young retorts that the trance was as deep as hypnotic trances usually are, and so the issue remains undecided. The question is really not vital, since during hypnosis as well as during waking states, success in carrying out our resolutions does not depend upon factors outside ourselves altogether. And the experimental procedures are not well adapted to discovering what the mental factors are which actually result in the carrying out of a resolution under ordinary circumstances. One of these factors is certainly a memory factor which enables us to recall a strong motive when it is needed. Another factor is the value which we consciously attach to the action which we are resolved to perform.

One thing seems evident from this discussion, namely, that past habits of will and of attention are very effective in controlling and directing a given course of action. A person does not gain any increase in will power by subjecting himself to the influence of suggesters and hypnotists. The psychoanalysts gave up the practice of hypnosis with their patients because they became too dependent upon the ministrations of the physician and thus could not learn to exercise their own powers. A doctor who had practised hypnosis upon neurotic soldiers in the last war related to the author that his subjects could, as a result of hypnotic suggestion, forget the terrifying experiences which precipitated the neurosis, and thus overcome it. He also observed that this treatment was successful only in those cases in which the person knew that there was no further possibility of his returning to the front lines. Apparently even hypnotic suggestion did not take effect so long as the subject's will to avoid danger was likely to be frustrated. Each person has to strengthen his own motives, it seems, in order to prepare himself for the difficult situations in life, and no other person can perform this task for him.

Certain groups of experimenters have attempted to test the strength of the human will in their experiments on hypnosis. They first put the subjects in a trance and then suggested various actions including criminal or unconventional acts of various sorts. Froebes reports that the freedom of the will is not totally unaffected by the suggestions of the hypnotist, but the subject does tend to resist those suggestions which do not agree with his own moral standards.[18]

There is so much uncertainty, however, about all these experiments that we would not like to suggest the practice of hypnosis as a means of discovering the real character and moral values of any person. As long as human beings are able to direct their choices by acts of voluntary attention, they will be able to take an active part in forming their own character and systems of values. Their character, once formed, will be a very decisive factor in determining their conduct when they are placed under the influence of hypnotists and powerful suggestions.

Readers who are interested in studying this subject further will wish to consult the larger works, especially Froebes' *Lehrbuch* and the works of Hull[19] and of Janet.[20] There is evidently a very intimate bond of relationship set up between the suggester and the suggestee, but there is also a very powerful force in every human individual which is operative in various degrees whenever a human being comes in contact with persons who try to act as suggesters. When this force is utilized effectively, it will enable each person to resist certain suggestions if he so chooses, and to carry out others which he deems worthy of his attention. McDougall's hints may serve as a warning to those who forget that they are somewhat suggestible.[21] He says that whatever quality of a person makes him seem to you powerful or impressive adds to his power of exerting suggestion upon you; and conversely whatever makes you seem weaker than the source of the suggestion favors your susceptibility to suggestion from that source. In applying this rule it is very necessary to think out for yourself the question of the source of the authority and power of the person who seems to you impressive and great.

CONCLUDING REMARKS

In using suggestion as a tool to secure some kind of action from others, the following techniques may be employed. The suggester appeals to the dominant interests and emotional weaknesses of the subject. He tries to inculcate a certain sense of security in the subjects by ostensibly encouraging them to determine their own actions while actually putting into their minds the things which he himself desires. He will, by reason of a personal influence over others, induce a bias toward certain actions and beliefs. Such action or belief may or may not be opposed to evidence and reason, but the persuasive suggester subtly combines suggestion with logical argument and emotional appeal. Effective verbal techniques are repetitions of stereotyped expressions and catchwords, such as "Science says," "Have you had your vitamins today?" etc. Even more effective than half-truths and exaggerations are analogies such as "Virtue grows by war's red rain." Other familiar but efficacious devices are flattery, or an appeal to cruder natural tendencies, such as is common in modern advertising. Often enough logical fallacies are employed, and most commonly the fallacy that generalizes from too few cases, or argues to causal sequence from mere temporal succession. People who are averse to reflective thinking will frequently be unable or unwilling to perceive the errors in such reasoning.

Provided no ethical principles are violated, both suggestion and persuasive·instruction ought to be employed as tools or instruments for establishing desirable and useful attitudes on the part of the members of society. It is deplorable, of course, that propaganda makers will distort these techniques to create attitudes which serve their own purposes but are socially dangerous.

For Accelerated Reading

SHORT SUMMARY OF THE CHAPTER

Language aids in the transmission of culture. Language must evolve in each individual separately. It serves to clarify and to convey ideas as well as to get action from others. Understanding precedes language expression; at the early stages of language formation emotional tone is associated with it because it serves to satisfy individual needs. Some emotional speech forms and gestures remain in the adult repertory of behavior patterns.

Suggestion means securing spontaneous action from others without mere persuasion or violence. Propagandizing today, if it can be distinguished at all from other social forces, implies suggestion along with a selective use of either truth or falsehood. The suggester appeals to deep-seated needs and tendencies and insecurities of the suggestees. Suggestions are made flagrantly attractive and aim at uncritical action to release the subjects from some tension.

Variable factors in suggestion are imagination and expectation;

prestige, power, and loquacity of the suggester. All persons have some suggestibility; the degree depends upon the mental attitudes and appreciations of the subjects some of which are voluntarily acquired. *Hypnotism* is a phenomenon of extreme suggestibility and the same factors are involved as in suggestion. Personal convictions and an unbiased desire for the truth can neutralize the effects of suggesters and hypnotists. Various techniques are supplied, with a necessary warning as to their moral implications.

Find Review Questions and Supplementary Reading at the end of the book.

CHAPTER 9

ATTITUDES, THEIR FORMATION AND MEASUREMENT

On Classification and Measurement — Meaning of Attitude; Measurements Applied; Allied Meanings of the Word Attitude; Divisions or Classes of Attitudes. *How Attitudes Are Formed* — Factors in Attitude Formation: (A) Home; (B) School; (C) Press; (D) Movies and Radio; (E) Advertisements; Some General or Universal Attitudes; Attitudes Found in Special Circumstances; Relation of Attitudes to Knowledge; Axioms on Attitudes.

ON CLASSIFICATION AND MEASUREMENT

MEANING OF THE TERM ATTITUDE. An *attitude* of will means a tendency or firm resolve to act in a given way under a given set of circumstances. It amounts to an habitual or virtual intention which carries through a whole series of actions without much advertence to its existence. Thus, a law-abiding citizen presumably has a fixed intention of observing the known precepts of the locality in which he resides. He may at times inadvertently violate some law or other, have to pay a fine, and try to be more observant in the future, without any real change of attitude toward the law and his intention of keeping it. Or again, in certain circumstances, he may decide to break his resolution deliberately. This change of actual intention need not affect his fixed attitude of approval of the law. But if he makes up his mind quite deliberately to violate the law whenever and wherever he can without being caught, then he has taken on a new attitude toward the law, an attitude of resistance. Because habitual frames of mind may be very detrimental to social order, social psychologists and sociologists are seriously interested in the formation and modification of attitudes.

MEASUREMENTS APPLIED. It would be very helpful to society if

161

someone could tell us precisely what attitudes people possess and how strong they are. Quite recently various technical devices have been invented for more accurate prediction and control of attitudes. *Attitude scales* have been prepared for measuring degrees of favorableness or unfavorableness toward the church, the Negro, the union, the government, and many other institutions, customs, and persons. Essentially these scales consist of a large number of statements which are to be read by the person whose attitude is to be tested. Among these statements are some which will agree rather closely with his own subjective leanings and preferences, and these the testee is required to check. In this type of scale, each item has a definite scale value, so that some of them will indicate a very hostile attitude and others a very favorable one, with all possible gradations between. Numbers such as one to ten may be used to designate this continuous gradation and a person's score will be the average value of all the items checked by him.

Thurstone and his associates have attempted to standardize these scales. They tried to make the meanings of the statements clear and objective by having the scale values of the various items assigned by a large number of judges whose attitude was not being tested. Whenever there was marked disagreement among these judges, the items were rejected from the test. The Murphys and Newcomb maintain, however, that the Thurstone method is not as serviceable as other methods, except perhaps for students who have already made their attitudes articulate.[1]

Murphy and Likert have compiled a simpler and less laborious method which is quite as reliable as that of the Thurstone scales. According to this method the testee merely records, on a scale of one to five, the degree of his agreement or disagreement with each of a series of statements. This allows of fewer statements and a much simpler method of scoring. The reliability of the test is checked by the criterion of internal consistency. The reader is referred to Likert's publications for a fuller account of the method.[2]

Some items from the Thurstone scale are the following: "I believe the church develops friendships and ideals that help one to reject low and evil purposes and acts"; "I think the church is a divine institution, and it commands my highest loyalty and respect." The former item would be somewhat less favorable but both would score very high on the favorable side. On the unfavorable side we have such statements as: "I think the church is unreservedly stupid and futile"; "I regard the church as a parasite on society."

All these attempts to measure attitude depend on the honesty of the person being tested, as well as on his grasp of the intended meaning of each item. If he is at all suggestible, he may accept a statement as his own, just because it is in print before him and no other printed item suits his fancy. It also happens that a person's behavior does not correspond with his declared attitude. Hence those who construct attitude scales must try to word the items in such a manner that they indicate the type of action in given situations, and endeavor to verify the person's statements from independent sources.

Perhaps the main source of difficulty is the inconsistency which most people manifest, not only between their better judgments and their actions, but also between their attitudes at one time and at another. Thus a rabid prohibitionist may be secretly engaged in bootlegging. And however enthusiastically a sincere prohibitionist may express his attitude against drink his inner convictions must tell him at times that there is a rational use of alcoholic beverages, even though it may be tainted with the rationalized desire to improve one's health.

Later on we shall see how readily these same attitude tests may be used to prove that a person's emotional attitude is at variance with his own intellectual convictions. Whether attitudes can be tested accurately or not, they are very important factors in social behavior, as can be seen from considering attitudes toward other nations and races, toward communism or labor unions or rationing.

ALLIED MEANINGS OF THE TERM ATTITUDE. The current use of the term attitude varies widely. It has been used to denote any kind of disposition or set, and on the other hand it sometimes denotes an emotional bias or preference. The simplest review of all its meanings would be the following: *an inner motive or intention, a preparatory bodily set or determining tendency, the probability that a certain act will be performed in the future.* The last meaning pleases the statistician, the second is favored by physiologists, the first is best suited to the psychologists, for it implies that one has acquired a pattern of action or adjustment, a tendency to act in given ways, because of his habitual outlook. Attitudes are always considered as something developed, and all writers agree that they denote a tendency to act, a latent adjustment. The terms "habitual intention" and "fixed resolve" seem more readily understood today than most of the newer technical terms which evade the notion of will. Hence we shall adhere to the older terminology. The reader must consult the journals for a complete history of the term.[3]

A difficulty is encountered when we look upon attitudes as tendencies or readinesses to act, because such a habit or tendency may be either bodily or mental or both at the same time. Every readiness to act consciously involves bodily activities, but confusion arises from the statement that a man who is impelled to act according to moral principles must first be physically ready to act before he can "think of the truth of the principles" and desire to apply them. In any discussion of attitudes it is important to make a clear distinction between the conscious ways of acting mentally, and the unconscious bodily sets or states of preparedness which result from past bodily activity. Failure to apply this distinction has led to the apparent implication that the bodily set predetermines all dispositions to act in any way. Let us briefly point out how this misconception may have arisen, and try to indicate the true significance for social psychology of such factors as "determining tendency," "preparatory adjustment," and "postural set."

In experimental psychology we can point out instances in which human beings follow a predetermined set or course of action over a period of time without realizing that they are doing so, that is without adverting to the existence of the factor which is directing them. For instance, a person gets "set" to cross out all the "o's" on a page and carries out this intention very effectively without consciously adverting to his previous resolve. Many other instances of the same sort might be taken from actions in everyday life. Experimenters will say that this "set" or initial posture determines the course of action automatically. But a social psychologist may profitably inquire why the person decided to begin the task at all, or why he yielded to the suggestion to get set here and now. The real reason would probably be that he wanted or determined to do so in his own mind, and it will be of some use to inquire under what circumstances people want to do certain things and what motives influence their desires.

Psychologically it seems evident that many of man's wants and desires are unpredictable; nevertheless, owing to their self-determined and unrevoked choices, they execute whole series of actions in a uniform way. Hence by studying the basis of such uniformity we may predict actions as long as the uniformity lasts. There will be a monotonous repetition in the behavior of all persons taking the same "o" cancellation test. The uniformity of the acts will be initiated by the subjects' willingness to begin the test and finish it. In any case, it is clear that the "preparatory set" leads to action, but quite differently from the way in which "motives to get set" lead to action. A person's desires and motives have something to do with "getting set," whereas an unrevoked habitual intention of doing what is expected results in a series of uniform actions, such as crossing out "o's."

Gurnee expresses the same facts by saying that the function of a "set" is to lower the threshold of activity for responses associated with it and to heighten the threshold for other incongruous acts. This technical circumlocution tends to conceal a very simple and straightforward fact, namely that a temporary resolve, formed sometimes reflectively, sometimes spontaneously, may direct the whole course of actions which follow upon this resolve. There will be a certain facility in doing this one thing, owing to the self-determination or direction, a facility which would not be had in regard to actions outside this specific course. Attempts to explain all behavior and attitudes in terms of thresholds merely show a leaning toward neurological explanations of all habits and tendencies.

There is doubtless a certain economy in getting set or determined or adjusted physically and mentally to perform actions which we wish to perform with ease and readiness. We establish habits of mind or frames of mind in regard to many circumstances of life. In regard to some things we have initiated useful and desirable habits. In regard to others we may find that we have to correct faulty attitudes and adjustments. Although social psychology cannot tell us what all the good and desirable attitudes of mind should be, it can indicate which ones are present in a given community and under given circumstances. It does a service to humanity in pointing out the fact that too many of these attitudes are *formed* unintentionally, that it is without full prevision of the consequences, often to the great detriment of individuals as well as of the group. This science ought to show men how to use their minds and motivate their wills in order to rid themselves of antisocial and disruptive social attitudes.

VARIOUS DIVISIONS OR CLASSES OF ATTITUDES. The various bodily tendencies and habits, such as good posture and habits of breathing, concern the hygienist rather than the social psychologist. We are concerned chiefly with the mental and volitional attitudes. It is possible to classify conscious attitudes as those which are dominantly *intellectual* and those which are dominantly *emotional*. In practice the two may be difficult to isolate, but each needs special consideration in view of the facts which we have stated in regard to language and suggestion. Since the human volitional power must operate in a single unified person, it is to be expected that the desires and emotions should be intimately related to a person's whole mentality. Our convictions as well as our opinions and beliefs may often be emotionally founded and reinforced, which is another way of saying that they are apt to be biased or prejudiced.

Prejudices are usually looked on as judgments formed without due investigation. When no ill will is presumed to be present, the mental state is called *bias*.[4] Biased opinions are likely to arise when the mind is not supplied with adequate knowledge for the formation of a reasonable conviction. When the reasons for the truth or value of a proposition or project are clearly and forcibly presented to us, we are convinced by the evident truth of the matter and desire its advantages. When such reasons are not clear to us we may still have an opinion in the matter because we are expected to have one, and we allow feelings to sway our judgment of approval, or we adopt a tentative attitude merely to avoid a state of indecision. In such cases we often accept and approve, or set up an attitude of favorableness toward various things, without clear evidence and perhaps in a conventional, irrational, or emotional manner.

This explanation is quite different from that given by Gurnee, Britt, and others,[5] who maintain, on the basis of poorly constructed questionnaires, that attitudes toward truth are largely based on what people wish to be true, in other words they are the results of wishful thinking. Though this is the case in some instances, there is no clear evidence that it is a general rule. The mere existence of high correlation between firmness of belief that a thing is true and strength of desire that it should be true cannot be used to establish this contention even for the items used in the inventory of Lund.[6] But there are persons in whom the will to believe in social matters is stronger than the inclination to investigate the truth.

Actions resulting from such beliefs and attitudes are apt to be rather emotional and impulsive. They may very well be motivated by feelings rather than by clear knowledge and reasoned certainty. One of the items on Lund's list was this: "Is slander wrong?" A person who had just been the victim of blackmailing might readily feel strongly in this matter and want badly to have the wrongs which he has suffered brought to right. He then will claim that he has a strong conviction that slander is wrong, probably because he wishes to appear consistent in his views, but it does not follow that he could give a sound reason for his conviction. If he could not, we must say that his views and his attitude of mind were being supported largely by emotional factors.

Again, it may be true nowadays that in many people the desire to believe and to accept the policies of socialism, radicalism, and communism is very strong. If a belief in the truth of these -isms is not augmented by clear thinking and evident proof of the real value of these systems, then it is probably emotional. If, on the other hand, the wish to accept these systems in their totality is accompanied by a conscientious effort to study all their aspects and to weigh their merits, then the systems themselves will probably be rejected, because they will be recognized as unreasonable and undesirable.

Perhaps the number of attitudes founded upon clear and logical thinking on the part of rational human beings in a given group is smaller than it should be. But it seems too much to say that all the beliefs and opinions of all men, those of scientists included, are solely the result of prejudice and emotional bias. The empirical scientists themselves are not at all inclined to admit that their own opinions and theories are biased, however ready they may be to attribute this quality to others.

From what has been said, it ought to be clear that emotionally toned public beliefs (sometimes called public opinion) should be given special consideration in studies of social processes. They are the "attitudes" which are of most interest to the social reformer. It is just as obvious that an enlightened public opinion and a rational attitude toward what is appropriate and good should be fostered by every possible legitimate means. Emotional reinforcement and enthusiastic support of convictions will be in order only when the rational basis for an attitude has been found. Thus a Protestant who believes all calumnies against Jews and Catholics without investigation has an emotional (or irrational) attitude. And the same may be said for the Catholic who uncritically accepts slanders and propaganda against Jews and Protestants.

HOW ATTITUDES ARE FORMED

FACTORS IN ATTITUDE FORMATION. The story of the formation of attitudes would require a complete account of mental development. We shall select certain features of this development which are characteristic of most persons in our era and culture.

A) The Home. The child usually acquires some emotionally toned ideas very early in life, some of which will turn into strong attitudes or evaluations later on. Whenever parents and responsible persons are thoughtless and inconsiderate of the rights of others, the tender mind of the child may be prejudiced against other persons and things before the child has had any opportunity to realize what is happening. Many prejudices and hatreds, even of innocent persons, appear to arise during early home training, and as the child matures he may do one of two things. He may passively and uncritically approve of all that he has learned, for instance, about other races, governments, and customs. Or he may begin to inquire into the meaning and true worth of all these things and in time come to decide for himself upon a reasonable and proper course of action. He should not deceive himself into believing that what he is doing is reasonable and proper merely because his elders have done it before him. The child's schoolmates, and especially his idealized friends and companions are probably the most fruitful sources of the formation of attitudes which require investigation in later life.

B) The School. In the schools, children need to foster attitudes of respect for law and order, interest in cooperative endeavors, and a willingness to further the ends of society by means of social justice, charity, honesty, and obedience to authority. These attitudes cannot be properly inculcated unless educators have a clear knowledge of the true nature of man and of his destiny. Through a mistaken ideal of patriotism, schools often prejudice the minds of youth against harmless though peculiar habits and customs of persons living in other regions. Undue boasting of the superiority of our own customs over all others may do much to foster antagonisms and dissensions later on; egotistic claims of race superiority have been known to result in wholesale group attitudes of aggressiveness.

C) The Press. Printed publications are very powerful tools for creating and controlling attitudes. Within recent years, however, the influence of syndicated newspapers has decreased, partly because of their policies, and partly because other sources of information are becoming more available and are at least equally reliable. The society pages, the want ads, and the sports sections are probably not very efficacious in forming disturbing attitudes. The Sunday Supplement and similar publications often aim at popularizing modern science. Since the accounts do not, as a rule, convey to the lay reader all the limitations of such discoveries as the lie detector and the lobotomy operation, harm is done both to science and to the public good by their premature disclosure. Criminal feature stories are generally admitted to foster unhealthy attitudes in the young, because of the tone in which they are written. False reports on the policies and activities of leading personages occur with deplorable frequency. Whenever a staff of reporters or editors deliberately distorts the facts and aims at wider circulation by disseminating false or inaccurate reports, they should be forced by public opinion to change their tactics or to resign. But as long as presumably intelligent persons continue to spend money in order to keep informed of the useless gossip which is paraded as good journalism, it is hard to lay all the blame upon the press.

Newspapers and periodicals can do much to foster favorable attitudes as well as to disturb or destroy them. Educated persons are probably less effected by them than others. A sounder and more widespread education is needed as a safeguard against the "tyranny of the printed page." How often it happens that the only evidence a person has about the supposed faults of some public personage is a biased account in the daily paper. The best way to insure the freedom of the press is to avoid abusing this freedom.

D) Movies and the Radio. Both these inventions are steadily becoming more influential in shaping public opinion as well as in furnishing recreational enjoyment. They are also rapidly becoming the lazy man's excuse for remaining illiterate. The same precautions must be heeded in accepting their propaganda as in yielding to the suggestions of public speakers and of the crowd. The greater effectiveness of radio and the movies in comparison with newspapers derives from the fact that they seem to appeal to deeper human interests and needs. Moreover they can project their entertaining and enlightening messages into our ears and — in the case of the talkies — into eyes and ears at the same time. Several analyses have been made of the motives which direct the choice of movies by the young today, and these motives appear to be selfish and childish. Whether this selfishness is something more than a desire for pleasant diversion cannot be stated with certainty.

The movies were found to be effective in changing attitudes for a time, at least according to several investigations.[7] It is useless to lament the fact that our youth is becoming too competitive and emotionally unsettled when we tolerate an educational and recreational program which fosters these very attitudes. Vivid portrayals of topics dealing with sex, crime, revenge, and selfish childishness are too often put before the public, regardless of their social consequences, because of their wide appeal and the financial returns connected with them. Producers and other responsible persons should see to it that the instruments at their disposal aid in building up healthy moral attitudes instead of destroying the physical and moral stamina of youth.

E) *Advertisements.* Without discussing topics proper to a special course in the psychology of advertising, we should here observe that advertisements can do much to foster attitudes of content or of discontent with present economic conditions. Most people seem to enjoy being reminded periodically of their need of a new car or of a radio. But when the specially trained salesman is intent on persuading the public to buy beyond its means, he is positively contributing to social unrest in a world of rapidly changing economic opportunities. A more intelligent and far-sighted grasp of the situation would lead salesmen to interest prospective buyers in commodities which are capable of giving complete satisfaction without fraud or deceit. They have been known to use such devices as false claims and seductive slogans — in a word, all the techniques which have been found effective in suggestion or in attracting attention.

The medical and legal professions, however, have always been opposed to advertising. Schools and churches generally do not indulge in high pressure advertising. The fact that the professions in general are able to serve the public without undue insistence upon their fitness to serve shows that they are accepted as rather necessary institutions. It is hoped that they will continue to serve the needs of humanity in such a way that cheap competitive advertising will be superfluous. The public could scarcely tolerate any notable increase in the use of a certain notorious and not too melodious type of radio advertising.

SOME GENERAL OR UNIVERSAL ATTITUDES. By a general attitude we mean one which the vast majority of persons in a group possesses. Such general attitudes seem to be few in our country, apart from moral attitudes and convictions about what is right and wrong, which are most difficult to measure accurately. The application of strict statistical methods reveals only three general attitudes:[8] an attitude toward other nations, toward the heinousness of crimes, and toward gainful occupations. Most Americans consider murder as the worst of all crimes, prefer to be on intimate terms with people of their own nation, and aspire to positions which will give them the highest salaries. Such attitudes are indicative of a certain degree of selfishness and a lack of internationalism on the part of our people, but in this we are not unique. People of other nations have the same preference for close social contact with those who belong to their own nation. Perhaps this nationalistic tendency is due to the solidarity or friendliness which develops along with patriotism and group spirit. As for selfishness in seeking the best-paid positions, it may be partly due to the American ideal of democracy, which makes it possible for the poorest and least important individual to rise to lucrative and honorable positions. Unless properly understood, this same ideal may lead to a chronic discontent with any lower rank of life.

ATTITUDES FOUND IN SPECIAL CIRCUMSTANCES. The Murphys and Newcomb present evidence to show that there are very few clearly defined and separable group attitudes, that is, attitudes which are found exclusively in one kind of group. They vary with different situations and environments. K.Young lists a whole series of "occupational attitudes" characteristic of lawyers, doctors, professors, mechanics, etc., but these would scarcely be measurable by the strict methods which the Murphys suggest. A somewhat more accurate method of identifying an attitude is needed in order to minimize the danger of vague and ill-founded speculations about them. For instance Young says in regard to the teaching profession: "The teaching profession is not well organized . . . develops no attitudes of the superiority of their calling as a profession. The public confirms their low opinion of themselves by continuing to regard the teacher as an inferior person. Most teachers feel a sense of inferiority. . . . Some compensate by flight into alleged superiorities of learning."[9] He also claims that the habit of correcting papers develops a mistake-hunting mental pattern in teachers, that driving an ox team develops a slow-moving mental pattern, etc. If these attitudes do really exist outside the mind of the student of sociology, they do not present any very great problems to the student of social order. A more reliable method of describing them will be required before it will be possible to suggest any remedies for them. Some professional attitudes are easier to describe, but since the members of the various professions have developed codes and techniques for controlling these attitudes, the reader is referred to the larger texts for an account of them.[10]

More important to discuss here are various attitudes which develop in characteristic environments. Before giving an account of the basic experiences and situations which normally lead to given attitudes, we may recall that most attitudes are subject to change under specific circumstances. The Murphys and Newcomb find that when a change of attitude in a given direction is desired, several factors are found to favor the process.[11] Among these are novel experiences, emotionally toned situations, and the use of prominent institutions and their insignia, which have prestige value for those persons who are to be influenced. Greater success will be had if there are no counter influences at work at the same time. Thus we may hope to induce more favorable attitudes toward other races if we can show that race prejudice is universally undesirable because it is based on misunderstanding and leads to persecution, and can point to prominent institutions and persons who do not have this prejudice. This is another example of the force of suggestion as an attitude builder, but we notice that it is effectual when counter influences, contrary convictions, have been eliminated. Though suggestibility functions through the emotions, it is contingent upon rational convictions. Thus a convinced instructor who at the same time inspires an affection for some hero or successful person, is already laying the foundations for attitudes of approval of all that these leaders stand for. A parent who can stir up sentiments of respect and admiration for a model of sanctity, is at the same time helping the child to form desirable attitudes toward moral virtues, and must take care to guard the child against harmful counter influences.

There are some life experiences common to all which normally lead to attitudes of a given kind. When given an opportunity to mix with members of other races and nationalities, most persons acquire more favorable attitudes toward them. In other words, acquaintance and contact tend to break down and remove prejudicial attitudes. Close association within the family leads to the formation of similar attitudes toward many things. These family attitudes tend to remain quite stable throughout life, regardless of all other factors. Newcomb summarizes the evidence on parent-child attitude relationships thus:

"At the present time parental influence upon some attitudes appears to be considerable, particularly at the lower occupational levels; the degree of such influence declines slightly but inconsistently with increasing age, and is to an unknown extent dependent upon personal relationships to both parents and siblings."[12] Family experience and training seem to be very powerful attitude determiners, and they influence later behavior in numerous possible ways. It is interesting to note how experimental social psychology emphasizes the true value of this age-old institution called the family.

Another common "life-experience" which will normally have some effect upon attitude formation is religious affiliation. Whereas it is commonly known that devout religious upbringing is generally but not always followed by adult religious belief, the real value of religion in establishing permanent attitudes has often been ignored. Many researchers who have used character tests on children and attitude tests on adults are inclined to belittle this influence. Or if they admit that attitudes are formed through affiliation with a church, they often claim that these attitudes are too conservative. Finally some report that religious influence has little to do with the present opinions of the young on matters of virtue or with their conservatism.[13] There must be a fallacy somewhere, for other competent investigators find very decided tendencies for religious groups to show characteristic attitudes. The influence of early training may be pronounced and yet a person will not be able or willing to state how his attitudes were influenced when he takes an attitude test. The Murphys and Newcomb admit that religious training exercises an influence which is permanent. We quote:

"Religious affiliation, among some groups, apparently determines whole clusters of attitudes; religious ties in general are strongest among conservative bodies, and hence these attitudes are characteristically conservative."[14]

Some of the attitudes which were tested in studies to which the Murphys refer, were attitudes toward militarism and pacificism, social distance attitudes, attitudes toward out-groups, and toward compulsory unemployment insurance. It was found that the effect of organized religions upon attitude was greater in the Orient than in Occidental countries. In the test of attitudes toward the church, using the Thurstone-Chave scale, Catholics were reported as approving the "Church" most. It is very doubtful, however, whether this test can tell much about the influence which any particular church has upon the lives of its members. The test items are not adapted to the measurement of such influence, nor do they make it possible to distinguish between understanding one's religion and desiring to engage in its activities.

THE RELATION OF ATTITUDES TO KNOWLEDGE. If attitudes grow up in a person on the basis of feelings and emotions, and if emotions are often in conflict with reason and better judgment, there should be very little correlation between what one knows about a thing and his attitude toward it. On the other hand, if attitudes sometimes develop because of rational convictions, we ought to find high correlations between information about a thing and attitudes toward it. Finally, if a person knows the truth and value of anything and can still choose to reject it in favor of something else, or for some other reason besides what he knows about it, we should expect no correlation at all between knowledge about a thing and strength of attitude toward it.

Certain experimental investigators have tried to study all the relationships which exist between knowledge and attitudes, with a view, no doubt, to suggesting methods for inculcating proper attitudes. They ought to be content with describing the relationships without trying to determine the causal connections, for it is a fact that knowledge is not the only factor which enters into the formation of attitudes. And when we discover, for instance, that "liberalism in general" is consistently correlated with intelligence but that "pacificism" is not so correlated,[15] we still do not know what action ought to be taken in the matter.

Common sense would suppose that human beings depend upon their knowledge in the formation of attitudes, and that people sometimes develop attitudes unreflectingly, that is without being aware of any good or convincing reasons for them other than custom or tradition. We see that common sense is not altogether wrong, for information about such matters as labor unions, prohibition, other races, or the church, has been known to produce a change in attitudes. On the other hand, when many subjects are tested first regarding their attitudes toward a given institution and then on the accuracy of their information about that institution, the knowledge does not correlate with the strength of their attitudes. Perhaps the attitude was at first rationally formed and the reasons for it were later forgotten, or perhaps the only reason for the attitude was the fact that others possessed it.

Unquestionably, many persons accept the attitudes of others on the authority of someone whom they trust. When there is a question of attitudes toward the church or toward ethical values, we should expect a believer in revelation to form strong attitudes without inquiring into all the reasons for his beliefs. He trusts others when he cannot find the time to study all the arguments, and in this case we might expect to find a high correlation between strength of conviction and strength of desire or emotional attachment to the church. Yet even in the case of attitudes toward the church, the emotional attitude and the intellectual convictions do not always run parallel, as we would expect them to do if all religious beliefs were merely emotional.

Applying the Thurstone-Chave technique of validating items and rewording Thurstone's items so that one half of them express intellectual convictions and the other half express emotional tendencies or feelings, we have found that the correlation between feeling and conviction is not high at all. (It is only plus .253 with a probable error of .078 for 65 cases randomly selected among Catholics.) It is quite probable that the search for a relationship between attitudes and knowledge will end in failure because individuals apply their knowledge differently and sometimes not at all to actual situations. Everyone knows of cases in which an emotional disturbance has resulted in some prejudice against the church or its ministers, without at the same time destroying the knowledge and conviction that the church is a worth-while institution.

All of us react uncritically at times to public beliefs, tradition, and custom, even in regard to important questions of politics and religion. But the ordinary religious believer and especially the educated Christian student of philosophy and theology probably has more critical arguments for the truth of what he believes than confirmed atheists and materialists have for what they believe. Scientific materialists who are specialists in their own branch of study may at times find themselves at a loss to give rational arguments for all that they hold as certain because they have given assent to propositions of cognate sciences without examining the evidence for the truth of these propositions. Thus the dogma of evolution is assented to by the physicist and by many psychologists who would make a poor showing at outlining the arguments in favor of it. Again the dogma of mechanicism (the machine theory of life) is accepted by many biologists who are incapable of giving good philosophical and scientific arguments to support it. Cases of this kind indicate a certain amount of wishful or emotional acceptance even on the part of careful and objective scientists.

AXIOMS ON ATTITUDES. We may conclude this chapter on attitude formation and measurement with two rather general observations, gleaned from a study of the social psychology of the child on the one hand, and the study of attitudes of adults on the other. The first generalization is that while the attitudes of children are easier to measure than those of the adult, they are also more susceptible of change or modification. They are therefore easier to catalogue and to describe because of the naiveté and lack of inhibition of the child, who usually tries to cooperate with the investigator. But because of the child's developing nature, its plasticity and educability, we are not in a position to make many predictions about its future behavior on a basis of attitude tests.

The second generalization is that the adult has more fixed and invariable attitudes probably because he has attained a state of contentment following upon a successful adjustment to life. It would be incorrect to say without qualification that adult attitudes are absolutely resistant to change. Owing to the subtlety and complexity of mental organization we cannot always be sure that we have described an adult's attitudes accurately. In other words, he may deceive even skilled observers who try to discover his true preferences and prejudices. If an adult is willing, he can effectively cooperate with the investigator and enable him to detect certain tendencies in attitude formation. On the whole, the adult attitude is rather inflexible when compared to that of the child, and this fact need not lead to any harmful consequences as long as the attitudes in question are suitable. With the adult, much more than with the child, the question of redirecting attitudes becomes a matter of individual motivation and interest.

For Accelerated Reading

SHORT SUMMARY OF THE CHAPTER

Attitudes are states of mind whereby a person is in favor of a thing or not in favor of it. Although the strength of approval or disapproval may not be measurable, it is important to know the fact that persons are either for or against an institution, custom, or law. Attitudes imply the existence of habitual intentions and tendencies which may have been acquired inadvertently. A fixed resolve or intention may be distinguished from a bodily set or drive. These *sets* or determining tendencies are capable of being voluntarily initiated and there is economy of action in acquiring fixed tendencies whereby a person favors socially approved and valuable institutions and laws.

Attitudes are not all *emotionally* toned. When they are not we speak of *intellectual* convictions. Not all our reasoning is wishful thinking, although conventions and customs are often accepted on grounds which involve feeling, or which involve inadvertence to future consequences; many convictions are also formed hastily and with inadequate knowledge of the grounds or reasons. Some satisfaction accrues to individuals when they accept the conventions without understanding their real value, but irrationally formed attitudes are often adapted on the basis of bias and prejudice, and these serve no useful social function.

Enduring though not immutable attitudes are formed in the *home* and often unreflectingly retained through life. *School* training need not foster antagonisms and dissensions among peoples. The *press* is an effective attitude former and should be safeguarded and corrected by enlightened public opinion. *Movies* and the *radio* are more effective but should be carefully sponsored.

Few attitudes are identical in all men, and the emotional attitudes especially can be changed through prestige *suggestion*. The family and the church foster the most stable mental habits, although knowledge does not go parallel with the favorableness of attitudes. Childrens' attitudes are easily measured but very variable. Those of adults are in many respects the reverse.

Find Review Questions and Supplementary Reading at the end of the book.

Chapter 10

THE SOCIAL RELEVANCE OF ATTITUDES

Attitudes and Motives — (I) Socially Approved Attitudes: (A) Cultural Attitudes; (B) Collective Attitudes; (C) Individual Attitudes: (*a*) Toward Sex; (*b*) Toward the Self. (II) Disapproved Attitudes: (A) Children's Attitudes Toward Virtues; (B) Adult Attitudes; (C) Aspects of Criminal Attitudes: (*a*) The Effect of Glands; (*b*) Mental Disorder; (*c*) Mental Defect; (D) Delinquent Attitudes.

ATTITUDES AND MOTIVES

In this chapter we shall present an account of those attitudes which are generally approved or should be approved in modern society for its own well-being. We are not concerned with the question whether they can be measured in terms of strong or weak, for we wish to stress the fact that the qualitative aspects of human social life are often as important as the quantitative. It is just as important to know, for example, whether or not a person has an attitude of approval of moral precepts, as to know how strong this attitude is. Of course, the question of attitudes is intimately linked with that of *motive*. We do not always approve or disapprove of a thing without reason, and we generally have to appeal to another person's reason and judgment before we can change his attitude, although this is not always true in cases of suggestion and of sudden startling experiences. When we suffer some disappointment or when we act impulsively we are apt to manifest certain attitudes which we did not know we possessed, or did not wish to manifest. Many persons never come to realize that they have formed unsuitable attitudes until they are confronted with some difficulty or other. They have never taken the trouble to study their own minds carefully.

Before they can hope to cultivate desirable social attitudes, they must strive to know their own inner intentions and preferences better. In this chapter we shall sketch the attitudes which society requires on the part of its members. We shall presuppose that each individual is sufficiently aware of his own tendencies and goals to understand why some attitudes are approved and others are disapproved in every well-ordered society.

I. SOCIALLY APPROVED OR DESIRABLE ATTITUDES

A) CULTURAL ATTITUDES. Human beings living in society are habitually predisposed in a certain way toward the traditions and conventions of their group, and their fixed ways of regarding these things usually result in fixed ways of acting. Many of these habitual attitudes have been acquired spontaneously by the mere fact of living in society. On the other hand, moral pressure is brought to bear upon a person who totally disregards all the social conventions of his group. Thus one is not readily tolerated in a group whose customs he fails to observe. Society everywhere makes demands for conformity in matters of food and dress; habits are prescribed within rather narrow limits by the group in which we live. Examples may be found to show that much of our behavior is defined as to time, place, and manner by the mere fact that we want to be well regarded by others, well received and respected by them, or even to be like them. Conformity is expected and is the rule with most people, as, for example, when they follow the norms regulating personal appearance and behavior before others. Nonconformists like nudists and faddists are perhaps partly motivated by a desire for notoriety, if they are at all aware of their real motives.

Allport and others[1] appear to have discovered a significant difference between behavior which conforms to customs (folkways) and that which conforms to moral codes (mores) and to institutional (legal) patterns. Since the interpretation of these results is still unsettled,[2] we may pass at once to a consideration of the attitudes which people possess in regard to customs, conventions, and institutions, reserving the question of attitudes toward laws for a later section.

Cultural attitudes are part of our cultural inheritance, in the sense that we come to acquire them through a process of learning which is largely predetermined. At the same time everyone comes to possess some personal appreciation for the various elements of culture. This fixed notion or idea of value becomes a guide, or a sort of symbol which may persist in the minds of individuals even after the true meaning of the element has been forgotten. Thus the real value of a college education is often overlooked by persons who merely see in education a symbol of all value. The idea that certain benefits are obtained from conforming becomes traditional, so that one generation after another accepts it without either questioning or attempting to change it. Such ideas lead to "patterning" of behavior as opposed to "culture change," both of which processes have been most interestingly described by M. Krout.[3] The reader may be disappointed with Krout's chapter because he does not give the individual in society credit for much independent thinking about the actual value of any and all social institutions.

It is interesting to ask ourselves how clearly aware we are of the particular advantages attached to following accepted conventions, such as table manners and various forms of etiquette. Often enough, we find ourselves conforming in regard to many of our actions without a clear appreciation of the real or original significance of the activity. Thus we never inquire how it happened to become proper for a gentleman to walk at the right of a lady, or to wear a hat in public, or to avoid the use of perfume. Many customs are holdovers from the past which have acquired a new significance, and these are often called "survivals." The "best man" at a wedding, for instance, is said by Krout to be a survival of the stalwart friend, who, in the days when brides-to-be were stolen, accompanied the prospective groom on his daring adventure.[4] Today he fills the important but prosaic role of a witness to the tying of the marital knot, though Krout jokingly says he only gives the groom courage to go through with the ordeal. These and other examples illustrate the fact that our social heritage includes many approved ways of acting, departure from which will often stigmatize an individual as an outcast.

We need not fully discuss here the psychological theories of "culture lag" and "change." Any fixed attitude indicates that there is a lag; in fact this attitude is itself the lag, and lags may be good or bad for society depending on the particular case in question. Social

approval, which is a latent motive affecting the attitudes and behavior of all of us at times, may be for some people a more powerful
motive than the desire to do what is morally right. Witness the
dejected feelings often connected with poverty or humble origin and
the natural repugnance which we all feel at any insinuation regarding the integrity of our past or the reputation of our ancestors. As
everyone knows, however, the process of conforming to moral or
conventional behavior out of fear of disapproval (human respect) is
an altogether different kind of experience from avoiding trangres-
sions which no one would ever be able to discover. Convention may
be a strong motive of action and choice, but it is definitely not the
only one.

Attitudes of conformity with the group are manifested in reactions of allegiance and loyalty toward our country and our flag, our
profession, our school, our church, and our family. The reward or
sanction for such loyalty is to be found partly in a heightened group
consciousness and a feeling of well-being. The more completely one
unites himself with the group and shares its burdens and responsibilities, the stronger must become the attitude of loyalty, and this attitude, in turn, makes the consciousness of participation in the group
a stronger motive. Group culture leads to social participation and organization, which in turn strengthens the organization. That is to
say, patterned behavior characteristic of family, school, profession,
or religion influences individual personality, and the life organization of individual personalities reacts to stabilize the organization
of all the social institutions. Individuals depend upon a hierarchy of
groups for certain outlets to their activity, and groups are constituted
by individuals so modified by group participation. This is social
action and interaction on a scale of ascending and descending complexity. Neither the individual alone nor the group alone may be
said to determine the nature and kind of attitudes of conformity
which are formed.

Cultural attitudes are especially stable in a well-developed group
and many of them live as long as the group maintains its existence.
They are indispensable for the continued existence of the individual-
in-the-group. Some necessary cultural attitudes are the will to foster
the various institutions necessary for a well-ordered society, such as
marriage, the family, religion, property, and education. Each of these

institutions will usually be so organized that certain clearly preconceived attitudes will be expected to result from them. The tenacity
of purpose manifested in adhering to those customs and institutions
which are specific to a given race or nation, though not necessarily
the very best ones, is one of the most powerful factors in resisting
change or domination by another people. The opposition between attitudes of the upper and the lower classes, or between various political parties or competitive enterprises, is largely responsible for
social unrest and conflicts of various sorts.

B) COLLECTIVE ATTITUDES. These are here arbitrarily limited to
the attitudes of smaller and more transitory groups such as sociable gatherings, lodges, audiences, and crowds. They are certainly
not always desirable attitudes, especially when the crowd or mob is
out of the control of a leader or blindly following an irresponsible
leader. Yet the spirit of *cooperation* and mutual dependence found
in a rally, a festive celebration, or church social is capable of producing strong impressions which favor the unity and well-being of
the group. The attitudes found in these temporary groupings may
be of a rather emotional sort, and individuals find themselves inclined to cultivate special distinctive attitudes for these occasions
which they are apt to lose later on. The organizer of a drive and the
promoter for the community chest know well that they must act
quickly after the rally or opening banquet if they hope to secure the
pledges, for collective attitudes have a way of disappearing after the
first enthusiasm diminishes. Although attendance at church service
calls for attitudes which are quite different from those of everyday
life, the work of the church could hardly be considered effective if
there were no carry-over from church to the other activities of life.
Leaders know how to use the occasions of casual meetings and
audiences in order to redirect the habitual inclinations of others
toward desired goals.

Perhaps it is largely through the mediation of these smaller temporary group attitudes that the larger cultural attitudes mentioned
before must be formed. It is amply clear to the author that rallies,
student unions, group discussions, and the like can be very effective
in producing deep-seated attitudes. Americans attending universities
in Nazi Germany even in peacetime sometimes found themselves
tending toward the acceptance of the radical principles presented to

them during the social gatherings which were held regularly for the purpose of enlightening the "foreigners." Some of the author's acquaintances stated later that they cannot imagine how they could have been so gullible as to accept the views presented to them in student rallies. When a foreigner decides to get a fuller understanding and appreciation of the habits and customs of the people whom he is visiting, he must participate in such gatherings. Such participation does lead to a change of attitude which is often imperceptible at first. If the visitor intends to return to his native land, he must be on his guard lest propaganda undermine his basic convictions or weaken the ideals and attitudes which have proved satisfactory in his home country.

That mysterious and elusive entity called "the public" is probably the agent responsible for many cultural, collective, and individual attitudes. It is through the channels of public communication that one is allowed to air his views. He has the opportunity of forming rational attitudes but is also in danger of forming emotional preferences which may bring on conflict. Just because attitudes of cooperativeness may be present in public-minded persons, this does not mean that they always avoid prejudice against minorities. On the whole, in spite of acute differences of opinion, the public usually succeeds in devising some rather unified plans of action and in settling vital issues to the satisfaction of the majority.

A calm and well-ordered public usually possesses morale. Leaders must labor diligently in order to make it conscious of the need of unity of purpose and co-ordination of efforts toward some goal. At certain times especially, the individuals must realize that their own wishes and needs must be subordinated to those of the group. They must identify themselves and their intentions with the representative of the group in order to attain that goal which both the leaders and followers have selected for themselves.

Public opinion is a term which has come to mean the dominant will or idea of the people. It seems to depend a good deal upon the expressed views of some one person, as when a popular editor or college president makes some important pronouncement to which a majority agrees. There are facilities in most journals and newspaper organizations whereby a person, who thinks that public opinion has been aroused against him unfairly, may make his own position clear.

This is one of the glories of a free press. When public opinion is not expressive of a firm conviction on the part of the public, then it does not as a rule indicate the existence of very fixed attitudes. In other words when people are merely inclined, for instance, to think that the police in a given locality are inefficient, or that there is graft in politics, they will not be aroused to action as effectively as if they were convinced. Public conviction, then, is an effective force in any group, and leaders know well how difficult it is to try to break down convictions and attitudes associated with them.

Belief, as used in social psychology, is hardly ever limited to mean the acceptance of a truth on the basis of authority, although it may include this meaning also. It usually refers to the state of mind resulting from insufficient evidence. It is more allied in meaning to the state of mind described in popular usage by the following expressions: "I believe it will rain today" or "I believe I am developing a neurosis." It is often taken to include superstitions, and since this is the case, it often happens that no other authority exists for some beliefs than public opinion or hearsay. One scientist will declare it his belief that much human suffering is caused by overcivilization, for instance, of the native Alaskans, whereas another will claim that only science can free men of all suffering. These are obviously beliefs founded upon the particular kind of evidence which the person in question had at hand. But when a famous flyer believed that disaster would result from flying a plane with the number 13 on it, and later found that another person who did take the plane up suffered disaster, his opinion was founded on too little evidence.

Belief has come to mean any judgment regarding the probable or possible cause or explanation of an event. Thus college students have been found to have erroneous if not superstitious beliefs regarding many things and these opinions generally arise because they have never investigated the matter fully. Twenty-eight per cent of one class thought brunettes were more serious minded than blondes, and 61 per cent thought that emotional expression in another person could be judged more accurately from the eyes than from the mouth.[5] These examples chosen at random show how important it is to discover the exact meaning intended by the authors whenever the term "belief" occurs in social psychology.

If belief is taken to mean opinion, it may be the result of scientific induction or it may be the merest surmise of the layman. But when a skilled investigator announces a certain view it may later become a scientific theory or hypothesis. Pasteur is said to have believed in the view that diseases are caused by living germs long before he adduced his scientific evidence. Other scientists believe that all thinking results solely from activity of the gray matter of the brain, and the evidence for their view is not yet available.

Emotionally toned beliefs and unverified assumptions often cause much disturbance in society because of the fixed attitude of the believer which may render him blind to further evidence. This has been known to happen to scientists and lay folk alike. Superstitious beliefs are more prevalent in the world today than one would believe, but they are probably not responsible for very much unsocial or antisocial behavior.

C) INDIVIDUAL ATTITUDES. All cultural and collective attitudes are at the same time individual attitudes. This is true in the case of those attitudes which can be clearly expressed, and are not just vague feelings or emotional tendencies permeating the group generally. Half-conscious racial sentiments in the sense of Jung's "Collective Unconsciousness" or of Durkheim's "Collective Representations" can scarcely be considered attitudes at all. We have already mentioned that some European psychologists consider all Americans possessed of a spirit of independence and hopefulness. If this is not just a vague impression of the European concerning a still more intangible national trait, we should be able to find a majority of individuals who actually possess these qualities in a high degree. Because the effects of certain individual attitudes may be different from the effects of the group attitudes, we give the individual attitude special consideration.

We should require a complete understanding of the genesis of ideas of any individual in order to describe his special attitudes perfectly. When we are able to describe and to express quantitatively all his attitudes and feelings, we shall still fall far short of the ambitions of some scientists, namely, to predict each separate action. An individual attitude differs from a group attitude chiefly because it resides in a single responsible person, whereas group attitudes, such as the attitude of discontent or of conformity to custom, may turn out to be merely a majority vote or statistical average.

Leaders of groups may at times declare themselves responsible for the attitudes of the members, but they cannot do this in a case of passive acceptance of some ancient custom whose origin no one takes the trouble to investigate: for instance, it would be hard to trace the origin of the preference of Americans for certain foods which Europeans dislike; or to attach responsibility to any one person for our acceptance of the American way of life. An individual is responsible for his attitudes because he can know them here and now and can take steps to change them. Group attitudes are too often taken for granted and it is often hard to decide whether they ought to be changed or not.

The tests described in the previous chapter are intended to measure the strength of individual attitudes in order to understand what the individuals taken as a group or the majority of persons may be expected to do. A social psychologist who has the true interest of each individual at heart will be seriously interested in studying those inner conscious processes which favor the development of desirable individual attitudes.

One of the most discussed efforts in this latter direction is the work of Thomas and Znaniecki on group opinion. Representative individuals were selected, and through interviews and case history methods much information was secured on personal reactions to the social situations characteristic of the group as a whole.[6] Bogardus and others have used the "Social Distance Scale" very successfully in measuring the attitudes of individuals in a group toward those in other groups.[7] It may be useful to know how distant people are from each other socially, whether they admit persons of other races to their own community or to their homes, but this is not enough for rational guidance of human behavior. Bogardus found that people are more favorably disposed toward those in their own locality than toward others and that they are better disposed toward members of in-groups than toward others. As a rule there was found a less intense feeling of friendliness toward persons farthest removed in space, provided there was any attitude at all toward them. Primitive peoples seem to have much stronger in-group attitudes than civilized persons do, perhaps because they lack information about other peoples and groups. It seems also that members of fraternities in our own society have very strong in-group attitudes, even though they are generally not far removed from the sphere of influence of other groups. It has been suggested that these strong in-group attitudes are fostered by the same techniques as those found in the secret societies of primitive peoples, such as initiations, rituals, ordeals, etc.

Societies with restricted membership undoubtedly contribute to the development of group consciousness among their members whether they be primitive or modern. In the discussion of in-group attitudes we often forget that their strength as manifested in any individual is but an expression of his degree of friendliness or charity toward others. Consideration for others requires that one person identify himself with others (amalgamate himself to his group) to the extent of sharing community burdens and responsibilities. This desirable attitude must be acquired by practising unselfishness from early childhood and by giving proof, as in primitive society, that an individual does not lack courage and willingness to cooperate. Whenever sufficient motivation is present, we find that human beings can learn to regard other men as their brothers at least to the extent of showing a friendly or favorable attitude toward them at times. Attitudes of "keep your social distance" cannot well foster a spirit of harmony in any group, but rather lead to forms of behavior which any student of social distance must deplore. Some of the ordeals which primitives have to undergo before they are judged fit for adult society could profitably be imitated by more advanced groups.

Taking men as we find them, conflicting and irrational attitudes are all too frequent among them. If the statistics thus far gathered enable us to suggest some remedies for the world, the most fitting suggestion at the present moment seems to be to prevent the formation of strong hostile attitudes toward out-group members of whatever sort.

Many of the individually acquired hostilities, it is true, may have been formed indeliberately; but others are due to easily perceived errors of judgment or to generalizations from too few instances. Some of these mistakes can be avoided if attention is called to them by proper educational procedures. Habits of belittling other races or religions, even if developed unintentionally, may be rendered innocuous by conscious efforts to learn the truth. Errors of judgment among men of authority need more careful handling, especially because when a person comes to occupy a superior position in any respect, he tends to consider his own judgments almost infallible and so expects others to agree with him. Workingmen are guilty of the fallacy of overgeneralization when they argue that, since day laborers are underpaid and discriminated against by their employers, the whole capitalist system should be eradicated at once. The voter who votes a straight ticket without knowing the character of the candidates for office is probably acting on an attitude which he has very uncritically accepted from others. When prejudice and bias enter in to distort judgments which were not well founded in the first place, much disorder may be occasioned in a society, and more than attitude testing will be needed to correct strong but mistaken individual attitudes in regard to ourselves as well as to our fellow men.

a) ATTITUDES TOWARD SEX. Every person possesses his own individual attitude of mind toward the function called sex, not only as it exists in other individuals, but especially toward his own conscious experiences with regard to the reproductive functions. Some of these attitudes have led to serious social problems. Attitudes toward the sexual functions are closely bound up with attitudes toward self as a moral agent.

In his "Training the Adolescent" Father McCarthy treats the problem of attitude toward sex in a masterful way, stressing the notion that young people especially need some clear-cut system of ethical principles, merely from hygienic considerations, to guide them in their efforts to evaluate the sex functions. Professor Britt points out that countless social factors often act as preparatory conditions, if they do not actually motivate much of the behavior which is ordinarily associated with sex and sex differences. Mere outward behavior does not necessarily indicate a strong "sex drive." Noting that many types of sex activity may be carried on in order to achieve such objectives as prestige, dominance, companionship, or money, Britt concludes that inner attitudes do not always square with outward behavior manifestations of sex. He says: "One person may, because of religious attitudes, early childhood conditioning, or a variety of emotions, restrain his overt manifestations of sex. Another individual may engage in a great many 'sexual conquests,' not so much because of an unusually strong sex drive but because licentiousness may be looked upon by others as an indication of dominance and superiority."[8] His examples also show the effect of social pressure upon the formation of individual attitudes.

Many scientific psychologists favor the formation of such attitudes toward sex as presuppose restraint and rational guidance. On the other hand, E. D. Partridge, in his "Psychology of Adolescence," apparently because he wishes to be objective and to avoid moral issues, contents himself with recounting the frequency of premarital incontinence today, and with describing the social factors which seem conducive to this breakdown of morals. In vindicating the right of youth to know what their elders are doing, he overlooks the question whether people have any qualms of conscience in this matter.

Such a treatise may be useful as a protest against undue secrecy in the matter of sex and may enlighten the younger generation in regard to the consequences of vice, but it is not very helpful in inculcating habits contrary to an attitude which even modern society disapproves. It will be difficult indeed for the future generation to develop strong attitudes in favor of suitable behavior if the educators themselves do not seem to know what attitudes are to be inculcated. While overcoming prudery and false modesty, young people should realize that the strength of the sex drive is largely a matter of acquired habit and self-persuasion, and that the real motive for much disapproved and antisocial sexual behavior is often a desire to find sympathetic companionship, or to imitate and excel others in a manner which lowers one's self-respect and respect for the dignity of man.

The topics of courtship, dancing, and recreation have been very ably handled by Father Daniel Lord in his "Guidance of Youth" and in various pamphlets which combine sound psychology with a popular appeal. Psychologists are well aware that proper attitudes toward reproduction must be inculcated in young people not only for their individual good but also for that of the group. Whatever hesitation they may feel in dictating what those attitudes should be, they ought not to conceal the fact that society itself does not approve of transgressions against human nature and right order. Psychiatrists as well as ministers of religion are beginning to see the need of instructing youth to strive for greater unselfishness in .controlling the fundamental sex urges. They inform those troubled youths who seek advice regarding the functions of sex that the sex act is destined to bring two persons of opposite sex into most intimate union, and that this kind of union of the whole person of two lovers can be fully realized only when they become lifelong partners in marriage.[9]

They point out that any other use of the sex functions tends to spoil the beauty and happiness of the future union, and that the sex relation in human beings is eminently personal and sacred, involving mutual respect as well as self-restraint. Young people who receive such instruction will have some incentive for trying, at least, to shape their attitudes and behavior accordingly. The man will learn to respect the role of the woman in establishing a family. Women will recognize the excitable nature of their masculine suitors and feel a certain sense of responsibility for making them respect their own individual rights and prerogatives. Individuals of both sexes can thus be helped to realize that any form of behavior indulged in before marriage which diminishes one's respectability in the eyes of the other party will surely not be conducive toward a happy and enduring partnership in later life.

Much confusion has been caused in the minds of young people by recent discussions about the effects of repression upon mental health. Psychiatrists are now attempting to clarify this question by teaching that sexual abstinence is not in itself a causal factor inducing nervous disorders.[10] The noted psychiatrist and psychologist, Dr. Rudolf Allers, has always insisted that young people be educated in such a way that they will be able to deal efficiently with their problems of sex.[11]

The widely accepted opinion of anthropologists that repression is characteristic only of civilized peoples and that primitives are wholly uninhibited and consequently are free from mental disorders is now being doubted or denied by competent observers.[12]

It is important simply to accept the fact that masculinity and femininity are easily distinguishable characteristics of human persons, and that each sex has a definite function which must be safeguarded by society. Feminine nature, however dominating and active it may appear in primitive or modern society, must still serve the biological purpose for which it was destined, namely, to elaborate the cells and tissues from which a new individual may develop. Masculine nature must supply the complementary activating cells. The fact that some people possess certain characteristics of the opposite sex does not mean that they will have compelling tendencies toward sexual perversions.[13] The opposite contention is upheld by those who confuse the sex urges with socially conditioned behavior patterns in the two sexes. Enlightened young people in our day will not only insist on knowing the whole truth about such matters but will also desire to direct their behavior according to reliable principles. The Catholic finds in his Church both the needed directives and the aids required to carry out her teaching.

b) INDIVIDUAL ATTITUDES TOWARD SELF. In the section on age levels we noted that at some time in the life of every person there is formed an attitude of appreciation or evaluation of himself as a worth-while object.[14] Perhaps the attitude of most people toward themselves is characterized by a degree of vanity and selfish exaggeration of their own perfections. This is not exactly desirable even though we often tend to strengthen this attitude in others by flattering them and minimizing their defects. If we adopt the attitude of expecting others always to praise our good deeds, we shall soon find ourselves acting solely from motives of human respect, that is, seeking to have others notice us more and more and to recognize in us not merely our actual worth but also the high-minded, efficient, and successful individual *which we would like to become*. Thus we may begin to seek unmerited praise and become dissatisfied when we do not receive as much as we think we deserve.

There is not much doubt that many of our actions result from an attitude of seeking to play a role or a variety of roles, or to secure status, or recognition — to use the terminology of modern social psychology. As a result we often appear to expect some of our friends to look upon us in one light and others in another, that is, to play a double role. Thus the behavior of some persons in their homes is so different from their dispositions and manner before outsiders that they scarcely seem to be the same individuals. The deliberately dignified manner of the professional man is quietly put aside when he is among equals or intimates. This change of role, however, is not traceable solely to the social environment, but results from a particular attitude toward oneself. Self-evaluation connotes that there is some way of ascertaining just what value or worth any given role actually possesses. Some persons reflect very little upon the real value of life and are content with acquiring a normal amount of self-criticism as well as some consistent degree of self-assurance or self-sufficiency. Errors in the matter of self-evaluation lead to undesirable social behavior. The person who is inclined to approve of himself too much and to undertake tasks beyond his powers, or the person who depreciates himself too much and becomes confused and hesitant in making decisions or in meeting crises, is apt to be unsuccessful as well as unhappy. A reasonable amount of appreciation of oneself aids in becoming successful with a given amount of talent, whereas undue self-depreciation may lead to misery and failure. Also, a mediocre man may succeed where the more talented person fails, provided he has that degree of initiative which the person who thinks well of himself usually possesses.

If it is true, as psychologists state,[15] that a person's conception of himself is linked with and grows out of his conception of his role, the precise significance of this term is worth noting. Each individual human being may be said to have two distinct but not necessarily opposed roles in life. If asked what they are he would probably hesitate to answer, because an answer would manifest his own secret thoughts and aspirations. There is a sense in which each of us leads a double life: the life of external actions which others observe and the inner life of ideals, which includes conceptions of what we would really be if we lived up to our ideals, if we were the kind of person we liked to be. There is within us, in our more reflective moments, a realization that what others observe and society approves in us may not be the thing which we ourselves know we *ought* to approve. We judge ourselves very often by what others think and say of us, but more deeply and indelibly imprinted upon our minds is the realized value of our actions in terms of what we think of ourselves in relation to our ideals.

This twofold role indicates that there are two sets of values which are dear to all of us. They are the value of attaining our ideal and the value of winning the approval of others. We have stated in Chapter 5 that an incentive for a given action has attraction for a person only in so far as it measures up to his aspirations, to his ideal. Some writers have a tendency to overlook the distinction between inner ideals and the winning of social approval. They do this either because they wish to avoid questions of moral values or more probably because they deny the existence of any real objective ideals of value and describe the subjective experience called value[16] as a "set toward obtaining what we desire," or simply "the thing which is desired." Both these definitions would make it appear that a thing has value, for example, social approval, only because it is desired. Some things are valued in our heart of hearts even when they do not merit recognition or approval.

One thing which thinking human beings desire is the possession of an upright, conscientious, and unselfish character. They know that this is something to be aimed at in a reasonable manner by forming ideals and pursuing them. On the other hand, because of social pressure or faulty education, some individuals may seek only the recognition of others, or positions of leadership and power for themselves, regardless of any consideration for the real good of society. This latter course always involves some misgiving and dissatisfaction in the long run. And if total selfishness is the motive of all action, the result will be definite discontent, because the self can never be adequately satisfied by itself in a social world where many similar beings have the same needs and tendencies. Whenever selfishness so dominates an individual that he acts as though the other person did not exist for him, there follows an unhealthy isolation and discontent, conflicts, suspicions, and fear of others, all of which indicate individual maladjustment. The person's system of values has been at fault because he did not discover any difference between the real value, even for himself as an individual, of social participation and social approval.

Just why human beings should be so dependent upon one another, and why extreme egocentrism should make them miserable, will probably never be explained in terms of the data of science. The existence of a soul destined for a happiness not of a temporal nature but contingent upon a life of real merit and service to others is certainly consistent with this mutual interdependence and striving. Through participation in social life we come to set a value upon the recognition and approval of our friends and associates, and we may often judge of our success in this matter by the norms and conventions of our group. We wish to be well received by others, respected and honored perhaps, and in one sense many things we do depend upon our culture setting. But there are some things we can do which do not depend on the setting in the same way. In our inner life of thoughts and aspirations, we all strive after an ideal of some sort, and we know that no other person, whether superior or inferior, can ascertain whether or not we are attaining this ideal. This personal scale of values or ideal, though vague at times, is no more so than the ideals placed for us by society and its conventions. We will judge ourselves according to it whether we reflect much upon it or not. This is true even of such ideals as the attainment of wealth, success, honor, and power at any cost.

Since our actions are evaluated in our own eyes in terms of what appears to be their real objective merit as judged by some standard, we are no less interested in acting as we *know* we ought to act, than in trying to secure the attention and recognition and approval of others. We cannot help asking ourselves at times whether we have merited the approval which we receive, and whether or not we respect the just claims of others upon our own attention. In a word, because of the ethical and moral concepts which every human being possesses, we all desire to have our actions evaluated in accordance with our intention of doing what is right and not merely according to their external effectiveness or apparent value. Since no other human being besides ourselves easily learns just what these intentions and aspirations may be, we cannot be satisfied with the mere approval of others. We must approve ourselves, and we do this every moment of our lives according to some real objective norm set up through a process of thinking.

When our intentions are in accordance with our ideals of value, our actions give us a special kind of satisfaction or complacency. And when our ideals of value include a sense of individual responsibility for the welfare of our group, or our community, we possess that kind of social adjustment which social workers believe is essential for preventing crime and furthering public welfare. It is evident, then, that the individual maintains self-respect throughout his efforts to participate in the group life largely because he has learned to esteem and approve himself for following an ideal. A college student, for instance, who knows that cheating is wrong and who tries to be faithful to his ideal in spite of the example of others, experiences a contentment which could never be obtained by cheating in order to win the approval of his fellow students or to gain a higher honor count at graduation. This inner complacency is experienced at times even in cases where persons are accused falsely, especially by those who ought to be better informed.

There is an ideal role which we all seek to play when we aim at suiting our actions to our own inner convictions and determinations. The degree to which we succeed in being loyal to our ideals is an indication of the strength of our convictions on the one hand and, on the other, of the amount of worth, in terms of approval, which we are accustomed to set upon ourselves as responsible agents in a world in which true merit is not always rewarded. This attitude toward ourselves as responsible agents is often more important in directing our behavior than any other attitude could be. An attitude of unprincipled and pleasure-seeking selfishness is not spontaneous, but we may be inclined in that direction all too easily. When a person fails to realize the importance of his inner role in life, he is likely to be discouraged at failure to win social prestige and favor. When he thinks that self-criticism and self-depreciation are never called for unless he fails to compete successfully with others in playing a famous role or in attaining some material advantage, he is allowing his desire for approval to become confused with ideals of value. The truth is that we must criticize and blame ourselves not merely for external social blunders or reverses of fortune, but also for other consequences of our deliberate actions. When we overlook this fact we suffer conflicts and moroseness which may lead to discontent and maladjustment.

The disparity between our own conception of our role and that which our friends assign to us has been grossly exaggerated by the social psychologists as a supposed source of conflict. The really disturbing conflicts are those which arise when our own appraisal of ourselves as moral agents disagrees with the judgments of others who cannot very often rightly appraise our moral worth. Knowing this, we can manage to bear such judgments without harboring a grudge, for we shall realize that the appraisal of others will seldom be perfectly in line with our just deserts. When we have trained ourselves not to expect adequate remuneration for our intended actions in the approval of others or in promotions, half the difficulty of resolving our conflicts about roles and status is eliminated, as competent observers of the workings of the human mind must admit. Here, of course, religion has a strong influence to assert and a true reward to offer.

Modern psychologists following Adler would have us believe that feelings of inferiority predispose to neurosis. Some of them seem to hold that the source of such feelings is the consciousness of lack of skill, talent, power, or social graces, which puts one in a poor light in comparison with others. Feelings of inadequacy do, of course, arise from these sources, but they also arise from the mistaken notion that others must be able to appraise us according to our true worth in every respect, and this notion is based on the impossible supposition that others know the inner workings of all our thoughts and desires. No one feels himself inadequate simply because he cannot secure every kind of social prestige and popularity. Each person rather selects some one object or goal and directs his "will to power" toward it, and his feelings of weakness are largely due to obstacles which hinder his progress toward that goal. Feelings of inferiority and guilt, which are a hindrance to real peace and contentment, arise from failure to attain the goal of one's ideals, and among these are ideals of moral value. Moreover, the embarrassments and emotional disturbances which one experiences at being blocked in his progress toward any goal cannot compare with that culminating deflation of one's ego which results when one has been caught taking undue advantage of the good will of others, or playing upon their sympathies in order to win their unmerited approval, because everyone knows that such dishonesty is not ideal. No one feels totally depressed because of such unavoidable habits as a lisp, or for mannerisms which might meet with approval in some other society, as, for instance, an affected accent, unless he unduly centers his attention upon such trifles and neglects to cultivate worth-while ideals. Respect for ourselves as responsible agents is shown by trying to live up to our ideals regardless of public opinion, whereas approval of ourselves as conventional and normal social beings may often be a matter of cultivating the friendship of others, or of being well received by them in order to flatter our vanity.

The importance of individual ideals as contrasted with conformity to the expectations of others is being recognized in social psychology on a scientific basis as a result of studies of delinquent children. The Murphys, quoting Piaget, hold that there are two kinds of morality in the child, one of constraint and one of cooperation. The morality of constraint is simply that of acceptance of adult standards, and in this the intention of the child plays a very small part. The morality of cooperation which is based on the principle of solidarity and which puts the primary emphasis on autonomy of conscience, and on intentionality — to use their own words — develops first parallel with the morality of constraint, and later in contrast to it.[17]

The Murphys think no more statistics are needed to prove the prevalence of bad living conditions or bad morals, but that we do need more fundamental analysis of faulty personalities and that we ought to inquire, with Piaget, whether a given child has *"known* clear and definite demands for conformity to elementary community demands." Among these "demands for conformity" might be included those basic ethical standards which apply to all men.

II. ATTITUDES WHICH ARE NOT APPROVED

We shall now enumerate some undesirable attitudes which are found too often in society. Certain attitudes are expected if right order is to be maintained. Favorable attitudes toward laws and certain social virtues are the normal outcome of a socializing process in the life of every individual who has not departed noticeably from the accepted norms. Hence the two chief kinds of disapproved attitudes are: (*a*) hostile attitudes toward law and the institutions of law and order; and (*b*) attitudes of resistance to and disrespect for the social virtues of honesty, truthfulness, unselfishness, and cooperativeness.

These attitudes could be called attitudes toward morality in the sense that laws impose moral obligations. It is not correct to limit the use of the word *moral* to those actions only which are sanctioned by positive laws. Morality can be predicated of any kind of human behavior which is intentional, or which involves deliberate choice. Many writers identify legality and morality, since they hold that the only act that can have moral significance is the one which society or the lawmakers of society prescribe. It is true that some actions have a moral quality because legitimate authority prescribes or forbids them, but there are also actions which are morally good, or morally bad, independently of positive laws regarding them, and some of these actions have not been regulated to any extent by legislation. In our discussion of attitudes toward law and the virtues we shall bear in mind the fact that morality has a much broader meaning than legality.

It is worth remembering, however, that a person who is concerned not only with gaining the approval of others for his actions, but also with living up to his own ideals will be very likely to have more clearly defined attitudes toward personal morality and toward laws for maintaining social order than he will toward mere conventions. Conventions and customs are often accepted in practice without much reflection. The requirements of punctuality, or of civility in manners and dress, for example, are rarely objected to, and conformity in these matters is generally not difficult. But when regulation of actions is brought forcefully to our attention, for example, through the speed laws, or through laws affecting the disposition of property or laws regarding sexual behavior, we are more consciously impressed with the need of taking a stand in the matter. Perhaps this is the reason for the distinction which Allport and his co-workers[18] found it advisable to make between conforming behavior of the conventional kind, and conformity or nonconformity to what they call "mores" and "institutional" patterns.

In the process of making up our minds about observing laws and moral principles we are generally quite conscious of ourselves as responsible agents. This reflective sort of mental disposition in regard to institutions and laws is an indication that the attitude toward the law or institution includes an implicit attitude toward ourselves. We picture ourselves as either observing or violating the laws, and may respect or despise ourselves in either case. If we despise ourselves for keeping the laws, or respect ourselves for breaking them, our attitudes toward laws are hostile. If, on the other hand, we respect ourselves for keeping them or despise ourselves for violating them, we have favorable attitudes toward laws. These are plain facts of experience which anyone will recognize by a little self-analysis. A gangster who is ever on the alert for new opportunities for circumventing the law must inwardly admit, on reflection, that he respects himself for his lawlessness, just as the social worker or reformer must be aware that he rather respects himself for his law-abiding intentions. It is possible that both of the above attitudes depend largely on a desire for the approval of others, and the ideals of gangster and reformer alike may have been socially conditioned to such an extent that little effort was ever made to subject these ideals to their own personal approval or disapproval. But the dishonest and criminally inclined person, even while respecting himself for his good reputation in spite of secret misdemeanors, must also despise himself at times for his duplicity. He is well aware that he would not maintain the approval of society as a whole if his intentions were to become publicly known. His complacency and self-respect in his dishonesty are the result of faulty ideals. Conversely the upright and respectable factory employee who is contented with his lot and avoids all dishonesty may pride himself on his spirit of contentedness and on his integrity, but his sole motive for so doing cannot be that society as a whole fully approves of his self-effacement and contentment. He must also have developed attitudes of self-respect which are necessary for citizens who desire to cooperate in the maintaining of a larger scheme of things.

All these considerations must be kept in mind when we discuss attitudes toward institutions, laws, and social virtues. Sociologists agree that laws are necessary for maintaining right order in society, and some exert themselves strenuously to inculcate, especially in young people, healthy attitudes of respect for and obedience to just laws and regulations. The fact that graft in politics and procrastination in court proceedings prevent many people from developing a better attitude should move public-spirited politicians and judges to correct these abuses.

A) Children's Attitudes Toward Virtues. The child must acquire notions of right and wrong by using his reflective powers in evaluating his experience. Children's attitudes toward various offenses such as swearing, cheating, and lying are often quite different from those of adults precisely because their understanding of the implications of these forms of behavior is so inadequate. When attitude or character testers use items in their questionnaires which children interpret differently from adults, their tests have not much validity. In order to eliminate this difficulty, a group of investigators carried on a gigantic test program with grade school children, in which the child was put in a concrete situation, and his behavior observed. This "overt behavior" method of studying attitudes led to some interesting results. Hartshorne, May, and Maller, who were in charge of the testing program, wished to discover what attitudes the children actually possessed, and not the attitudes which they should have possessed. For this purpose the test situations were so arranged that these children had ample opportunity to cheat, to be cooperative, or to be self-controlled.

The first conclusion of these investigators was that there is no evidence of general factors of morality like the general factors of intelligence, athletic ability, and mechanical ability. They thought that morality depended on the type of training a child received in the home and at school more than it depends on inherited constitution or fixed traits. We quote: "The conduct trends and their relations to one another in individuals are the precipitates of specific experiences and are functions of the situations to which they have become attached by habit."[19] In particular they held that no special virtue such as honesty or truthfulness manifested itself, and that behavior was situationally determined. On the basis of a later investigation independently of the above authors in which he applied special mathematical techniques, Maller made the following statement: "Apparently such aspects of character as honesty, cooperation, inhibition, and persistence seem to be positively related and to go together to some extent."[20]

The results of the first investigation, therefore, cannot be regarded as definitive. When we remember that children's attitudes are very variable, the inconclusiveness of these attitude or character tests will not surprise us. The understanding and appreciation which children have of all these social virtues is certainly very much modified by training. Moreover, the overt behavior of children affords no certain evidence that they possess a clear understanding of moral principles. Even if we were able to demonstrate the fact that they possess a knowledge of principles at a certain age, we could not expect that they would act on them in the same way under similar circumstances, unless we assume that freedom of choice means nothing.

The Character Education Inquiry clearly indicated that children up to the age of 12 or 14 are very naïve and unsuspecting in the presence of adults. They readily allowed themselves to be caught cheating, for instance, under circumstances in which more experienced persons would have been rather more cautious. It was seen from the scores that brighter children were less likely to be dishonest than duller ones. Perhaps the brighter children, because of their wider experience, did not so readily allow themselves to be detected in their dishonesty. If so, the test did not really give a score for honesty but rather for cleverness or some similar quality. It was also apparent that emotionally stable children were less inclined to be dishonest than were the emotionally unstable, perhaps because the fear of failure which characterizes emotionally disturbed children made them less capable of perceiving the value of honesty. Children from better homes did less cheating than those from poorer families, which would suggest to some that economic security is a cause of honesty and truthfulness. From these correlations alone it could just as well be argued that honesty causes security. This correlation alone is incapable of establishing any valid argument unless it is also demonstrated that dishonesty is always correlated with insecurity arising from poverty of circumstances.

B) ADULT ATTITUDES. Cattell and others have tried by means of what they call "Temperament Tests" to discover whether there is any such trait as will power or strength of character in adults. They tried to discover the existence of externally observable qualities, but it may be presumed that if a trait or complex of traits existed in the persons tested, there was also a fixed attitude of mind in regard to it. Since the testers wished to avoid the danger of self-inflation on the part of the persons tested, they preferred to use the "overt behavior" method rather than the self-rating inventories. Obviously the situations described above for testing children could not be used for adults, and so Cattell[21] made use of specially trained college students as judges of the external traits of some sixty of their acquaintances. The judges were instructed to be as objective as possible and not to expect any particular cluster of traits to be found together before they made their prolonged observations. The judges had not taken any courses in psychology which might be thought to bias their judgments. They rated the subjects on such traits as persistence, energy, kindness, and willingness to forego pleasure.

Cattell made an analysis of these data and found that certain traits seemed to go together to form character complexes which were independent of intelligence. Of course, there was a possibility that the judges were mistaken in their appraisal of the persons tested. Granting for the moment that their judgments were reliable, it is not at all certain that real will habits, that is, actual frames of mind in regard to virtues, were being studied. This is because the inner attitudes of a person toward the above qualities are never fully manifest in his overt behavior. As a matter of fact the temperament testers were not at all interested in the inner attitudes of their experimental subjects. But other authors interpret the findings of the testers as if there had been question of real personality traits and attitudes.[22]

We may prescind from the question of the inner attitudes of the children and of the adults whose character traits were studied and make a comparison between the published results. We notice that intelligence as measured by the intelligence tests is not correlated with "goodness" of character in the sense in which Cattell uses this term in regard to adults, but that it is correlated with the virtues of honesty, truthfulness, cooperation, and self-denial in the cases of the children who were tested. In recent investigations on the intelligence of criminals, Cattell's findings are substantiated in the sense that adult criminals are just as intelligent as the average citizen, if not more so.

There is only one way in which all these conflicting data concerning the relationship between intelligence and virtues may be interpreted consistently. Intelligence may be developed along certain lines without any apparent corresponding change in the habits which are attributable to the will. Attitudes and will acts require a normal use of intelligence, but the quantity of the thing called intelligence today seems to have no particular determining influence upon the quality of the will acts. A person who is highly intelligent may direct his actions either along the lines of useful and cooperative social participation, or along the lines of socially disruptive and criminal activity, just as he sees fit. In other words he is able to choose what appears suitable under certain circumstances and in order to do this he needs to consider motives of value which will direct his choices along socially desirable lines.

C) CRIMINAL ATTITUDES. A crime in the technical sense is the intentional commission of an external act prohibited by law (for example, willful murder) or an intentional omission of an external action prescribed by law (for example, evasion of the income tax law). It does not refer to illegal actions which were intended but for some reason or another not executed. Usually the intention of violating the law is the decisive element in any particular case of criminal investigation. The intention of violating the law actually does exist sometimes in the minds of human beings, along with the awareness of the fact that a given action if performed would violate some particular law. All those below a certain age, which varies in different localities, are technically incapable of committing a crime in the strict sense. This is because they are presumed to be incapable of realizing the consequences of their actions for society. The same is true for mentally deficient and deranged persons. Our practice thus seems to support the common-sense view that a rational attitude toward the law takes time in which to develop. During the earlier years and in cases of mental defect, since there can be no clear awareness of the full meaning and implications of criminal offenses, there can be no real criminal violation.

Before children reach a certain age, their defections from right order are known as delinquencies, and special methods of handling delinquents ought to be devised in accordance with the distinction which we have just indicated. The main factor contributing to delinquencies and to delinquent attitudes is an erroneous personal view which the wayward child takes toward himself and society. Should the child become convinced, from one cause or another, that he is of no use whatever to himself and to others, or never come to realize that he can gain self-respect and the approval of others by accepting *personal* responsibility for the public welfare, his attitude is definitely unhealthy.

Christian education undoubtedly aids greatly in establishing in the mind of the child the proper attitudes of respect and esteem for his own dignity and the rights of others. These attitudes are absolutely prerequisite for enabling the child adequately to meet emergencies and to solve problems that arise. A Christian education will stress the fact that every man has a dignity and a destiny, and it does not lower any man to the level of a machine or a cog in the wheel of human society. Christianity is not a doctrine of "rugged individualism," nor does it teach that any person loses his identity and individual responsibility by merging in the group. It aims at motivating individuals to a proper understanding of the value inherent in social virtues, whether they are prescribed by positive law or not. It furnishes motives besides human respect and social approval for the formation of strong attitudes of appreciation of the qualities of honesty, truthfulness, cooperativeness, and unselfishness.

Unfortunately, the effectiveness of this traditional teaching in regard to the necessity of fostering strong favorable attitudes in the young toward social virtues is impaired by the efforts of certain writers. We may now consider the basis for the arguments used by these writers.

a) THE EFFECT OF GLANDS. There has been much theoretical discussion on the influence of glands and of the general physique upon the attitudes and tendencies of the child. The evidence for glandular abnormalities among prison inmates suggests a correlation between criminal attitude and glandular functions, since glandular disturbances have been reported to be present in a larger degree among the inmates of prisons than among the general population. How frequently they occur among the general population no one has seriously attempted to determine, but many research projects have been carried out by endocrinologists upon the prison population. We have already pointed out that the life led by these inmates is generally such that it does not predispose toward a healthy functioning of the glands which play a part in the emotional life. It is evident also that prison occupants are often disturbed by such psychological factors as hatreds and fears and morbidity. The malfunctioning of the glands could perhaps be traced to the new environment and to the consequent unhealthy attitudes of the inmates, and we have no grounds for ruling out this possibility until tests have been made upon individuals both before and after they enter the institutions. The notorious attempts of Lombroso to detect the "criminal body type," at any rate, have been considered by able research workers to have ended in failure.[23]

b) MENTAL DISORDER. Under this heading are included the psychoses and psychoneuroses. They are of two main kinds: those whose origin is chiefly organic, such as paresis; and those whose origin is chiefly functional, such as paranoia, schizophrenia, manic-depressive psychoses, and obsessional and compulsion neuroses.[24]

Certain traits which are present in all of these disorders produce a tendency toward criminal acts. For example, the exaggerated delusion that one is being persecuted may suggest assault or vengeful acts to the one who suffers from it. In a certain stage of the epileptic seizure, uncontrolled fury and deeds of violence are apt to be indulged in. In cases where obsessive thoughts and imaginations regarding sexual activities torment a person, there will be corresponding tendencies toward disapproved behavior. Lastly, instances are on record in which children developed sudden impulses to steal which were probably traceable to their desire to attract attention and to feel important, and these impulses carried over into adult life. Because the child did not get the normal amount of attention due him at his age, he lost confidence in himself and others and became unmanageable. The advice of a parent or of a prudent counselor might have spared him much of his later difficulty.

Again, the tabulated figures seem to show that mentally disordered persons are found in much greater abundance in prisons than in the general population. Authorities do not agree on the exact figures,[25] but a life spent in evading the law and terminating with a prison sentence may scarcely be said to favor the development of an emotionally stable personality or to make possible an adequate adjustment of any personality to its surroundings. As yet we do not know just how frequently psychopathic personalities are to be found among the general population. There is little agreement as to the meaning of the term, but J. F. Brown is of the opinion that one person in ten is at one time or another psychopathic. The confusion which we find in the figures results in large part from the recent attempts to include under the term "psychopathic" all character defects of whatever kind, such as inferiority complexes and unsociability.

If we assume, for the sake of argument, that about 20 per cent of first entrants into penal institutions, on the average, are somewhat mentally disordered upon entrance, whereas only 1.3 per cent of the general population is so afflicted,[26] we must remember that only a small percentage of all real criminals have actually been placed in custody. Countless others who have escaped detection or have had criminal intentions without putting them into execution are free among the general population, which latter, on the above assumption, is only 1.3 per cent mentally disordered. If the unconvicted and also the criminally minded persons are added to the class of the actual criminals detained in the institutions, it will be seen that the total percentage of disordered persons in the institutions drops considerably. Until we are better able to detect real criminal intentions and attitudes, there is very little use in trying to predict the effect of mental disorder upon criminal tendencies.

c) MENTAL DEFECT. This term now means a lack of normal intelligence,[27] and persons who are so deficient will be relatively incapable of developing the habit of restraining their emotional life according to accepted norms. Lack of intelligence is always relative, and in this country we arbitrarily designate as feeble-minded those persons who, though actually much older, have not reached the development of an average 10- or 11-year-old child, including many who have been retarded on a much lower level. There are persons so retarded in their development that they are not able to care for the necessities of the body without assistance. Being under the care of guardians, these persons will not, as a rule, become dangerously criminal. But the case is different for the upper class of defectives and the likelihood of their coming into conflict with society is all the greater because other more gifted persons will exploit them for vicious purposes. Then, too, the failure of mentally retarded children to attain success in school often makes of them chronic malcontents. They come to resent the normal restrictions placed upon them by the ordinary routine of life, and when they become totally antagonistic toward the society in which they live, they sometimes take revenge in acts of delinquency or crime. There is a real need here for the cooperation and protection of friends and benefactors, who will be able to give such defective persons a chance to spend their time usefully without coming into conflict with the group. Those who have intelligence quotients below 50 and those whose emotional life is completely upset can best be cared for in institutions.

Thus juvenile delinquency occurs more frequently in the case of mentally defective persons than among the normal persons, and this supports our former claim that moral development depends upon the use of the rational powers of man. But when we turn to the question of adult criminality we see a different picture. Although the literature on this topic is very extensive and inconsistent, there is no clear indication that the intelligence quotients of criminals are inferior to those of the general population. Hence the growth of healthy attitudes toward law and the social virtues requires the normal use of the intellectual powers, but the full use of these powers, no matter how superior they may be, does not indicate that suitable moral attitudes will necessarily follow.

d) SALIENT FACTORS IN DELINQUENT ATTITUDE FORMATION. The full treatment of the social factors conducive to delinquent attitudes belongs to the study of sociology. Chief and foremost of these, as we mentioned above, is the home atmosphere and example. The sad cases of delinquency with a history of broken or unhappy homes should be published in the daily papers for the benefit of those about to marry. Another factor which need not here be enlarged upon is the inculcation of moral standards and strengthening of motives. Finally, there is the question of adequate supervision and choice of companions. Parental neglect is a subject of grave concern to social workers, who believe that parents need a fuller realization of their responsibilities. The question of neighborhood influences, which is closely connected with choice of companions, can be properly treated when we remember the meaning of free will and rational motivation. Although the environment tends to pull a child down to the level of the baser elements in a group, a properly formed and motivated child in a poor environment will tend to elevate the moral level of the group as a whole. As for public opinion and group attitudes in regard to delinquency, their importance is so great that psychologists can sometimes predict a group reaction from a knowledge of the prevalent attitudes in a group. Public convictions and attitudes are capable of being directed along desired lines when leaders take the trouble to enlighten the public by appealing to their sound judgment and not merely to their sentiments and feelings. Reform measures should of course be inaugurated by choosing an adequate ideal standard and directing men toward this ideal.

FOR ACCELERATED READING

SHORT SUMMARY OF THE CHAPTER

Certain favorable attitudes toward society and right order are needed in every group. The motives for cultivating these attitudes must be considered by individuals lest they develop and persist in antisocial preferences and prejudices. Uniform ideas and sentiments regarding some customs and necessary institutions conduce toward a cluster of cultural attitudes. Social pressure fosters and insures the right attitudes, but individually evaluated motives of loyalty to the group and of social participation strengthen group unity and lessen the danger of petty strife among members.

Collective attitudes are fostered by small transitory groups — clubs, lodges, etc. — and these should harmonize with the attitudes of the larger unity. Public opinion is a cross section of all attitudes. Rational convictions are not all emotionally toned, but hastily formed opinions are often not founded on any real values — much less so are superstitions. They have little social significance unless they beget prejudice or delay needed progress.

Attitudes ultimately reside in the individual because he can accept the responsibility. Each one must find reasons for developing healthy favorable attitudes toward right order in the use of reproductive functions. Social approval cannot be the only motive in fostering unselfish and cooperative desires in men. An attitude of evaluating self is required in order to maintain self-respect in following ideals. External actions alone appear to the public and self-approval is not necessarily lost when some group disapproves or approves of a given type of action. We seek to be well received and respected by others, but also to see value in and attain satisfaction from following objective norms.

Hostility toward the restrictions of society is in itself disapproved. Each person has better awareness of his attitude toward laws than of his state of mind toward mere conventions; an attitude toward self is involved in every moral obligation. Intelligence directs formation of attitudes, but does not guarantee that they will be favorable to social order. Delinquency patterns indicate failure to esteem the self as a responsible participator in group life. Mentally defective persons lack this sense of responsibility, but they probably do not contribute to the delinquency problem as much as do broken homes, or irresponsible parents and educators.

Find Review Questions and Supplementary Reading at the end of the book.

CHAPTER 11

HUMAN NATURE AND DESIRABLE OR APPROVED PERSONALITY

Nature in General — False Impressions of Human Nature Analyzed; Consequences of the View That Society Confers Human Nature; True View of Human Nature; The Dilemma of Culture Determinists; Our Purpose in This Chapter. *Traits Which Make for Distinctiveness and Are Approved* — (I) External Traits: (A) Special Skills and Self-Evaluation; (B) The Social Graces. (II) Life Interests and Total Outlook: (A) Practical Values and Interests; (B) Outlook on Life or Philosophy of Life. (III) Some Selected Traits: (A) Intelligence; (B) Tenacity and Energy; (C) Self-Assurance and Decisiveness; (D) Sociability and Progressiveness; (E) Sublimation and Altruism. *Retrospect.*

NATURE IN GENERAL

FALSE IMPRESSIONS ANALYZED. A typical modern view of human nature is that proposed by M. Krout[1] according to which we are individuals by birth and become persons by acquiring social status. Every individual has some conception of himself, some role to play upon the social stage. The normal person, it is claimed, adopts that status which society and culture approve. Thus if his own conception of his status is at variance with other people's conception of it, as when he thinks himself to be a genius whereas others regard him as a moron, he is called a psychotic; but if his own conception of himself agrees with that of society, he thereby is said to become a person, having been made a person by society's determination and approval of his status.

A slightly different notion is to be found in LaPiere and Farnsworth.[2] According to it we are born animals, but receive human nature from society. Deviations from the norm of the social group give personality once we have acquired human nature by normal behavior. But if these deviations are excessive, the result is not

210

personality but psychotic individuality, or even that kind of individuality which we find in criminals and other socially unpopular types.

Such notions as these have been developed by the attempt to define personality and human nature in terms of what society and culture confer upon the individual. They both neglect to take into account the individual's own active participation, although, as a matter of fact, Krout recognizes that there is a difference between the social history of the group and that of an individual. Instead of trying to define personality in purely social terms, we should define it on a basis of sound philosophical principles regarding universal human nature.

Born of human parents, each individual receives through them his human nature and is, like them, a human being. Since this nature includes the power of reason, which develops normally in all individuals along with the power of sense, and gives direction to the instincts and to the natural social tendencies, it is recognizably a rational nature. By human nature one ought to mean the basic principle of operation within man, the fundamental cause and source of the specifically human activities of judging and reasoning, of reflecting and choosing, of behaving like a responsible individual. Since these activities are found at least to some extent in every human being, they indicate the existence of a common and specifically human nature. But the fact that human beings clearly manifest at least a minimum of rational power does not alter the fact that they also possess other qualities characteristic of the infrahuman species.

Owing to the many differences between human beings, there are within the totality of those possessing human nature very many subdivisions or smaller groups of individuals with their own special features that characterize their groups. These smaller groups, such as civilized groups, psychic and neurotic groups, or racial groups, all share in the specific qualities which are inseparable from human nature, and we may say that the individuals in them have a special and socially modified "group nature." Thus we speak of the excitable superstitious nature of the primitive, or of the irresponsible nature of the child. The term "nature" in such phrases has a limited sense, for we surely do not intend to exclude the infant or the primitive from the human family as such.

Most of the modern sociopsychological notions of human nature derive either from the view that there is no such thing as a common unchangeable rational nature, or from the view that human nature as it now exists evolved from prehistoric animal ancestors, and is still evolving. Both these views assume that animal nature is not essentially different from human nature. Students of culture must admit, however, the existence at present of certain specifically human features, at least in all healthy adult human society.

Many writers retain the term "human nature" without agreeing about what it means. One author holds that human nature appears at about the age of six and that before this age the children of the human family are simply animals. Hence he concludes that human nature is conferred upon us by the group. Yet the socializing process undoubtedly begins long before the age of six, and many natural animal tendencies manifested after that age have evidently not been conferred on the individual by human society. The composite nature of human beings involves the presence, in each person, of cognitive and appetitive powers that are rational as well as sensory.

Any one who maintains that evolution has produced a strictly human individual without any remnant of animal nature, must account for the origin of the new or emergent human quality which could obviously not have been produced by the social environment prior to the evolution of that environment itself. Even in childhood all human individuals possess the capacity for reason; primitive peoples, however retarded, have the same basic powers which characterize the human race in general. Rational power is the characteristic property of human beings exclusively, and yet it is only one of their many powers.

The view which holds that human nature is derived fully through a process of biological evolution is losing favor of late, partly because it leads logically to the myths of race superiority and to race persecution. As we shall see, serious consequences also follow from the view that society confers human nature upon us, and hence the proponents of the latter view are liable to the same charge of rationalization which they allege against the supporters of the evolutionistic view, precisely because it leads to myths of group minds and to special group distinctions. There is actually no ground for the assertion that human nature is conferred upon individuals either by heredity alone or by the social environment alone. Some social leaders have succeeded in inducing profound changes in social trends, without deserving to be called psychotic or neurotic in their deviation from group norms. Individual differences can be found everywhere among leaders and followers alike and occasionally at least the use of planned and rational methods is effective in guiding human beings to a desired goal. In spite of the apprehensions of LaPiere and Farnsworth,[3] it is even possible to develop a dynamic and outstanding personality without becoming psychopathic.

CONSEQUENCES OF THE VIEW THAT SOCIETY CONFERS HUMAN NATURE. According to this view, "human nature" means the sum total of those attributes which approximate the normal for a given group, while individuality traits are experiments with new modes of behavior, involving deviations from the normal.[4] Since only by measurement of traits is it possible to discover the normal, what is here meant by human nature is expressed in terms of a *statistical average,* a point on a curve. Now the utility of statistical averages as a means of predicting behavior is quite well established, yet a twofold danger needs to be guarded against in the application of these figures. It is misleading to suggest that in order to acquire individuality and status, one must experiment with new and disapproved modes of behavior; and there is also the danger that after comparing their averages from different groups, the investigators themselves, having failed to study *basic* human traits, may conclude that there is no common basis for human nature in the different groups.

Professor Krout is a typical case for, having denied that human beings are superior to the brutes, he also fails to find a common basis for human nature in the different cultures, each of which imposes its particular roles or codes upon the members of the group. He seems rather inconsistent, however, when he is discussing the meaning of culture.[5] For here he says that whereas the content of culture is actualized in overt behavior, the *form* of culture represents the meanings or attitudes involved in individual acts. How human beings in any culture could develop attitudes and understand meanings without having been endowed with a power of intelligence remains a natural mystery for all those who deny the existence of any common basis for human nature. Again, Professor Krout holds that, if psychosis is considered to be the disparity between an individual's status and his own conception of his status, then maladjustments (deviate behavior) are as prevalent in one society as they are in another.[6] Maladjustments and all sorts of deviate behavior, he claims a few pages farther on,[7] result from nonrational acceptance of culture patterning and not from a functional failure of hereditary factors or of social organization.

Now if society actually did confer human nature on the individual, society would by that very fact have the right to prescribe the rules for all human actions. If society alone is responsible for endowing human beings with their basic social properties she should also take all the responsibility for regulating their activities. This is the most serious and destructive consequence of the theories we are discussing. For as soon as some hypothetical sort of entity called society is regarded as the carrier of the laws of morality, which are considered to be different for different groups because the statistical averages of their behavior tendencies are different, then the doctrine of the relativity of morals seems plausible, because normal or average behavior alone appears to be the natural behavior, the kind which society approves. This implies that there are no principles of morality founded upon universal human nature, and that all and only those things are right which society approves. Such speculations are, indeed, quite outside the realm of positive science, and tend to create a certain distrust of the scientists who thus set themselves up as moralists after insisting that they have nothing to say about morals.[8]

When scientists refer to desirable personality traits as those which society approves and to undesirable traits as those which society disapproves, the implication is that society is a being which assumes all the responsibility for individual acts, even though the existence of a group mind is explicitly denied. Moreover, undue stress is placed upon the importance of social approval as a motive of behavior. Social approval is indeed a motive, and the attainment of social order must be desired as a goal, but neither of these two objectives can be attained simply by expecting people to accept a role passively and unreflectingly.

Human beings need to be convinced of their personal responsibility for their role if they are to be guided in their efforts to secure status. Those actions and habits for which a person knows that he is responsible and which he strives to incorporate into his plan of life must be guided by sound principles, unless one's only goal in life is to become an uncritical imitator of what he observes in his social environment. The Nazi leaders were fully aware of this fact; and hence, though they appealed to mob psychology or to the sentiments and prejudices of the masses, yet when possible, in order to secure quick action, their university professors were expected to provide logical and scientific arguments in support of their views. The works of Rosenberg are typical of this sort of scientific propaganda.

The burden of social reform cannot be placed upon some mythical entity called society, since the individuals taken together make their own society, and each one has an active role to play in the group. It is often said that society owes us security, status, recreation, etc. From whom shall we claim these advantages? Our cooperation in group activity and our attitudes of loyalty to what is right, whether it is approved by our little group or not, will give us the only status and security which can endure. Instead of attributing all delinquencies to the faulty organization of society, we must realize that the responsible heads in society are trying to direct our actions according to principles which derive their efficacy from something besides mere custom and convention. We know that human nature is shared in common with individuals of all groups, and that the legislators of separate groups are trying to give satisfaction to the majority of people most of the time by appealing to their sense of duty, not merely by urging them to conform to the patterns of behavior of the group for fear of delinquency or of neuroticism. A sense of security comes from regulating our needs, as far as possible, in accordance with the available means for satisfying them, not from aiming at selfish gratifications which in due time will fail to satisfy.

TRUE VIEW OF HUMAN NATURE. We all possess powers of intellectual insight, of foresight, and of rational choice, even though we do not always make the most efficient use of them. They are rooted in our nature, and they develop separately in each individual, contingently upon the following factors: (1) inherited qualities and dispositions; (2) training; (3) opportunities of a given social environment; (4) free use of these opportunities along with the helps which religion can and does supply. The concluding portions of this chapter will deal with those habit systems which develop in our society and contribute to the individual's development as a responsible self-directing person, a distinctively human individual.

The notion of individuality is very important here because the experiences of each person are eminently his own. Though similar to those of others, they are never identical with them. Customs and the example of others tend to produce a similarity between persons, but this is never absolute, for there are in almost every group degrees of nonconformity to rule. And even if the conformity is as perfect as it can possibly be, there is individual consciousness of taking some active part in producing and maintaining it. Group influence may not be said to produce the uniformity any more than it may be said to produce the nonconformity, for there exist many kinds of smaller groups, and these will have an influence upon a person in so far as he elects to join them or to participate in their activity.

Group influence depends, quite concretely and understandably, upon the habits and dispositions of each responsible person, and upon his attitudes of mind toward conventions, customs, laws, and himself. Sometimes an individual acts deliberately with prevision of consequences, but at other times he acts hastily with neither foresight nor reflection upon the full consequences of his actions. Yet it is never true to say that his actions have no meaning apart from the social context in which they are found, or that he never determines their meaning for himself. This view, which discounts the role of the member or part, developed, as we have seen, out of generalizations from the Gestalt theory. Each individual person comes to recognize the meaning of his actions as often as he directs his habits toward those goals which he approves for himself and others.

THE DILEMMA OF THE CULTURE DETERMINISTS. Professor Krout is a good example of a writer who tries to adhere to the teaching that an individual makes his own environment but that this same individual is culturally determined in all his actions. He insists that specific cultural material does not reach any two individuals in exactly the same way, and that it does not reach any one individual all at once. Yet he says that all human behavior, as a sociocultural fact, may be explained in terms of the way in which the social institutions of a group become manifested in human behavior. He describes at some length the manner in which the behavior of the infant, the youth, and the leader are patterned in primitive society; how marital rituals, death rituals, manners, moral attitudes, conscience, sense of shame and guilt, and reactions to the sacred are stereotyped in all societies. Throughout his description he fails to note that the way in which a particular individual accepts this cultural material really makes a decided difference to the group in which he lives. Professor Krout is concentrating upon the influence of the group and apparently overlooks the fact that individuals contribute anything special to the process. He has already, in other parts of his book, denied that human beings possess any power that would distinguish them essentially from animals. Finding that his culture determinism, no less than Allport's theory of hereditary determinism, fails to account for the deviations from the normal in any group, he admits that there is no clear proof for the assumption that individuals must act like other individuals. He then reviews the evidence in favor of uniformity, and finds, contrary to Mead and others, that there is proportionately as much deviate behavior, even of the psychotic sort, among preliterates as there is among civilized groups. Almost in desperation, he repeats that culture can explain the deviations as well as the conformities, and that these differences or deviations are only a special aspect of social patterning. There are, he believes, about eight factors arising in the sociocultural milieu which could account for the deviate or nonconforming type of behavior. Among these factors he lists the lack of rational acceptance of the culture patterns on the part of certain individuals. In the end, he admits that the individual must do something to make the group what it is, that culture alone does not make him all that he is.

LaPiere and Farnsworth state explicitly that "the individual does not make his Society."[9] He is culturally determined in all his actions, and sometimes conforms to the norms, sometimes deviates somewhat from them, sometimes deviates so widely from the accepted norms that he segregates himself from society. This subtle doctrine leads the authors to state that the only difference, from a sociological point of view, between criminal and psychotic persons is the degree to which they deviate from the norms. All these manifestations, they say, are merely experiments, on the part of various individuals, with new forms of behavior which make a person an outstanding individual,[10] for human nature plus individuality constitute personality.[11] It may well be doubted whether any individual consciously and deliberately strives for the attainment of a psychopathic personality, but the factors of consciousness and deliberation do not enter into the discussions of behavioristic writers. They ought to find a place in textbooks which outline the types of adjustment possible for human beings.

It is not sufficient for understanding human behavior to state that all deviations from the norms are mere departures from the accepted ways which society disapproves. True it is, society does not approve of psychotic behavior. But its disapproval is of an altogether different sort from its condemnation of criminal behavior. Society and her responsible heads do not assume that distinctiveness of behavior of the psychotic kind is aimed at deliberately by any individuals in order to disturb the common good. Our officials rightly realize that maladjustment can occur without direct intent to violate an approved norm, whereas criminal behavior occurs at times precisely because of this intent. They recognize the distinction which we have made in this book between the inner life of values which must guide a person in his choice of actions, and that tendency to drift along in the approved manner until some striking conflict results in maladjustment. We have reason to expect that they will continue to act on this distinction in spite of the doctrines of modern social psychologists.

OUR PURPOSE IN THIS CHAPTER. A complete description of the social personality in all its aspects is beyond the scope of this book. Our task will be merely to emphasize, without evaluating from an ethical standpoint, certain traits which are generally thought to be useful for understanding social interactions. Under our discussion of attitudes we outlined the relation which exists between motives, attitudes, and action. One motive of action is the example of others, and hence there will be some benefit in indicating the approved personality traits which are readily observable and likely to be imitated. The habit of accepting approved ways, or of seeking to acquire desirable traits merely because they are culturally defined or approved, undoubtedly places a limiting condition for the exercise of choice. Such a habit is not to be considered the inevitable consequence of living in any group. Conventional behavior which is enforced by social pressure may be useful in bringing conformity into certain groups, yet a person does not develop a strong character simply by allowing himself to be carried along with the group, and he does not conform to customs and laws in an unreflecting manner all the time.

Habit formation follows upon the use of volition conditioned by social pressure, but not in such a manner as to take away all personal responsibility. There is an active participation on the part of the members of society, and this activity of the individual must never be lost sight of in discussing the effects of social pressure. Sometimes a person may be more strongly motivated, it is true, to avoid such things as "social blunders" than to follow his ideals, but that is a matter for each individual to decide for himself. It is a known fact that an individual's actions can usually be made to change their course provided he is sufficiently interested in bringing about a change and his motives lead him to take some action.

Sometimes a person will not be fully aware of the factors which are effective in bringing about a certain habit tendency in himself, or of the advantages which accrue to himself and to others from such a habit. There is often an implicit assumption that we all gain security and power from conforming to customs and from cooperat ing in a group, from checking the will to power against the will to community. But to describe all human striving in terms of a conflict between the real desires of the individual and the lagging or un-progressive restrictions of the group and of group authority is an exaggeration. Some kinds of authority are respected everywhere because leadership is admittedly necessary in every group. Whatever one may hold as regards the relative advantages of a changing rather than a static environment, it is easy to see that the safety and security of the group will be furthered by individual habits of submission to legitimate authority. That authority which is respected because it is legitimate is the only kind capable of forming attitudes conducive to right order. Most thinking persons realize that the personal happiness of individuals is not inevitably frustrated by the necessary restrictions of group life.

By studying the individual in relation to his group without for-getting that he is an individual in his own right we shall be able to sketch the approved traits which give a person status as well as distinctiveness. There are, of course, approved styles in any occupation or profession, and success in life often depends upon acceptance of these styles and roles. While conforming to these norms we do not forget that there are certain more fundamental objectives toward which we strive. We realize that we have our ideals of value which we cherish and approve even though others do not observe them and approve them. The fact that most thinking persons do actually approve of unselfishness, truthfulness, honesty and cooperativeness indicates that there is some universally approved set of norms. We can gain status by living up to these norms.

It is significant that the qualities of fair play and consideration for others are judged by the social psychologists to be required for the leader. It has also been pointed out in this book that individual effort is required of a person if he wishes to acquire the distinctive qualities of a leader. Since society will always be in need of leaders, efforts will have to be made on the part of all persons to adjust themselves to the situations involving leadership. One can acquire that distinctiveness and outstandingness which are required for leadership without deviating from the fundamental norms of morality which regulate human actions, and without becoming either a psychopathic personality or a criminal.

APPROVED DISTINCTIVE TRAITS

I) EXTERNAL TRAITS

A) *Special Skills and Self-Evaluation.* Every person possesses some attractiveness for somebody, because of the things which he can do. He must not allow himself to contract the habit of talking and thinking about himself as if he had no abilities or status at all, for this is not true. Nor should one for a moment think that he possesses all possible skills and aptitudes. Self-inflation can be as detrimental to success as too much self-depreciation. One must try to realize his own limitations, yet not worry too much if his friends do not recognize what he sees in himself. If he does, he may easily be led to suspect that others are unfair to him. In fact, their mistaken judgments will more likely be due to other factors than unfairness. Their standards of value may vary, and therefore they will form different judgments according to these various standards.

Judgments of moral worth are often mingled with appraisals of usefulness and success, so that a complete and correct evaluation even of a person whom we know well is very difficult. The same holds for both sides of the mutual judgment process.

B) *The Social Graces.* Since a leader must be outstanding in some way in order to gain the attention and respect of his followers, it is well to note the various reasons why a person can be regarded as outstanding or singular. Some think that even physical defects, extremes of size or figure, make for attractiveness in a leader or in an influential person, but there is no evidence that this is generally true. When one allows his natural talents and good manners to manifest themselves, and aims at gentlemanly behavior, there will be little need of cultivating peculiarities in order to attract attention. Whether others approve of us or not, and whether they are susceptible to our influence, will depend on many things besides attention-causing eccentricities of behavior and perfection of physical form. Persons who are afflicted with physical defects have often acquired a pleasing and attractive personality in spite of their handicaps. Their total effect upon others depends largely upon their own attitude toward their own abilities. It is well known that physically handicapped individuals easily develop hostile attitudes or attitudes of dependence upon others, no matter how carefully their tutors and associates avoid anything that would encourage such attitudes. Cases of this kind are effectively dealt with by informing these persons that their own attitude must be corrected by themselves. Again, we may readily fancy, at times, that others look down on us for such defects as a foreign accent, or for stolidity of disposition or for social blunders, when, as a matter of fact, they may respect us highly for not showing any embarrassment because of them. We are very easily deceived as to the intentions of others. Fearful and suspicious attitudes regarding their reactions cause many unpleasant experiences on our part which are quite unnecessary, and the best way to avoid calling attention to peculiarities which are unmistakably disapproved is to avoid showing embarrassment over them, in case they cannot be removed.

The attainment of a pleasing and attractive external appearance thus depends upon a combination of mental and physical qualifications. Doubtless also a natural pleasantness of manner and cheerfulness of disposition (the extrovert manner) will make us more attractive, but since standards of value regarding attractiveness are so different for various groups and nationalities, we ought not to place too much stock upon mere appearances. It has been said that blonds prefer brunettes as marriage partners and that a sanguine person prefers one of the choleric type. So long as we are able to indulge our preferences, everyone may be satisfied and contented. But when companions are thrust upon us, we may have to modify our preferences in the interests of sociability. So too, when appearances are all against us in a given group, one may make up for this by cultivating skills and a pleasing manner of address and of welcome, and above all, by not being a bore. It is well to make a point of avoiding those traits which most annoy us when we notice them in others.

Perhaps our tendency to look with favor upon the efficient and energetic personality is a reflection of our habitual attitudes of unrest and excitement. Persons in other countries, at any rate, seem to be mildly surprised or even displeased at our constant display of activity. Taking the situation as we find it, it seems possible to please the majority the most of the time by conforming to the approved customs in the matter of deportment, etiquette, and manners. It may be argued that this state of affairs is deplorable; that if one does not approve of and conform to what others desire, he will be considered queer, whereas if he does conform he must do violence to his feelings and can never hope to effect a change. The facts of history are all against such a conclusion, for change actually does take place in various localities. We would suggest that the impatient reformer or pacesetter in the matter of conventions should await an opportunity to exercise the influence which alone will bring about the desired change. And it will require the courage, tact, and decision of a leader to redirect any deeply imbedded human tendencies.

Similarly, when a person goes from one stratum of society to another, he may be required to change some of his conventional forms of behavior, and may be judged harshly if he does not change them. It is even possible that his capacity for adjustment, which today has come to mean mental ability, will be judged by his external manners. If he cannot succeed in changing these to suit the occasion, he may have to face the unpleasant consequences of being denied a position, because he cannot adjust himself to change.

In addition to traits which naturally attract a majority of persons, we can all aim at cultivating those *special traits* which our friends desire. Our motive is not entirely unselfish in such a case, since, by winning the favor of others, we are also improving our own status. In order to rid their clients of certain disturbing symptoms, some clinical psychologists today urge the acquisition of more and more skills and the broadenings of interests so that one's circle of friends and acquaintances may be enlarged. And they say that the method works very well, although, no doubt, as Professor Link remarks, it would be even more successful if religious motivation were stronger. The same writer emphasizes the need of effort if we wish to extend our influence over others. He would have us become proficient at bridge, tennis, singing, dancing, dramatic performances — in a word, in social accomplishments. Perhaps it is just the effort to get out of oneself and the appreciation of the real value inherent in oneself and others that make his methods socially effective.[12]

II) Life Interests and Total Outlook

A) *Interests and Values.* We often judge a person on the basis of his dominant interests and the unity of purpose manifested in his endeavors. Such interests are indicative of attitudes of value toward various kinds of occupations and projects. They have practical importance because they increase one's usefulness to others and prevent him from becoming apathetic or indifferent toward major social issues. Spranger has divided the main interests into six groups, and investigators have found some consistency within various professions in regard to them. Thus psychologists and students of medicine report themselves interested in theoretical problems such as the value of education or of a philosophy of life. Students of economics and engineering show interest in problems relating to manufacturing and trade. Business men and students for the ministry prefer socio-political and religious topics, such as relief of the poor, or improvement of morals in politics and diplomacy.

The dominant topic of a person's conversation is often an indication of his outstanding interests. However, many persons of wide interests have at least a superficial acquaintance with topics as widely different as foreign policy and child guidance, or dietetics and surrealistic art. A broad and thorough education can foster interests of all sorts. Clever entertainers are adept at picking up information which will make them more confident of themselves and more capable of reaching a large audience. Talented specialists may cause annoyance to others by talking exclusively of their special interests, just as the superficial dabbler in all sciences may at times become the laughing stock of the specialists. An attempt to impress others by pretending to have more knowledge than one actually possesses will seldom meet with real success. A middle course between interests which are too broad and those which are too narrow seems to be the approved pattern to follow. A modest estimate of our own ability as well as a not overcritical appraisal of the ability of others will often secure a more friendly reception from our associates.

B) *Philosophy of Life.* The well-balanced individual who is contented in a group, and who can at the same time add something to the enjoyment of others, will usually have a definite outlook on life. He will have integrated his thoughts and expressions in such a manner that he is consistent in his views and yet not too intolerant of the views of others on every conceivable subject. He will gain prestige in many cases without seeking it intentionally, and will be liked because he inspires confidence in those whom he meets by the wisdom of his opinions and his sympathetic understanding of the needs of others. He will find that, in order to influence others successfully, it will be more suitable to try to understand them than to use mechanical devices for winning their approval, and he will be pleased with himself for his success in understanding and appreciating others.

Persons of this type work for the most part according to a preconceived plan of their own. Out of the jumble of ideas found in books or derived from conversation concerning problems of human welfare and the remedies for social ills, each individual may develop a well-defined system of principles and convictions to guide his thinking, and he usually does formulate some kind of consistent and integrated outlook on life. The Germans call this system of principles or values a philosophy of life or a Weltanschauung. No student in a German university is considered mature unless he is able to express his Weltanschauung clearly in words, and adheres to it consistently both inside and outside the classroom. The most interesting insights into the character of a German youth can be had by observing him casually outside of class, and by showing deference for his opinions in matters of science. He will nearly always be willing to state his views on such erudite subjects as Hegelian philosophy or the cultural differences between Europeans and Americans.

One gets the impression that students in European universities have more clearly defined outlooks on life after they finish their course of studies than do Americans. Perhaps this is only a reflection of a national characteristic whereby the young people mature somewhat earlier, or incline to be more inflexible in their views partly because they attempt to form all-embracing working hypotheses before they have had the time or opportunity to investigate pertinent sources of information. The declared opinion of many Europeans in regard to Americans is that the latter narrow their views too soon by a process of overspecialization, so that they are not capable of viewing all the facts in their proper perspective. Perhaps there is room for improvement on both sides.

With a little training it is not difficult to detect the dominant outlook which a person has on life. One can also ascertain whether or not he has succeeded in establishing and adhering to some fixed outlook. Since a person's philosophy of life, once established, may influence all his preferences and choices, it is advisable that some caution and prudence be exercised in forming and adopting it. The facility with which some persons solve all problems and take a stand on issues which should normally require maturer consideration is often surprising. Yet one must not adopt an indifferent attitude which may prevent him from showing interest in anything. Why such confirmed indifference or nonpartisanship should be considered undesirable is difficult to state. We rather expect a rational thinking person to be alert to the problems of his time and to know where he stands in regard to such vital issues as capitalism versus labor or the race question. We do not generally approve either of too much optimism or of too pessimistic an outlook with regard to such matters as relieving human sufferings and discovering an ideal or perfect form of government. Most persons do not reach a definite attitude in these matters until adult life, and then they may be susceptible to change. We may safely follow the pronouncements of the experts on questions which we ourselves have not the leisure to investigate fully, making sure, however, that the expert is not dealing with something outside his own special field. We should not consult the student of politics for the solution of a theological problem, any more than we should consult a lawyer for advice in medical matters.

The advice and assistance of prudent counselors will be of service, especially to young people, and in dealing with matters of conscience. Religion supplies the answers to many personal problems in a way that nothing else can. Hence, when a person is guided by religious principles as well as by a personally elaborated philosophy of life, he will be more securely oriented toward all of life's problems, and will be better equipped to cope with perplexing situations. This proves to be the case because the outlook on life of a Christian philosophy takes cognizance not only of the changing temporal needs of human beings, but also of the intrinsic moral value of human life and suffering. Consoled and directed by such a philosophy of life, one can more easily be aroused to deeds of valor in a transitory cause, and will be actively interested in the promotion of permanent justice and charity among those who have no religious outlook to guide them.

III) Some Selected Traits

Long lists of the so-called personality embellishments may be found in various textbooks of social psychology. It is customary to list physical and temperamental traits, as though they were operative independently of aptitudes, attitudes, and ideals of value. Such artificial classifications do violence to the fact of the total unity of personality and the interdependence of all our operations. It must be remembered that all the characteristics and functions of a person are fused into one concrete rational emotional personality. Each single experience of his daily life makes a definite contribution to his formation.

The outstanding traits not yet discussed which are often considered capable of giving us influence over others are intelligence and imagination, energy and tenacity, self-assurance and decisiveness, sociability and progressiveness. A word of caution is needed in regard to each of these, apart from the fact that each trait is in some way integrated into the total personality pattern.

A) *Intelligence and Imagination.* Intelligence is probably the most envied of all human traits, for reasons which are not altogether clear. Yet it may actually not be the most significant one from the standpoint of successful social personality. Generosity of spirit is often more attractive than intellectual acumen, though for some strange reason high intelligence is more often praised. Ability to mix with people and to sympathize with their difficulties is sometimes impaired by cold reasoning and analysis of facts. Intellectual persons tend to become irritating sometimes because of their fondness for academic discussions in which they display extreme dogmatism and an utter lack of practical sense, as well as a surprising ignorance of the actual problems which confront humanity in general.

The attempted division of all men into two mutually exclusive types, called the practical-emotional and the abstract-intellectual type, is an artificial division originated by German investigators which has not received much recognition in America. Each one of us has, as a matter of fact, intelligence enough to learn to be somewhat practical, and practical skills in dealing with people are acquired by social participation rather than by abstract reasoning and theorizing about personality types.

However, both extremes of intelligence, the low and the high, seem to have their limitations in everyday life. The person who is too talented for his job becomes discontented and the one who is not gifted enough fails to give satisfaction to his employers. Brightness and dullness are not the only factors which determine social success or failure. Although the unintelligent person may be at a certain disadvantage in our complex society, hardly anyone is so lacking in mental accomplishment that he cannot realize any of the social consequences of his actions. Even a naïve individual can ultimately learn to adjust himself to situations in which sophisticated persons try to exploit his ingenuousness for their own selfish ends. Intelligence of a much lower than average level is usually enough to enable a person to attain some success, to contribute something to the common good, and to avoid being altogether overwhelmed by unfavorable and unfair criticism. The aptitude testers can render a real service to all persons if they help them to discover that occupation for which each one is best suited, and their recent findings support the view that intelligence alone is no guarantee for success in every enterprise.

Imagination often aids intelligence in supplying original and provocative solutions for problems. But something more is needed to make a person an outstanding social figure, in spite of the apparently simple instructions of the personality popularizers, according to whom anyone can become a successful organizer merely by reading the latest brochures on this subject. The reader will have to experiment with these suggestions on how to get up a party in order to find out how many of them are practical. If they were all carried out in full, great courage and perseverance as well as superhuman tact would be required of the experimenter.

B) *Energy and Tenacity.* Most of us approve of a certain amount of energy or drive in others, and may marvel at the way in which certain individuals can so constantly maintain their high level of energy output. Perhaps higher motives and a lively interest, strengthened by the feeling of expansiveness which results from the recognition of others, have aided these persons in sustaining their energy and in replenishing their lost stores. As for tenacity or fixity of purpose, it is not always an unmixed advantage, because it may lead to stubbornness and stereotyping of behavior. On the other hand, it supplies endurance and forbearance, and enables one to pull himself together after suffering some defeat, thus making him a more influential and effective individual. To cultivate an attitude of persistence may indeed be the best way to avoid feelings of depression and inadequacy. We need to sustain ourselves in striving toward a goal, and to be sustained by others, so as to be neither altogether flighty and visionary nor sullen and dull.

C) *Self-assurance and Decisiveness.* A person who cannot make up his mind is one from whom we tend to draw away spontaneously. Although he who hesitates may not necessarily be lost, he will generally be so far behind others in the contest for success that he will virtually be out of the race. Still more generally disapproved is the habit of vacillation, of abruptly changing from one decision to another without apparent cause.

Yet it would be a mistake to suppose that all indecisiveness is unwholesome, or that great self-assurance and determination is always beneficial. This is because misinformed and highhanded persons, who often possess extremely strong attitudes of self-approval and decisiveness, are thereby prevented from becoming enlightened, and their habit of making decisions hastily or rashly is not ordinarily calculated to inspire others with confidence. New situations may require different decisions, according to their peculiar circumstances. One reason why the decisive and self-confident person is likable is that we expect him to handle such new situations effectively without later going back on his judgment. Hence, although overconfidence and stubborn tenacity are distasteful, a normal amount of self-assertiveness and determination suggests to others that we are predictable and reliable.

It may be objected that perfect predictability of behavior characterizes only abnormal and stilted individuals; for such people often have allowed their judgment to become so disturbed by emotional factors that they cannot appraise new situations properly and hence take on the appearance of automatons. Yet a totally unpredictable person is apt to appear very abnormal too, for he not only does the most unexpected things, but seems quite unable to adapt his behavior to the demands of others and to regulate himself according to a plan. Prolonged states of indecision and timidity, especially when there is question of adjusting oneself to change or of facing life's problems realistically, are generally a source of annoyance to others.

D) *Sociability and Progressiveness.* If we are keenly alive to social demands, we tend to cooperate readily with others, and to yield to the opinions of the majority where no moral principles are at stake. Argument and bickerings are often a hindrance to concerted effort and they often indicate unsocial or antisocial attitudes. On the other hand, positive antipathy for social situations or a lack of desire to participate in group life may be, though they need not be, signs of egocentrism. The unsociable individual who feels no need of others will find satisfaction in solitary occupations. Instruction and example go far toward changing a child from an unsocial and uncooperative individual into a friendly and likable person. A great crisis in a person's life may have a similar effect. It is interesting to notice, in this connection, that monks in their cells may be isolated from human society and yet not be unsociable. They have often displayed an amazing capacity for understanding and dealing with others after years of leading a secluded life. Religious persons who are not contemplative realize as well as anyone else that there is need, at times, to develop a more sociable and attractive personality by means of group participation and conscious effort.

As for progressiveness, it is difficult to lay down any general law. On the whole, this quality is to be considered desirable only when the older and conservative methods have been definitely proved inadequate. Much of the injudicious tampering with the existing methods of education is the result of our modern trend toward experimentation, and often begins with the faulty conviction or belief that nothing old can be good, and that only the changing and progressive methods can be efficient and useful. To what lengths the cult of pure progress can be carried is suggested by the following motto which was displayed for the edification of the public on the notice board of a prominently located church: "Anywhere — so long as it's forward." This type of progressivism is definitely dangerous to society as a whole; and moreover, many who declare themselves imbued with progressivist principles are really antisocial at heart. They seem to direct all their efforts at destroying the older institutions and, although in doing so they may gain prestige, their gain is a hardship to others.

If sociability is defined as amenability to social regulations and a willingness to cooperate, it is clear that extreme progressivism in matters of morality and religion would tend to upset rather than support social order. Progressivists in morals are actually evading their social responsibilities, for they often dictate a change without any ground for supposing that the proposed change will benefit anyone. Radicals sometimes admit quite openly that they are willing to be bound by social regulations only when doing so contributes to their own advantage. Personal gain seems to be their only motive for cooperating with others, and such selfishness is rarely approved even by social psychologists. If this kind of progressivism is the result of modern science, then old-fashioned conservatism is much to be preferred, and society will not really make progress until we become less modern in our outlook on life as a whole.

E) *Sublimation of Desires and Altruism.* Social psychologists in their treatment of unadjusted and maladjusted personalities often refer to compensations and escape mechanisms as causes of faulty development.[13] They observe that when a person, for instance, engages in daydreaming, lying, or stealing, he may be filling in the gap caused by some inadequacy or inferiority feeling; that he is providing mental substitutes for social reality; and that when he develops functional disorders such as aches and pains, or habits of conventional forgetting and feelings of persecution, he is evading some reality which he cannot tolerate. They admit that in actual practice it is hard to distinguish between a compensation and an escape reaction, but they agree in regarding certain aspects of both these reactions as very undesirable especially when they become extreme. The habit of rationalizing seems to be present in them, and this tendency is manifested in efforts to find plausible reasons for justifying one's defects before others and in projecting the blame for failures upon others. The unwholesome aspects of the habit of rationalizing appear to derive from the fact that the rationalizer fails to face reality squarely or to understand his own traits clearly. Students who habitually neglect schoolwork on the plea that they need relaxation and social contacts are probably guilty of rationalizing. The drunkard who tells himself that he needs to flee from the trying situations of real life by the expedient of losing consciousness is, no doubt, trying to escape from the unpleasant realities of life.

When such compensative and evasive forms of behavior lead to slothfulness and untruthfulness they are certainly indicative of a faulty personality development. Thus the student who constantly shirks the distasteful duties involved in school work and blames the teacher for all his failures will need a more wholesome outlook on life if he is to become successfully adjusted to any role in life. He will, perhaps, begin to see himself as others see him only when some friend tells him that he appears to have two reasons for everything he does, the good reason which he gives others, and the real reason.

Professor Anable[14] appropriately points out that there is a difference between such reactions as blaming others or shirking duties and reasonable substitution reactions. He says that compensations involve the acceptance of *equivalent* substitutes for certain unpleasant experiences, for example, the pleasure of recreation for the annoyances of duty. On the other hand, the process of sublimation means the acceptance of a substitute form of behavior which is deemed more valuable for ourselves and others. Thus the religious person who wholeheartedly dedicates himself to the complete service of God must willingly forego much that would be pleasant and agreeable to him in some other walk of life. Social workers may be motivated, at times, with a desire for a more noble outlet for their energies and thus substitute the promotion of social welfare for the satisfaction of pursuing purely personal interests. Religious motives can impel a person to engage in difficult tasks because religion trains a person to see the highest value in relinquishing temporary pleasures, and hence religious sublimation is the highest type because of the permanent values inherent in religion itself. Far from being a mere compensatory or escape reaction, this type of sublimation is healthy and wholesome and does not necessarily involve any escape from reality or indicate self-deception or rationalization. Since there are real objective grounds or reasons for preferring certain types of action to others, and since these reasons can be understood and appreciated at their true worth, sublimation cannot be said to result from mere unconscious mechanisms of self-defense.

A desire to labor for the betterment of society involves something of that quality known as altruism. The totally egotistical individual will not be capable of sublimating his desires very long in such a manner as to appreciate this quality. Long before the arrival of Professor Adler, the greatest Altruist of all times told us to love our neighbor as ourselves, declaring that we could not love God without loving our fellow man. This doctrine, so strongly supported by some social reformers, has been described by the psychoanalysts in such misleading terms that it is scarcely recognizable. They tell us that our failure to direct our psychic energy toward others results in egocentrism or fixation of the love energy upon the ego or self, and that when we cannot any longer hate others, we hate and condemn ourselves immoderately.[15] This seems to imply that we have not enough energy for loving both our neighbor and ourselves at the same time.

We do, as a matter of fact, often experience a state of satisfaction which results from altruistic endeavors. We are often pleased with ourselves for striving to benefit others, just as we are displeased with ourselves for hating and opposing others. We can love ourselves while loving others, and hate ourselves for hating others. Our convictions as to the real worth of other persons and of their actions will often determine the direction which our love energies take. When our ideals of value are co-ordinated and unified about some satisfying ideal or principle, we learn to respect both ourselves and others for what is truly respectable and valuable in both.

A love of self is consonant with a love of our neighbor, and when the affection for him is reasonably sympathetic and courageous, it is possible to detest that which is undesirable in others without hatred for the offending person, and without increasing selfish desires. We can hate the wrong that is done us without hating the evildoer. If social reformers do not accept this view of human relations, grave consequences can be expected for society taken as a whole. Fortunately our people recognize the possibility of taking this stand in so crucial a matter as our attitude toward enemies in war. When William Allen White posed the question to the readers of Coronet in September, 1942: "Should we organize a hate Hitler campaign?" 70 per cent of them replied "No," adding that this war must destroy hate and not foster it, that we are not fighting against individuals, but rather against the ideas which have enslaved them.[16]

This same mistake, of hating persons who do evil instead of loving the doer while detesting the thing done, is discovered on analysis to be the starting point of the egocentrism and antipathy for others displayed by psychopathic individuals. They impute evil intentions to others without cause, gradually separate themselves from those whose activities have aroused suspicions, and then invent excuses to justify such behavior in their own eyes. The more they disapprove of others, the more they seem to disapprove of themselves and the more incapable do they become of thinking through the tangle of affairs which led to their disturbed state of mind. The theory that the loss of affection from others inevitably causes an increase of self-love will suggest no method of helping such individuals to overcome their difficulties, any more than it suggests how to improve the condition of society as a whole. But the individual and society will both be helped if the individual is led to overcome his egotism by realizing the value of social participation and of his own role in society.

FOR ACCELERATED READING

SHORT SUMMARY OF THE CHAPTER

The doctrine that "society confers human nature upon individuals," besides failing to explain how the specifically human properties arise, implies that some groups are more irrational than others owing to their close proximity to the animal species. It denies the Creator, the unity of the human family, and the existence of any universal norms of morality. The view which holds that "deviations from average behavior constitute personality" destroys the unique dignity of the human person and with it all individual responsibility if these deviations are the result of culture patterning. Both doctrines seem to presuppose that society is some sort of separately existing entity apart from the individuals who make up the social group.

Society as such, by its approval or disapproval of certain actions, does not assume all responsibility for individual acts of conformity or nonconformity to rule. Individuals as members strive for friendship and recognition but these are not their only goals. Membership in a group may entail restrictions and even frustrations, but these are not the only obstacles to individual striving. Some conformity is necessary and conflicts are inevitable in the present state of man partly because he strives for partial and contradictory goods in this life.

External traits which are approved are skills and aptitudes; attention-causing peculiarities are not needed for acquiring distinctiveness and the social graces. *Special interests* enlarge our sphere of influence and a philosophy of life gives consistency to our efforts; all traits are radicated in the total personality, and real character qualities are more attractive than mere intellectual sagacity, diffuse energy, or affected sociability. The cult of pure *progressivism* defeats its own purpose; desires which are directed toward higher goods make for healthy, happy, and efficient adjustment; some *altruistic motives* are required of individuals in any society whereas total egocentrism founded on hate of other individuals leads to conflict between individuals as well as to maladjustment of the individual himself.

Find Review Questions and Supplementary Reading at the end of the book.

RETROSPECT

The writer is not convinced that he has attained that ideal of perfection toward which he strove in writing this treatise. But he experiences few regrets and little remorse on this score because of the great satisfaction derived from the attempt to recount the story of social relations. He will be forced, by convention and social pressure, to rely in great part upon the benevolent attitude of his readers, and upon social approval or disapproval for determining the influence this work may have upon the lives of others.

In various ways he has set forth the thesis that although we are all profoundly influenced by others in ways which we do not always foresee, many kinds of interaction depend entirely upon the deliberately formed and consciously modifiable attitude of the individual. This holds true particularly in regard to behavior prescribed by laws and customs, perhaps to a lesser extent where there is question of purely conventional behavior. Hence children and adults who passively accept every suggestion from others without weighing the consequences are most susceptible to being influenced unintentionally. There are those who would seek to reform everything, to disturb the existing social order without any clear prevision of the direction in which social change should progress. Intelligent leaders are needed, equipped with the knowledge and skill requisite for influencing others along the lines prescribed by safe principles. The less reflective and the passively indifferent among us will not qualify for such leadership. If no more than a few potential leaders receive inspiration and guidance from these pages, the writer will consider his efforts abundantly rewarded.

L. D. S.

APPENDICES

APPENDIX A: QUESTIONS AND PROBLEMS FOR DISCUSSION

CHAPTER 1. INTRODUCTION

1. Discuss the purposes of social psychology.
2. Give two meanings of the term "adjustment."
3. Why is the view which makes social approval the norm of a good adjustment likely to mislead the student?
4. Distinguish between convention and moral value.
5. Why cannot deterministic science discover the nature of moral values?
6. Name some factors which cannot well be controlled in experimental social psychology.
7. Criticize the division of all social reactions into external and internal.

CHAPTER 2. METHODS OF INVESTIGATION

1. Criticize the anthropologists' conception of method in social psychology.
2. What two aspects of man's nature must be taken into account in any good method?
3. What dangers are to be avoided in making observations and reports?
4. What limitations have life histories and self-inventories?
5. What advantages and disadvantages have rating scales?
6. Mention some benefits and some cautions connected with the use of correlations.
7. Have we any need at all to study correlations?
8. Of what usefulness is the distribution curve and the average deviation?

CHAPTER 3. THE GROUP AND ITS BEHAVIOR

1. What is the fallacy of the Gestalt-topologists' view of man?
2. Mention factors which might help Marie Dionne to become less dependent socially in later life.
3. Sketch the main aspects of the development of responsibility during late infancy.
4. What new features must be added during adolescence?

5. Comment on the expression: "the irrational behavior of the mob."
6. What is meant by the polarizing effect on an audience?
7. Contrast the properties of the riotous crowd with those of the co-active group.
8. Discuss the causes of the panic following the "Invasion from Mars."
9. Evaluate this argument: A race must be identical with a nation since mental differences are more important than geographical.
10. Why is there not the same relationship between the "soul of the people" and their society as there is between the soul of man and his body?
11. Explain why people ordinarily select leaders who are in some way superior and popular.

CHAPTER 4. SOCIAL LEARNING

1. Mention some motives which often direct the learning of social customs.
2. What motives may seem to be quite universal, if an observer fails to consider the conscious report of individuals?
3. Give an example of an attitude in one of your friends, of which you think he is unaware.
4. Compare adult learning with early childhood learning in regard to motive.
5. How does "emotional immaturity" in adults indicate that they need to learn by methods different from those of children?
6. What is meant by preparatory set?
7. What chief differences do the experiments show between human and animal conditioning?
8. What specifically human activity enters into the process of conditioning to make results unpredictable?
9. What social importance attaches to a study of conscious reconditioning of unconscious processes?
10. What is meant by trial-and-error learning?
11. Comment on the statement that all learning is by "imitation."
12. In what instances could the "reflex-arc" theory of learning be applicable and what practical value has the theory for social study?
13. Explain how learning self-adjustment by means of insight involves the abstracting of relations.

CHAPTER 5. SOCIAL MOTIVES AND MOTIVATION

1. What is the difference between motives in the strict sense and motivating factors?
2. Differentiate between instinctive and intellectual activity on the basis of introspective evidence and of uniformity of behavior.
3. What is the reason for saying that predictable human behavior is not necessarily instinctive?
4. Criticize the division of human motives into inner bodily drives (the instincts) and outer incentives or goals (the motives).

5. Give some examples to show that physiological drives in human beings may be made subservient to other motives.
6. Why is an experimenter not justified in concluding to the presence or absence of the maternal instinct from his questioning of pregnant mothers?
7. Why is it illogical to argue from an increase of maternal affection following upon fondling the child to the conclusion that this increase is caused by the sensual pleasure of contacts between mother and child?
8. What one desirable aspect do the following incentives have in common: social approval, security, rewards, and success?
9. Do you think that feelings of insecurity arise from our inability to satisfy extravagant needs? From what source do they arise?
10. If you were to investigate the effects of rewards or of success upon the schoolwork of a child, how would this investigation differ from a study of animal behavior following upon rewards?
11. What is meant by an altruistic motive, and why should submissiveness and cooperativeness be found together normally?

Chapter 6. Affective Social Life — The Emotions

1. Why is the study of the energizing effects of the emotions so important in social psychology?
2. What difference is there between saying that a certain reaction is desirable and saying that it is ethical?
3. What techniques of practising psychiatrists today show that they admit the need of intelligence for emotional guidance?
4. Why are we justified in studying the animal reactions which are analogously emotional? Why do the child's early reactions seem to be instinctive and emotional?
5. How can we be helped toward a conscious control of emotions by classifying them according to their bodily effects? Why is this merely physiological classification inadequate in practice?
6. Explain the value of emotions, without holding that they are all harmful or that they are all beneficial.
7. Show how the experimentalists' objective description of fear responses differs from an introspective account.
8. Why is it bad psychology to advertise the fact that frustrations are all harmful?
9. Under what conditions might sympathy help to promote social justice and altruistic behavior? Discuss.
10. How can one effectively prevent the human sentiment of love from degenerating into selfish passion? Is the motive of social approval apt to be effective in this connection?
11. Why may jubilant laughter, even boisterous hilarity, and "college humor" be considered specifically human rational reactions?
12. What do you think of a leader who tries to keep morale high by

preaching the doctrine of hatred of our enemies? What alternative practice is there which has been known to be very effective?

CHAPTER 7. THE SOCIAL TEMPERAMENT AND DISPOSITION

1. State reasons for the emphasis upon distinctiveness and individuality in modern studies of personality.
2. Why is it likely that the scientific study of personality will continue to emphasize the desirability of behavior instead of real character?
3. Taking desirability to mean agreeableness or attractiveness, how would you distinguish it from character?
4. Why would you say that a person's attitudes toward moral values are far more important to him than what is called desirable adjustment?
5. Mention some traits which would probably differentiate Americans from Europeans, and state whether these are predominantly physical or mental.
6. Explain how the distribution curve may be employed in a search for types of temperament.
7. What evidence can you give that emotional temperament is pliable and plastic?
8. Why are most tests of temperament traits always apt to be unreliable?
9. Explain a way in which the common reaction tendencies to sluggishness and restlessness may become the basis for a division of temperaments.
10. Comment on the assertion that emotional temperament is simply a matter of glandular functioning.
11. Because we have not yet any reliable and valid tests for the total temperament of a person, must we despair of ever knowing the real traits of our friends? What criterion do we use in our judgments of these?
12. Mention a few unwholesome temperament trends of your friends and tell why you consider them unwholesome.
13. Recall a person of your acquaintance who seems to be emotionally immature and name some of his "spoilt child" attitudes.

CHAPTER 8. SUGGESTIBILITY, GESTURES, AND LANGUAGE

1. Mention some motives which might impel persons to communicate with each other by means of language. Specify which of these motives are at least partially indeliberate.
2. What feature distinguishes language from gestures and emotional expressions?
3. Define suggestion. Comment on the definitions of propaganda and of education given by LaPiere and Farnsworth.
4. Mention the conditions which are essential for securing high suggestibility.

5. What conditions on the part of the suggester and of the suggestee make for a high degree of suggestion?
6. What facts indicate that suggestibility depends to a great extent upon certain attitudes and emotions of the suggester and the suggestee?
7. Discuss the existence of a special trait called suggestibility. What other variable factors such as age and intelligence are related to it?
8. Show that the process of becoming hypnotized is similar to that of receiving suggestions.
9. What facts show that the individual does not act altogether passively under the influence of powerful suggestions and of hypnosis?
10. Mention some techniques which might be used by others in order to influence you inadvertently, and tell how you would prepare yourself to resist this influence.

CHAPTER 9. ATTITUDES, THEIR FORMATION AND MEASUREMENT

1. Illustrate by an example what is meant by an attitude.
2. What is meant by saying that it is economical to establish "sets" or fixed attitudes of mind?
3. Why is it necessary to distinguish emotional from intellectual attitudes?
4. What is meant by emotional or wishful thinking? Give examples.
5. What special attitudes should be formed in school? Why?
6. What faulty attitudes are apt to be fostered by the movies and the radio?
7. What conditions are requisite for bringing about a change in a group attitude?
8. Mention the three attitudes which most people in this country possess.
9. What institutions seem to be the most powerful of all organized attitude determiners?
10. Give evidence to show that attitudes depend upon knowledge but that information does not necessarily determine what kind of attitudes develop.
11. Compare the attitudes of children with those of adults.

CHAPTER 10. THE SOCIAL RELEVANCE OF ATTITUDES

1. What are some attitudes which people have as a result of social pressure? Which ones more usually result from personal conviction?
2. In what sense is public opinion a cross section of individual and group attitudes?
3. Distinguish between superstitions and faulty inferences in regard to their origin.
4. What factors clearly distinguish individual attitudes from public opinion?
5. Give instances to show how social pressure and self-persuasion can come to motivate courtship behavior.
6. Describe two roles which a person sometimes strives to play which may cause him to experience conflict.

7. Analyzing your own experience, point out how attitude toward laws differs from attitude toward conventions.

CHAPTER 11. HUMAN NATURE AND DESIRABLE SOCIAL PERSONALITY

1. Mention some consequences of the doctrine which holds that human nature is conferred by society.
2. What outstanding difference must be stressed between deviating behavior contrary to laws and that which results in maladjustment?
3. Point out certain instances in which social patterning does not produce perfect uniformity. What factors account for the presence of both conformity and nonconformity to customs and rules?
4. What advantage is there in acquiring an outstanding personality in the sense of distinctiveness or external effectiveness? Comment on the definition of personality commonly met in sociology: the social stimulus value.
5. Are the social graces more the result of temperament than of character? Give reasons for your answer.
6. Are dominant interests necessarily pleasing to others so that they belong to an outstanding personality? Why?
7. Under what circumstances may intelligence, persistence, self-assurance, and progressiveness be called undesirable traits?
8. What do you mean by rationalizing? Are all habits of compensating and defending oneself against criticism conducive toward an unwholesome personality structure? Why?
9. Give reasons to show that some sublimation is necessary if egocentrism is considered undesirable. Why is altruism approved?

APPENDIX B: LITERATURE CITED
(Numbers refer to superscripts in text)
CHAPTER 1 (PAGES 1 TO 15)

[1] Krout, M. H., *Introduction to Social Psychology* (New York: Harper and Bros., 1942), p. xiv.

[2] McLean, F. C., "The Happy Accident," *Scientific Monthly,* July, 1941, pp. 63–64.

[3] Ruch, F. L., *Psychology and Life* (Chicago: Scott Foresman and Co., 1937), pp. 9–16.

[4] Morgan, J. J. B., *Psychology* (New York: Farrar and Rinehart, 1941), pp. 150–151.

[5] James, F. C., "Science and Society," *Scientific Monthly,* July, 1941, p. 59.

[6] Confer Reference 4.

[7] Jensen, H. E., "Science of Human Values," *Scientific Monthly,* September, 1941, p. 761.

[8] Fletcher, J. M., "Science and the Problem of Human Values," *Scientific Monthly,* March, 1942, p. 263.

[9] Krout, *op. cit.*, pp. 369, 383, and ff.

[10] Murphy, G. and L. B., and Newcomb, *Experimental Social Psychology* (New York: Harper and Bros., 1937), p. 759 and ff.

CHAPTER 2 (PAGES 16 TO 34)

[1] Flugel, J. C., *A Hundred Years of Psychology* (London: Duckworth, 1933), p. 105 and ff.

[2] LaPiere, R. T., and Farnsworth, P. R., *Social Psychology* (New York: McGraw-Hill and Co., 1936), p. 36 and ff.

[3] Bernard, L. L., *Instinct: A Study in Social Psychology* (New York: Holt and Co., 1924), p. 522 and Chap. XX.

[4] Werner, H., *Comparative Psychology of Mental Development* (New York: Harper and Bros., 1940), pp. 8, 9, and passim for ethnopsychological views.

[5] Brown, J. F., and Menninger, Karl A., *The Psychodynamics of Abnormal Behavior* (New York: McGraw-Hill and Co., 1940), Chap. VIII and passim for psychoanalytical views.

[6] LaPiere and Farnsworth, *op. cit.*, p. 360; gives further references on the conflict theory of mental disease.

[7] See Chronological List of Textbooks on Social Psychology, Appendix C.

[8] Myerson, A., *Social Psychology* (New York: Prentice-Hall and Co., 1934), especially Chapter VI for social psychology of the nervous system.

[9] Klineberg, O., *Social Psychology* (New York: Henry Holt and Co., 1940), pp. 330–331 and passim for a moderate Gestalt view of society.

[10] Compare reference 6 with Lowie, R., *Primitive Society* (New York: 1920), and Siebert, S., and Müller, F., *Social Life of Primitive Man* (St. Louis: Herder, 1941). Siebert belongs to the Vienna School of Anthropologists and studied under Schmidt-Koppers.

[11] Ruch, *Psychology and Life*, p. 51.

Harmon, F. L., *Principles of Psychology* (Milwaukee: The Bruce Publishing Co., 1938), p. 559.

CHAPTER 3 (PAGES 35 TO 59)

[1] Brown, *Psychodynamics of Abnormal Behavior*, passim and p. 143.

Lewin, K., *A Dynamic Theory of Personality* (New York: McGraw-Hill and Co., 1935), pp. 19–20, 30–31.

[2] *Basic Writings of St. Thomas Aquinas;* edited and annotated by Anton C. Pegis (New York: Random House, 1945), Vol. I, Chap. VI; Vol. II.

[3] Krout, *Introduction to Social Psychology*, p. 230 and ff.

Wheeler, R. H., *Readings in Psychology* (New York: Thomas Y. Crowell and Co., 1929), Chap. I.

[4] Moreno, J. L., "Sociometry in Relation to Other Social Sciences," *Sociometry*, 1938, No. I, pp. 206–220.

[5] Blatz, W. E., *The Five Sisters* (Toronto: Wm. Morrow and Co., 1938), p. 185 and ff.

[6] Furfey, P. H., *Social Problems of Childhood* (New York: The Macmillan Co., 1929), a classic.

[7] Lehman, H. C., "Optimum Ages for Eminent Leadership," *Scientific Monthly*, February, 1942, p. 162.

[8] Hollingworth, H. L., *Mental Growth and Decline* (New York: D. Appleton-Century Co., 1927), p. 321.

[9] Cantril, H., *The Invasion from Mars* (Princeton: The University Press, 1940), passim for an analysis of the panic.

[10] Britt, S. H., *Social Psychology of Modern Life* (New York: Farrar and Rinehart, 1941), p. 439 and Chap. VII.

[11] Britt, *ibid.*, p. 231 and ff.

[12] Klineberg, O., *Race Differences* (New York: Harper and Bros., 1935), p. 192 and ff.

[13] Hurwicz, El., "Die Seelen der Völker," cited by J. Froebes in *Lehrbuch der experimentellen Psychologie*, Band II, Herder, Freiburg, 1929, S. 516.

[14] LaPiere and Farnsworth, *Social Psychology*, p. 214; some stereotyped notions of racial differences are given.

[15] Froebes, J., *Lehrbuch*, 1929, Band II, S. 517.

[16] Gurnee, H., *Elements of Social Psychology* (New York: Farrar and Rinehart, 1936), p. 336.

[17] Werner, H., *Comparative Psychology*, passim, esp. pp. 8–9.
  Herr, V. V., "Gestalt, Psychology: Empirical or Rational," *The New Scholasticism*, XVII, 4.

[18] Britt, *Social Psychology*, Chap. XIV, esp. p. 280.

[19] Thorndike, E. L., *Man and His Works* (Harvard University Press, 1943), p. 117.

CHAPTER 4 (PAGES 60 TO 81)

[1] LaPiere, *Social Psychology*, pp. 3, 23–24; esp. p. 66.

[2] Krout, *Introduction to Social Psychology*, Chap. VII, esp. p. 378.

[3] McDougall, Wm., *Social Psychology* (Boston: Luce and Co., 1923), passim.

[4] Bogardus, E. S., *Essentials of Social Psychology* (Univ. of Southern California Press, 1920), passim. In the 1931 edition the author accepts behaviorism completely in explaining social learning.

[5] Gurnee, *Elements of Social Psychology*, Chaps. V and X, esp. p. 239.
  Britt, *Social Psychology*, Chap. 9.

[6] LaPiere, *Social Psychology*, p. 355.

[7] Thorndike, E. L., *Human Nature and the Social Order* (New York: The Macmillan Co., 1940), pp. 5–6.

[8] Lewin, *Dynamic Theory*, Chap. II, p. 51 esp.

[9] Shafer, L., Gilmer, B., Schoen, M., *Psychology* (New York: Harper and Bros., 1940), whole of Chap. II.

[10] Freeman, E., *Social Psychology* (New York: Henry Holt and Co., 1940), pp. 152–153.

[11] Young, K., *Social Psychology* (New York: Crofts and Co., 1930), p. 84 and ff.

[12] Murphy, *Experimental Social Psychology*, pp. 161 and 167.

[13] Freeman, G. L., *Introduction to Physiological Psychology* (New York: Ronald Press, 1934), p. 399 and ff.

[14] Greene, J. S., *I Was a Stutterer* (New York: The Grafton Press, 1932), in *Stories from Real Life*.

[15] Woodworth, R. S., *Experimental Psychology* (New York: Henry Holt and Co., 1938), p. 621.

[16] Herr, V. V., *Die isolierende Einstellung bei Kontrast-Erscheinungen*, a dissertation (Koellen-Verlag, Bonn, 1939).

[17] Britt, *Social Psychology*, p. 116; author approves Thorndike's conclusions.

[18] Woodworth, *Experimental Psychology*, pp. 753 and 762; for theory of form, p. 624;
Woodworth, R. S., *Dynamic Psychology* (New York: Columbia University Press, 1925), for learning by imitation, Chap. VIII.

[19] Ellwood, E. A., *The Psychology of Human Society* (New York: Appleton, 1926), p. 342 and ff.

[20] Murphy, *Experimental Social Psychology*, p. 181.

[21] Allport, F. H., *Social Psychology* (Boston: Houghton Mifflin Co., 1924), p. 169 and ff.

[22] Woodworth, *Experimental Psychology;* for insight in animals, p. 756 and ff.; in young children, p. 763 and ff.; problem solving in adults, p. 768 and ff.

[23] Buschan, G., *Illustrierte Völkerkunde* (Stuttgart, 1922), Band II; a classic.

[24] Graubard, M., "Food Habits of Primitive Man," *Scientific Monthly*, Nov., 1942, p. 453 and ff.

CHAPTER 5 (PAGES 82 TO 104)

[1] LaPiere, *Social Psychology*, p. 46.

[2] McDougall, Wm., *The Energies of Men* (London: Methuen, 1939), p. 69 and ff.

[3] Krout, *Introduction to Social Psychology*, pp. 109–114.

[4] Kellogg, W. N., and L. A., *The Ape and the Child* (New York: McGraw-Hill and Co., 1933), full account of the experiment.

[5] Krout, *Introduction to Social Psychology*, p. 102; comments on Kellogg's experiment.

[6] Wyatt, H. G., "Volition in Scientific Psychology," in *Readings in Psychology*, edited by C. E. Skinner (New York: Farrar and Rinehart, 1935), p. 652.

[7] Morgan, J. J. B., *Psychology*, p. 150 and ff.

[8] Krout, *Introduction to Social Psychology*, p. 339.

[9] Murphy, *Experimental Social Psychology*, pp. 86–87.
Woodworth, *Experimental Psychology*, p. 753, on awareness of relations in men and animals.
[10] Murphy, *Experimental Social Psychology*, pp. 130–131.
[11] Ruch, *Psychology and Life*, p. 131.
[12] Woodworth, R. S., "A Justification of the Concept of Instinct," *Journal of Abnormal and Social Psychology*, XXII (1927), pp. 3–7.
[13] Gurnee, *Elements of Social Psychology*, p. 63.
[14] Bird, Charles, *Social Psychology* (New York: D. Appleton-Century Co., 1940), pp. 29 and 32; also Chaps. III, IV, and V.
[15] Murphy, *Experimental Social Psychology*, p. 99.
[16] Bird, *Social Psychology*, p. 29.
[17] Aldrich, Dr. and Mary, *Feeding Our Old-Fashioned Children*, Third Edition (New York: The Macmillan Co.), p. 13 and ff.
[18] Morgan, A. F., "Vitamins and Senescence," *Scientific Monthly*, May, 1941, p. 416; on some harmful effects of manufactured foods.
[19] Murphy, *Experimental Social Psychology*, p. 508.
[20] Brown, *Psychodynamics of Abnormal Behavior*, p. 244.
[21] Gurnee, *Elements of Social Psychology*, p. 80 and ff.
[22] Bird, *Social Psychology*, Chaps. IV and V.
[23] Murphy, *Experimental Social Psychology*, p. 94.
[24] ——— *ibid.*, p. 99.
[25] Buehler, K., *Die geistige Entwicklung des Kindes* (Jena: O. Fischer, 1930), passim.
Buehler, Charlotte, *Kindheit und Jugend*.
[26] Murphy, *Experimental Social Psychology*, pp. 425–442; importance of aspiration level.
[27] Thorndike, *Man and His Works*, Harvard Lectures; all of Chapter VIII.
[28] Husband, R. W., *General Psychology* (New York: Farrar and Rinehart, 1940), Chaps. VII and VIII; pp. 152 and 154.
[29] Murphy, *Experimental Social Psychology*, pp. 754–756.
[30] Allers, R., *The Psychology of Character*, Translated by E. B. Strauss (London: Sheed and Ward, 1931), p. 77 and ff.; p. 119 and ff.
[31] LaPiere, *Social Psychology*, p. 72.

CHAPTER 6 (PAGES 105 TO 123)

[1] Low, A. A., "Lost and Found," Chicago, March, 1939, Vol. II. No. 2, p. 16.
[2] LaPiere, *Social Psychology*, p. 350.
[3] Valentine, W. L., *Experimental Foundations of General Psychology* (New York: Farrar and Rinehart, 1941), p. 235.
[4] Valentine, *ibid.*, pp. 248–249.
[5] Brown, *Psychodynamics of Abnormal Behavior*, p. 244.
[6] Allen, A. H., *Pleasure and Instinct* (London: Harcourt Brace, 1930),

p. 60 and ff. Author is Aristotelian; writes for International Library of Psychology, Philosophy, and Scientific Method.

[7] Murphy, *Experimental Social Psychology*, p. 198.

[8] McDougall, W., *The Group Mind*, Cambridge University Psychological Series, 1928, passim.

[9] Allport, *Social Psychology*, whole of Chap. X; author attacks McDougall's "Group Mind," Chap. I.

[10] Gurnee, *Elements of Social Psychology*, p. 109.

[11] Murphy, *Experimental Social Psychology*, p. 388.

[12] Husband, *General Psychology*, p. 208.

[13] ———— *ibid.*, whole of Chap. X.

CHAPTER 7 (PAGES 124 TO 139)

[1] Kretchmer, E., *Physique and Character* (New York: Harcourt Brace, 1925).
Brown, *Psychodynamics of Abnormal Behavior*, summarizes this, p. 264.

[2] Britt, *Social Psychology*, p. 148.

[3] Shafer, etc., *Psychology*, p. 21.

[4] Schneiders, A. A., "The Unity of the Human Person in the Light of Evidence from Abnormal and Dynamic Psychology," Proceedings of Amer. Cath. Phil. Association, 1942, Vol. XVIII, p. 112.

[5] Murphy, *Experimental Social Psychology*, p. 684.

[6] Morgan, *Psychology*, p. 547.

[7] Murphy, *Experimental Social Psychology*, p. 865.

[8] Thouless, R. H., "Test Unreliability and Function Fluctuation," *British Journal of Psychology*, XXVI, 1938.

[9] Gurnee, *Elements of Social Psychology*, p. 163 and Chap. VI.

[10] ———— *ibid.*, pp. 170–173.

[11] Harmon, *Principles of Psychology*, p. 464.

[12] Murphy, *Experimental Social Psychology*, p. 775.
Gurnee, *Elements of Social Psychology*, p. 173.

[13] Murphy, *Experimental Social Psychology*, p. 776.

[14] ———— *ibid.*, pp. 772–777.

[15] Gurnee, *Elements of Social Psychology*, p. 178 and ff.

[16] Morgan, *Psychology*, p. 558 and ff.

[17] LaPiere, *Social Psychology*, p. 339 and ff.; pp. 344 and 350.

[18] Morgan, *Psychology*, p. 541.

[19] Murphy, *Experimental Social Psychology*, p. 777.

CHAPTER 8 (PAGES 140 TO 160)

[1] Gurnee, *Elements of Social Psychology*, p. 193 and ff.

[2] Allport, *Social Psychology*, p. 147 and ff.

[3] Valentine, *Experimental Foundations*, p. 404 and ff.; tries to revive subconscious vocalization theory so as to include muscles of whole body.

[4] Woodworth, *Experimental Psychology*, pp. 782 and 789; rather explicit in opposing associationism and simple conditioning; holds imageless thought.

[5] Buehler, K., *Abriss der geistigen Entwicklung des Kindes*, 1935, p. 52 and ff.

[6] Gurnee, *Elements of Social Psychology*, p. 202 and ff.

[7] Allport, *Social Psychology*, p. 187 and ff.

[8] Gurnee, *op. cit.*, p. 208.

[9] Thorndike, *Man and His Works*, Chap. V, a new theory of the evolution of language.

[10] Britt, *Social Psychology*, p. 476, for definition of propaganda; p. 216, for notion of suggestion.

[11] LaPiere, *Social Psychology*, p. 454.

[12] Britt, *op. cit.*, p. 474 and ff., for nationalistic propaganda.

[13] Gurnee, *Elements of Social Psychology*, p. 236 and Chap. IX. Murphy, *Experimental Social Psychology*, p. 168 and ff.

[14] Murphy, *ibid.*, p. 179 and ff.; subjective factors in suggestion.

[15] Allport, *Social Psychology*, p. 406; also McDougall and LaPiere who speak of special brands of religious emotionalism.

[16] Valentine, *Experimental Foundations of General Psychology*, Chap. XIV; Gurnee, *Elements of Social Psychology*, p. 226; Husband, *General Psychology*, p. 493.

[17] —— *op. cit.*, pp. 287–291.

[18] Froebes, *Lehrbuch der experimentellen Psychologie*, Band II, p. 556 and ff.; fine summary.

[19] Hull, Clark, *Hypnosis and Suggestibility* (New York: D. Appleton-Century, 1933), passim.

[20] Janet, P., *L'automatisme psychologique*. An older authority.

[21] McDougall, Wm., *Energies of Men* (London: Methuen, 1939), p. 253.

CHAPTER 9 (PAGES 161 TO 178)

[1] Murphy, *Experimental Social Psychology*, p. 904 and ff.

[2] Likert, R., "A Technique for the Measurement of Attitudes," *Archive of Psychology*, 1932, No. 140.

Likert, R., Roslow, S., and Murphy, G., "A Simple and Reliable Method of Scoring the Thurstone Attitude Scales," *Journal of Social Psychology*, 1934, 5, 228–238.

[3] Droba, D. D., "The Nature of Attitudes," *Journal of Social Psychology*, 1933, 4, 444–463.

—— "Topical Summaries of Current Literature: Social Attitudes," *American Journal of Sociology*, 1934, 39, 513–524.

[4] Stafford, J. J., "Psychology of Bias and Prejudice," *Proceedings of American Catholic Philosophical Association*, Vol. XVIII, 1942, p. 66 and ff.

[5] Britt, *Social Psychology*, p. 114.

[6] Lund, F. H., "The Psychology of Belief," *Journal of Abnormal and Social Psychology*, 1925, 20, 63–81 and 174–196.

[7] Peterson, R. C., and Thurstone, L. L., *Motion Pictures and the Social Attitudes of Children* (New York: Macmillan, 1933). See Britt, *Social Psychology*, p. 113.

[8] Murphy, *Experimental Social Psychology*, whole of last chapter.

[9] Young, K., *Social Psychology*, p. 340 and ff.; p. 347.

[10] Brown, L. G., *Social Psychology: The Natural History of Human Nature* (New York: McGraw-Hill, 1934), passim for occupational roles.

[11] Murphy, *Experimental Social Psychology*, pp. 979–1000.

[12] —————— *ibid.*, p. 1006.

[13] Horton, P. B., "Sources of Influence on Courtship Values," *Alpha Kappa Delta Quarterly*, XII, Oct., 1942, pp. 19–20.

[14] Murphy, *Experimental Social Psychology*, p. 1022.

[15] Murphy, *ibid.*, p. 930.

CHAPTER 10 (PAGES 179 TO 209)

[1] Allport, F. H., "Rule and Custom As Individual Variations of Behavior Distributed Upon a Continuum of Conformity," *American Journal of Sociology*, 1939, 44, 897–921.

[2] Krout, M., *Introduction to Social Psychology*, pp. 404–409.

[3] —————— *ibid.*, Chaps. VII, VIII, and IX.

[4] —————— *ibid.*, p. 439.

[5] Ruch, F. L., *Psychology and Life*, pp. 14 and 39.

[6] Thomas, W. I., and Znaniecki, F., *The Polish Peasant in Europe and America* (Chicago: Univ. of Chicago Press, 1918–1927).

[7] Bogardus, E. S., *Essentials of Social Psychology* (Los Angeles: Univ. of Southern Calif. Press, 1920; revised edition: Appleton-Century, 1931); also many articles by the same author in *Journal of Applied Sociology*.

[8] Britt, *Social Psychology*, p. 260; also pp. 261, 268–273.

[9] Bonnel, J. S., *Pastoral Psychiatry* (New York: Harper and Bros., 1938), p. 113.

[10] Bonnel, *ibid.*, p. 113 and ff.; Brown, J. F., *Psychodynamics of Abnormal Behavior*, p. 358.

[11] Allers, R., *Sex Psychology in Education*, transl. by Raemers (St. Louis: B. Herder Book Co.), p. 166 and ff.

[12] La Piere, *Social Psychology*, p. 360.

[13] Dunlap, K., *Civilized Life* (Baltimore: Williams and Wilkins, 1935), p. 94; also La Piere, *Social Psychology*, p. 325.

[14] Allers, R., *Psychology of Character*, transl. by Strauss (London: Sheed and Ward), p. 316 and *passim*.

[15] Krueger, E. T., and Reckless, W. C., *Social Psychology* (New York: Longmans, Green and Co., 1932), p. 336 and ff.

[16] Murphy, *Experimental Social Psychology*, p. 198. Explains value first as a complete process of fixation on an object, then as the "world of objects to which it (an organism) is fixated." On p. 199 he says that value

is a "statement of preparation for a response"; p. 200, it is not merely a satisfier but a "potential satisfier." Does he mean that there are any objective values or are they all subjective?

[17] ———— *ibid.*, p. 684.

[18] Allport, F. H., "The J-Curve Hypothesis of Conforming Behavior," *Journal of Social Psychology*, 1934, 5, 141–183. Author argues from the similarity of curves depicting moral and nonmoral behavior to the predictability and determination of all behavior.

[19] Hartshorne, H., May, M., Maller, J., *Studies in the Nature of Character;* I. Studies in Deceit, p. 411. II. Studies in Service and Self-Control, p. 445. Part I was prepared by Hartshorne and May alone, published by Macmillan, 1928.

[20] Maller, J., "General and Specific Factors in Character," *Journal of Social Psychology*, 1934, 5, p. 99.

[21] Cattell, R. B., "Temperament Tests: I. Temperament," *British Journal of Psychology*, 1933, 23, 308–329.

[22] Ruch, F. L., *Psychology and Life*, pp. 105–106.

[23] Brown, J. F., *Psychodynamics of Abnormal Behavior*, p. 260.

[24] ———— *ibid.*, p. 300 and ff.

[25] ————*ibid.*, p. 274.

[26] Gurnee, *Elements of Social Psychology*, p. 371.

[27] ———— *ibid.*, p. 372.

CHAPTER 11 (PAGES 210 TO 235)

[1] Krout, *Introduction to Social Psychology*, p. 398 and ff.

[2] LaPiere, *Social Psychology*, pp. 199, 290, 304; society as source of human nature; nature plus individuality equals personality.

[3] ———— *ibid.*, p. 355.

[4] ———— *ibid.*, p. 287.

[5] Krout, *Introduction to Social Psychology*, p. 364.

[6] ———— *ibid.*, p. 401.

[7] ———— *ibid.*, p. 409.

[8] See Chapter 2 of this book, and LaPiere, p. 289.

[9] LaPiere, *Social Psychology*, p. 66.

[10] ———— *ibid.*, p. 287.

[11] ———— *ibid.*, p. 201.

[12] Link, H. C., *The Return to Religion* (New York: The Macmillan Co., 1938), p. 135 and *passim*.

[13] LaPiere, *Social Psychology*, p. 344–355.

[14] Anable, R., *Philosophical Psychology* (New York: Fordham University Press, 1941), pp. 157–158.

[15] Brown, *Psychodynamics of Abnormal Behavior*, p. 160.

[16] *Coronet*, January, 1943, p. 178.

APPENDIX C

ANNOTATED LIST OF TEXTBOOKS ON SOCIAL PSYCHOLOGY IN CHRONOLOGICAL ORDER

ALPHABETICAL ARRANGEMENT OF AUTHORS CITED

Name	List Number
Allport, F. H.	8
Baldwin, J. M.	3
Bernard, L. L.	10
Bird, C.	32
Bogardus, E. S.	5
Britt, S. H.	35
Brown, J. F.	22
Brown, L. G.	23
Cooley, C. H.	1
Dunlap, K.	13
Ellwood, C. A.	4
Ewer, B. C.	17
Faris, E.	29
Freeman, E.	25
Gault, R. H.	7
Gurnee, H.	24
Judd, C. H.	12
Karpf, F. B.	19
Klineberg, O.	33
Krout, M. H.	36
Kreuger, E., and Reckless, W.	21
LaPiere, R., and Farnsworth, P.	26
McDougall, W.	11
Mujkerji, R., and Sen-Gupta, N.	16
Murphy, G. and L. B., and Newcomb, T.	27
Myerson, A.	20
Partridge, E. D.	30
Reinhardt, J. M.	31
Ross, E. A.	2
Smith, J. J.	18
Sprowls, J. W.	15
Thorndike E. L.	34
Thouless, R. H.	28
Williams, J. M.	6
Young, K.	14
Znaniecki, F.	9

1. Cooley, C. H., *Human Nature and the Social Order* (New York: Scribner and Sons, 1902, 1922); also *Social Organization,* 1909, and *Social Processes,* 1918. (Cf. No. 11 of Appendix C).

   Functionalist like Baldwin but more psychologically inclined; differs from him in regard to the recapitulation theory and imitation. An anti-individualist, because he thinks sociality does not follow individuality in time; and that therefore the individual in the naïve sense has no separate existence.

2. Ross, E. A., *Social Psychology: an Outline and Source Book* (New York: The Macmillan Co., 1908).

   Predominantly sociological approach; draws heavily on Tarde and LeBon; rational empiricist in ethics; environmental determinist; says that conventionality and custom passively imitated make for stagnation, whereas discussion, contact, conflict, and invention make for progress because then the individual dominates society.

3. Baldwin, J. M., *The Individual and Society* (Boston: R. Badger, 1911).

   Founder of the sociopsychological viewpoint by his appeal to genetic and evolutionary principles in studying children and animals; emphasizes early development of personality, the so-called organization-in-the-group; says that play, imitation, and organic selection bring about or conduce to the total societal organization of the individual.

4. Ellwood, C. A., *An Introduction to Social Psychology,* 1917; *Psychology of Human Society,* 1925 (New York: D. Appleton and Co.).

   Predominantly sociological approach; functionalist who tries to apply the principles of psychology and of biology to sociology but later modifies this a priori or deductive view; claims to allow for free choice.

5. Bogardus, E. S., *Essentials of Social Psychology* (Los Angeles: University of Southern California Press, 1920); Second Edition (New York: D. Appleton-Century Co., 1931).

   Predominantly sociological approach; environmental determinist who was formerly a functionalist but later shifts to behaviorism because he thinks conditioning of reflexes is a useful concept. He also made the concept of "social distance" and of "mental distances" popular.

6. Williams, J. M., *Principles of Social Psychology* (New York: A. Knopf, Inc., 1922).

   Predominantly sociological; uses modified concept of instinct now called dispositions; does not treat all social processes but gives a good analysis of economic conflict and of conflict of dispositions through the process of social organization in the concrete; thinks that subconsciously man adjusts conditions to himself and himself to them, but that conscious common-sense adjustment or the control of stimuli which bombard our overtaxed dispositions is much better, for it alone brings out the latent possibilities of personal development.

7. Gault, R. H., *Social Psychology: The Basis of Behavior Called Social* (New York: H. Holt and Co., 1923).

Psychosociological approach with definite anti-instinctivist views; for him this means that there is no "fixed human nature"; stresses the individualistic or personalistic aspects of development, saying that motivation is subconscious formation of predispositions and complexes; denies the "social mind" and explains co-ordinated behavior in terms of response to identical stimuli.

8. Allport, F. H., *Social Psychology* (Boston: Houghton Mifflin, 1924).

Predominantly psychological approach; the first of this kind, and a stanch opponent of the theoretical approaches of Bernard and the sociologists; sponsors behaviorism and psychoanalysis somewhat but prefers behavioristic expressions like "prepotent reflexes" to the psychoanalytic. Strongly anti-instinctivist; individualist always attacking McDougall's "Group Mind"; humanitarian in ethics, physiological-environmental determinist; favors experimental or at least empirical approach to all social problems.

9. Znaniecki, F., *The Laws of Social Psychology* (Chicago: University of Chicago Press, 1925). Collaborated with W. I. Thomas on *The Polish Peasant*, 1918–1927.

Predominantly sociological-ethnological approach; Dewey functionalist; formerly biological instinctivist, then shifted to Dewey's concepts of habits, attitudes, values, and wishes, all acquired from society; opposes H. Spencer's evolutionary-anthropological views; claims to deduce all his laws from case material, seems often to be fitting the cases to preconceived theories.

10. Bernard, L. L., *Introduction to Social Psychology* (New York: H. Holt, 1926).

Sociological approach though eclectic; environmentalist, personalist, hereditarian with something like a functionalist-behaviorist determinism; maintains that all behavior is product of environment-times-set or attitude of the organism; makes use of terms "choice" and "rational adjustment processes."

11. McDougall, W., *Introduction to Social Psychology*, 1908. Rev. (Boston: J. W. Luce and Co., 1926). Also, *The Group Mind, Psychoanalysis and Social Psychology.* Easily *first* on this list.

Psychological tendencies stronger; was first to publicize a widely accepted instinct theory to explain social process; changes theories of instinct-emotional patterns upon criticism; repudiates any approach to the study of soul or will which is not positivistic, yet claims to be opposed to mechanism; a hormic psychologist; a "Group Mind" theorist.

12. Judd, C. H., *Psychology of the Social Instincts* (New York: Macmillan, 1926 and 1931).

Sociological-educational approach, Wundtian tradition; opposes "individual psychology" with concepts of "social consciousness and collective will" which transform the individual; functionalist-evolutionist, though he claims that in the process, man's adaptations became essentially superior to those of animals.

13. Dunlap, K., *Social Psychology*, 1927; *Civilized Life*, 1935 (Baltimore: Williams and Wilkins Co.).

Psychological tradition, reputed to have settled the issue about instincts; mechanistic-configurationist in general psychology, dynamic environmentalist in social psychology; author thinks that all human reactions will eventually be described in mechanistic or response-to-situation terms; anti-Freudian; though apparently deterministic, says that ideas and reflection can direct the course of action and desires; actions are total responses to pattern stimulations; education furnishes the patterns; its moral codes are usually conventional.

14. Young, K., *Source Book for Social Psychology*, 1927; and *Social Psychology: An Analysis of Social Behavior*, 1930 (New York: F. S. Crofts, Inc.).

Sociological approach; opposed to purely physiological and experimental approach because "Content of Mind" is neglected; favors the case history method; furnishes a good list of these with interpretations; environment of sociocultural stimuli is responded to by individuals; this directs the course of personal and social development; uses behavioristic and psychoanalytic terminology freely.

15. Sprowls, J. W., *Social Psychology Interpreted* (Baltimore: Williams and Wilkins Co., 1927).

Critical review of schools of thought and of such theories as "Group Mind," "Collective Consciousness," etc.

16. Mujkerji, R., and Sen-Gupta, N., *Introduction to Social Psychology: Mind in Society* (Boston: D. C. Heath and Co., 1928).

Eclectic approach with many examples taken from Oriental cultures; authors speak of voluntary and purposive actions, reflexes, instincts, habits; these are all unconsciously determined for the most part by heredity and social environment; while opposing "Group Mind" they describe the patterning of the individual evolutionistically.

17. Ewer, B. C., *Social Psychology* (New York: Macmillan, 1929).

Eclectic method; opposes the emotionalistic leanings of other writers; one of the few who stresses the importance of reason as a guide to human behavior; apparently tries to synthesize Ross, McDougall, Dunlap, Bernard, and Allport.

18. Smith, J. J., *Social Psychology: The Psychology of Attraction and Repulsion* (Boston: R. G. Badger, 1930).

Follows psychological tradition, notably of McDougall and Bergsonian cast; cognitive elements, especially reason, function complexly in guiding the affective and conative states which make higher sentiments enjoyable; altruistic friendship and sublimated love for welfare of self and group are the best motives for adjustment; gives fine analysis of the sentiments and motives in their egotistic-altruistic setting.

19. Karpf, F. B., *American Social Psychology: Its Origin, Development, and European Background* (New York: McGraw-Hill, 1932).

Historical guide to most of the authors listed above; all are critically compared and related to respective philosophical systems and originators; stresses need for more objective studies and less attempts to apply preconceived theories to the facts of observation.

20. Myerson, A., *Social Psychology: An Introduction to the Study of Personality and Environment* (New York: Prentice Hall, Inc., 1934).

Neuropsychological approach with stress upon the forebrain (inhibitory) and visceral (emotional) processes; opposes the oversimplifications of behaviorists; doubts scientific value of Freudian theories; holds that conduct is determined by man's nature and social environment, but that there must be choice between alternatives, since contradictory stimuli compete at the same time for possession of the same motor pathway; adequate social choice of behavior develops personality; assumes evolution and relativity of morals.

21. Kreuger, E. T., and Reckless, W. C., *Social Psychology* (New York: Longmans Green Co., 1931).

Eclectic or sociopsychological approach; anti-behavioristic and anti-Freudian; approves case history method and supplies good collection; favors Stern's personalism; admits importance of ideas of value and especially of value of self in social development; straddles the question of instincts versus attitudes.

22. Brown, J. F., *Psychology and the Social Order,* 1936; *Psychodynamics of Abnormal Behavior,* 1940 (New York: McGraw-Hill).

Psychiatric-psychological approach; environment-times-heredity determines behavior; changes Freudian concepts to fit Gestalt-field notion of the individual-in-the-group; psychopathology needs no behavior traits which are solely biologically conditioned, that is, hereditarily instinctive; thinks Freud's self-preservation and self-destruction tendencies are not basic instincts; some behavior patterns may be innate and teleological but activity of every sort is a function of the organism in its social, psychological, and political environment; a good reference for the viewpoint of a psychoanalytic field Gestalt psychopathologist.

23. Brown, L. G., *Social Psychology: The Natural History of Human Nature* (New York: McGraw-Hill, 1934).

Sociological approach; character determinist with arguments against the older hereditary and environmentalist determinists; modified behaviorist with emphasis on formation of patterns and attitudes determining human nature and type of society; functionalist tendencies shown in explanation of adjustment, which is the sole result of a person's past experience with human objects and his systems of value whereby he redefines objects.

24. Gurnee, H., *Elements of Social Psychology* (New York: Farrar and Rinehart, 1936).

Psychological approach with emphasis upon experiment and induction; good and rather easy text with behavioristic terms used generally; reason and insight differ from conditioning, but language itself has evolved from lower forms; some psychoanalytic concepts used but they are rejected in the question of the evolution of religion.

25. Freeman, E., *Social Psychology* (New York: Henry Holt Co., 1936).

Eclectic but dominantly psychological approach; examines psychological basis of values of individuals and cultures; individualistic and claims that the good of the individual can be achieved only by cooperation, that leaders prescribe stereotypes of belief and value which are always accepted; opposes "Group Mind" fallacy on grounds that there is no group nervous system and that it leads to nationalism (fascism); mind means the aggregate of perceptual phenomena conditioned by external forces, organic structure, drives, and life functions; morals must be relative and education can only be impartial by leading students to find truth in tentative theories; refers to the new type of conditioning called "pattern" or Gestalt learning.

26. LaPiere, R. T., and Farnworth, P. R., *Social Psychology* (New York: McGraw-Hill, 1936).

Predominantly psychological treatment, Neo-Platonic and anti-instinctivist; still Freudian but modified; Gestalt-personalistic concepts used; opposes the overrationalistic concepts of those who distinguish between reason and nonreason, between individual and the group, between good and evil, and between faculties or traits of personality; holds that free will is a postulate of theology which majority of men hold today, having rationalized their behavior accordingly; successful social adjustment means adjusting human nature to social changes, crime and psychopathic behavior are merely disapproved maladjustments; human nature in normal persons is the outcome of social pressure, individuality means deviation from average behavior; morals are merely relative to time and place; uncivilized persons have their norms as well as repressions resulting from them.

27. Murphy, G. and L. B., and Newcomb, T., *Experimental Social Psychology* (New York: Harper and Bros., 1937). (First edition by Murphys alone, 1931.)

Experimental psychological approach; allows some margin of human freedom since actions are spontaneous (nonpredictable); modifies the older behaviorism as well as psychoanalysis to bring them in accord with physiological and experimental findings; heavily laden with citations to all current periodicals; gives the fairest and broadest interpretation to all these findings in existence to date; especially common sense in views about motivation, child training, personality, and attitudes.

28. Thouless, R. H., *General and Social Psychology,* revised from *Social Psychology* (London: Univ. Tutorial Press, 1937).

Psychological approach; Gestalt-functionalist, but allows for the existence of the individual in a group; admits faculty psychology in order to avoid difficulties of associationism, structuralism, behaviorism, and of psychoanalysis, but appeals to evolution to explain transmission of social changes; clearly holds that volitional effort of the ego can direct his inner forces and effect behavior, just as in the original Gestalt theory any inner force or part or attitude is a partial determinant of any given energy pattern; gives good analysis of "size-constancy" in relation to Gestalt theory and the traditional sensist views.

29. Faris, E., *The Nature of Human Nature; Other Essays in Social Psychology* (New York: McGraw-Hill, 1937).

Like Thomas and Znaniecki in that ethnological data is stressed; Dewey functionalist in stressing attitude functions; rigid antiinstinctivist calling on attitudes to explain all acquired predispositions (called concepts) to ways and modes of response; points out that actions are often at variance with these dispositions and hence cause conflict.

30. Partridge, E. D., *Social Psychology of Adolescence* (New York: Prentice-Hall, 1938).

Sociological-educational approach; uses field theoretical Gestalt concepts in treating individual in the group; holds that a combination of human nature and the social field causes delinquency; field relationship should be changed, that is, bad home surroundings and delinquent's own conception of his place in the field; stresses recent letup of morals from the purely descriptive-inductive standpoint and urges enlightenment of youth, but suggests no norms according to which sexual behavior is to be regulated.

31. Reinhardt, J. M., *Social Psychology* (Chicago: J. B. Lippincott Co., 1938).

Socioethnological approach with extensive use of case histories; holds relativity of morals and the heredity-times-environment theory of determinism; mentions will and mental qualities and individual value systems but thinks early training determines their subsequent patterning; favors Gestalt-personalistic conceptions and some psychoanalytic (Adlerian) methods and principles; concludes that "culture patterns" necessarily and by their very nature cause conflicts of various sorts.

32. Bird, Charles, *Social Psychology* (New York: D. Appleton-Century, 1940).

Psychosociological approach; gives the best single account of methods and results of attitude testing; very aptly stresses the difference between rational thinking and random or unconscious learning or conditioning; eclectic in regard to other questions, conciliatory and usually interesting.

33. Klineberg, O., *Social Psychology* (New York: Harper and Bros., 1940).

Comparative psychological approach making wide use of anthropological data and experimental (animal) material; Gestalt-functionalist, but concedes that the individual is quite important as such, with all his interacting dynamically with the social field (thus avoiding the difficulties of the "Group Mind" theorists); thinks morals are relative to time and place, that aboriginals also do not lack social repression; that race differences in intelligence are unreliable; advocates more attitude and personality tests in controlling prejudices.

34. Thorndike, E. L., *Human Nature and the Social Order* (New York: Macmillan, 1940).

Educational-psychological approach; behavioristic experimentalist but mingles empiricism with aprioristic theory; for this author the hypotheses of science are as imaginative, abstract, and subtle as the ramblings of the poet or of the philosopher; for him the fact of having actions stamped in by pleasure is as scientific as the fact of inhibition for the physiologist; thus science claims respect and commands belief in what the plain man sees or perceives, whereas philosophy and theology command belief in what is "comfortable" for men to think; opposes Gestalt theory with his Stimulus-Response Connectionism; man's nature is the list of responses which he would very probably make to whatever stimuli could possibly happen to him. If Thorndike finds the stimulus-response theory more comfortable than the Gestaltists find their total responses to total situations, perhaps this is due to the law of effect also operative in his case to give satisfaction to his efforts.

35. Britt, S. H., *Social Psychology of Modern Life* (New York: Farrar and Rinehart, 1941).

Sociopsychological approach with emphasis upon emotions (the background of conscious life); tries to reconcile psychological and sociological methods; claims that there is little rational thinking and conviction, but that by means of discussion and information strong irrational attitudes and prejudices may be changed; proposes no philosophy of life but urges students to examine all facts scientifically before accepting any philosophy. Having examined all the facts regarding social processes, this author closes with the suggestion that the reader must evaluate these facts himself and not allow himself to be indoctrinated by anyone. He insists on the need of objective evidence in studying social processes, and freely makes use of some very subjective interpretations of behaviorism and psychoanalysis. He makes no mention of Gestalt theory.

36. Krout, M. H., *Introduction to Social Psychology* (New York: Harper and Bros., 1942).

Sociological (cultural) approach; sources for this empirical study are taken from cultural anthropology, experimentation, and history; a typical Gestalt-topological-cultural viewpoint and deterministic; claims to aid students in adjusting themselves to changing mores which engender conflicts or at least confusion of ideals and attitudes; mores and folkways determine morals; the individual can do little more than accept rationally. This doctrine is claimed to be the fundamental groundwork for all further investigation into the nature of social change and progress; it denounces authoritarian leadership, stresses the need of followership, recommends purifying language of its vague and emotional content by developing the sciences of semantics and syntactics along the lines of pure behavioral meanings. It is claimed that this method alone will avoid the dangers of distorting the meaning of language because of misinterpretations of "symbols in the context." Behaviorism has a new task to perform, namely to reform the use of language — readers of Krout are made to feel this need all the more by the author's quaint use of newly invented operational concepts and still quainter forms of expression.

Imprimi potest: Rev. Leo D. Sullivan, S.J.
Nihil obstat: H. B. Ries, Censor librorum
Imprimatur: ✠ Moses E. Kiley, Archbishop of Milwaukee
May 25, 1945

INDEX